Marita Linton

THE SHAPING OF LIBERAL POLITICS
IN REVOLUTIONARY FRANCE

THE SHAPING OF LIBERAL POLITICS IN REVOLUTIONARY FRANCE

A COMPARATIVE PERSPECTIVE

Anne Sa'adah

PRINCETON UNIVERSITY PRESS   PRINCETON, NEW JERSEY

Published by Princeton University Press, 41 William Street,
Princeton, New Jersey 08540
In the United Kingdom: Princeton University Press, Oxford

Library of Congress Cataloging-in-Publication Data

Sa'adah, Anne.
The shaping of liberal politics in revolutionary France : a
comparative perspective / Anne Sa'adah.
p. cm.
Includes bibliographical references.
ISBN 0-691-07824-6 (alk. paper)
1. France—Politics and government—Revolution, 1789–1799.
2. Liberalism—France—History—18th century. 3. Jacobins—France—
History—18th century. I. Title.
DC155.S23   1990
320.5′1′0944—dc20   90–30700   CIP

Publication of this book has been aided by the Whitney Darrow Fund
of Princeton University Press
This book has been composed in Linotron Baskerville

Princeton University Press books are printed on acid-free paper,
and meet the guidelines for permanence and durability of the
Committee on Production Guidelines for Book Longevity of the
Council on Library Resources

Printed in the United States of America by Princeton University Press,
Princeton, New Jersey

10 9 8 7 6 5 4 3 2 1

For My Parents ───────────────────────────

MY MOTHER, MARJORIE ABRAHAMIAN SA'ADAH, AND

MY FATHER, MOUNIR RAPHAEL SA'ADAH

Contents

Preface

CONFLICT is the stuff of politics. The character assumed by or assigned to conflict varies from country to country, and more importantly, from one type of political system to another. Different types of political systems are defined by the identity of the political contestants, the stakes of the competition, the rules of the game, and the resources used by the players. But while conflict is basic to political life, a sense of community is crucial to the survival of any polity. The character of community, like the character of conflict, helps define a political regime.

Liberal politics, because of its emphasis on the individual and its legitimation of self-interest, poses the problem of conflict and community in a particularly interesting way. This book examines how the tension between conflict and community was played out in the revolutionary crucible that shaped liberal politics in England, America, and France. This, then, is both a study of seventeenth- and eighteenth-century politics and a reflection on a problem of political theory. It did not begin that way. When trips to France first became an important part of my education, World War II still loomed as the event that had shaped the lives of many of the men and women who became my friends. They spoke, directly and indirectly, of the decisions and dangers they had faced during those difficult years, and also of the choices they had confronted during the Algerian War (1954–1962). The questions their experiences raised fueled my interest in those historical moments when political conflict becomes so deep and so basic that it threatens to destroy the political community within which it arose. That such moments should be the rule in so many contemporary developing countries seems—alas—normal; that profound political conflict should so regularly rip at the fabric of the French political community—as it did between 1934 and 1944, or again during the concluding phase of the Algerian War, from early 1958 to the summer of 1962—seemed more perplexing.

In the early 1970s, the events of the war years were still a delicate topic.[1] The Battle of France had been quickly lost in the summer of 1940. The Armistice provided for the military occupation of the

---

[1] By way of illustration, see the response to Marcel Ophuls's documentary, *Le Chagrin et la pitié* (*The Sorrow and the Pity*), which French television declined to air. See also Henry Rousso, *Le Syndrôme de Vichy* (Paris: Le Seuil, 1987).

northern half of the country by German troops. The other half—the so-called Free Zone—remained unoccupied until November 1942, and was officially ruled until the Liberation by an authoritarian government.[2] The Vichy regime had been installed by the last elected Assembly of the Third Republic and could therefore claim formal legality, but it owed its existence to the defeat of French arms. The hostility of its leaders and chief apologists to the "old regime" was patent. Some had become estranged from the Third Republic during the difficult years of the 1930s; others had always condemned the republican tradition and the Revolution that had produced it. The men who succeeded one another in power at Vichy did not always share the same immediate policy preferences, nor did they all agree in their vision of the ideal state or France's proper place in the international system. Yet despite their differences and the brevity of their tenure in power, they did all endeavor to recast France's political institutions, reshape her social and political life, and remold the national character. Predictably, if not inevitably, they soon found themselves ordering arrests, organizing mass deportations, and deciding the fate of hostages the Nazis were only too eager to shoot. By late 1943, the country was in a state of virtual civil war.

At the Liberation, the Provisional Government of the Republic brought treason charges against many accused of wartime collaboration with the Germans. Philippe Pétain, Head of State at Vichy, was sent to prison for life. Pierre Laval, who had served as Prime Minister, poisoned himself after being sentenced to die. Laval was revived because it was considered—and quite possibly it was rightly considered—symbolically important that he perish before a republican firing squad and not by his own hand.

Another man who fell before a Liberation firing squad was Robert Brasillach. After attending the prestigious Ecole Normale, Brasillach had emerged as a talented writer and critic. He was also a political journalist whose outspoken fascist sympathies antedated France's defeat—a chronology he proudly and repeatedly recalled between 1941 and 1943.[3] Returning to his desk in occupied Paris after an abbreviated stay in a German prisoner of war camp, Brasillach immediately sought to put the occupation of his country to political use. Germans had fought Frenchmen in 1870, 1914, and 1940, but for Brasillach,

[2] For an analysis of the Vichy government and collaborationism, see Stanley Hoffmann, *Decline or Renewal? France since the 1930's* (New York: Viking, 1974), part I; and Robert O. Paxton, *Vichy France: Old Guard and New Order, 1940–1944* (New York: Knopf, 1972).

[3] For Brasillach's own account of the 1930s, see Robert Brasillach, *Notre avant-guerre* (Paris, 1942).

Germany's current ideological attractiveness outweighed—indeed, erased—all past rivalries. For Frenchmen who, like Brasillach, had greeted the Popular Front with cries of "Better Hitler than Blum," France's military defeat created an unexpected political opportunity. In column after column of the weekly newspaper *Je suis partout*, Brasillach did more than advocate new political institutions; he also vociferously demanded that France be purged of its human contaminations. Jews were not the only "foreigners" against whom Brasillach railed. Other categories on his long list of unwanted compatriots included communists, socialists, and even mere republicans: in short, the millions of people who had sustained the Popular Front, and a few more besides. Brasillach would have replaced what he saw as their rotten, decadent Republic with a "new," "purified," "virile"—favorite adjectives in the French fascist vocabulary—France. Only that new France would Brasillach acknowledge as his own.

Brasillach spoke for very few of his countrymen. If moral courage, political lucidity, and the material prerequisites of resistance were in short supply in a country disorganized and disoriented by defeat, outright fascist convictions were even more rare. Thousands of Brasillach's undesirables were nonetheless deported under Vichy's more "moderate" auspices,[4] and other French men and women fell in the struggle against a regime whose existence they considered a moral and political calamity. Thus, at Brasillach's trial, the government prosecutor summarized a national drama when he said to the defendant, "The France which now brings you to account is not that one [the purged France of Brasillach's fascist dreams]. The true France was the other one, the one you excluded, the one you betrayed."[5]

The words of the republican prosecutor have only one point in common with the stream of despicable prose that Brasillach had published between 1941 and the end of 1943:[6] they tell us, in much more graphic terms than any political scientist will ever coin, what political polarization can ultimately mean. The stark choices they suggest, rather than the more refined questions to which we will shortly turn, provided the original impetus that led me to write this book. I wanted to say something that would illuminate the constellation of social, political, and ideological factors that militated persistently against ideo-

[4] See Paxton, *Vichy France*; and Michael R. Marrus and Robert O. Paxton, *Vichy France and the Jews* (New York: Basic Books, 1981).

[5] Transcript of the Brasillach trial in *Quatre procès de trahison* (Paris: Les Editions de Paris, 1947); cited passage appears on p. 172.

[6] Toward the end of the War, Brasillach apparently had second thoughts regarding his earlier political positions. Unlike many of his associates who fled the country and escaped execution, Brasillach chose to turn himself in at the Liberation.

logical moderation, stable institutions, and the general legitimation of
political opposition—and this in a country we rightly include among
the liberal democracies of the modern world. I did not want simply
to explain a single crisis—the unraveling of the Republic in the late
1930s or the turmoil that accompanied decolonization. I wanted to
identify and explore a more global pattern of politics and thus make
sense out of a type of crisis that recurs, in more or less attenuated
form, rather frequently in French political life. How does such a pattern work, and in what ways can it seem advantageous? What consequences does it entail for the more general forms of social and political life? Why did a different pattern emerge in England and
America?

In answering these questions, I have generally used gendered
nouns and pronouns. This usage reflects historical realities. Political
elites in the seventeenth- and eighteenth-century settings I analyze in
this book were composed almost exclusively of men. In David's famous sketch of the Tennis Court Oath, the few women present watch
the scene through the room's open windows. Women, did, of course,
play political roles before they acquired political rights, but they did
not play primary roles, and in France, women did not even vote until
1944. To use gender-neutral nouns and pronouns would therefore
be inaccurate and misleading and would obscure the achievements of
our own era. The early liberals who claimed to speak in universal
terms were men; they were also white and propertied. But because
they formulated their claims in what they thought of as universal
terms, later it was possible for poor men and people of color and
women to argue that the "Rights of Man" were their rights too. Were
this not the case, the patterns explained in the pages that follow
would have a quite different historical significance.

Hanover, New Hampshire
August 1989

Acknowledgments ─────────────────────

THIS BOOK began life as a doctoral dissertation at Harvard University. After earning a bachelor's degree in Social Studies, I remained at Harvard as a graduate student in the Department of Government. At Harvard and then at Middlebury College, where I taught from 1981 to 1984, and at Dartmouth College, where I have been on the faculty since 1984, I benefited from more forms of material and intellectual support than I could ever acknowledge. A National Science Foundation Graduate Fellowship and a Sheldon Travelling Fellowship provided much-needed and greatly appreciated support while I was in graduate school. I accepted a job at Middlebury before finishing my dissertation, and a Faculty Research Fund grant facilitated continued research trips to Cambridge. The intelligence and inexhaustible good humor of my friend and typist, Claire Wilson, were a godsend in the last, hurried months before my defense. After I moved to Dartmouth and began to prepare the manuscript for publication, computers (and the helpful people who understand them) took over, but on another and more important level, my intellectual and professional growth has been enhanced by the good fortune of belonging to a cohesive, lively Department.

For the errors of fact and judgment that remain in the pages that follow, I, of course, assume full responsibility. Those errors would certainly have been more numerous and more serious had I not benefited from the assistance of several people. My undergraduate adviser and dissertation director, Stanley Hoffmann, indelibly shaped the way I think about French politics without ever promoting the sense that the important questions had already been answered. As Chairman of Social Studies and then as my second reader, Michael Walzer made the important issues of political theory matters of ongoing concern. He also prodded me to include England and America in a study I had originally planned to limit to France. Charles Maier and Georges Lavau have for years served as reliable sources of encouragement, insight, and criticism. To the many other friends, now increasingly dispersed and diversely employed, with whom, throughout and beyond the years of my undergraduate and graduate education, I learned and talked about politics, European history, and social theory, I am happy to acknowledge my debt. Richard Freeland, Pauline Maier, and Cheryl Welch responded to different parts of this manuscript in ways that allowed me to improve the quality of the whole. Finally, I am grateful to the late George Armstrong Kelly and to Nicholas Wahl for their helpful comments on the manuscript; I am also grateful to my editor, Sandy Thatcher, and my copy editor, Lyn Grossman, for their assistance.

This book is dedicated to my mother and father. They taught me (among other things) to love books, to take ideas seriously, and to pay attention to politics.

General Note on the Sources

CHAPTERS II AND III make extensive use of primary source material. In order to avoid unnecessarily cumbersome and/or obscure notes, I have adhered to the following guidelines in acknowledging sources. Except for the surname of the person quoted, information already specified in the text (for example, the date on which a speech was delivered) will not be repeated in the note. Where a speech is concerned, the name of the speaker will be followed by the place where the speech was given (for example, Constituent Assembly, Jacobins, Convention, etc.), the date of the speech, and the published source. Except where it seemed crucial to read a speech in its context, I have usually tried to cite easily accessible modern editions of speeches and documents rather than original sources. All translations from French into English are mine unless otherwise noted. The awkwardness of the translations often reflects the equally awkward constructions used by the revolutionary orators.

When the source of a primary source citation is a secondary source, the note will refer only to the secondary source unless there is a compelling reason for including further information.

THE SHAPING OF LIBERAL POLITICS
IN REVOLUTIONARY FRANCE

Introduction _____

Liberalism in England, America, and France: Problems and Approaches

In ENGLAND, America, and France, liberal politics was shaped by revolution. In this book, I will present two different patterns of liberal theory and practice as the product of different types of revolutionary competition. I will then analyze how each pattern "worked": what each looked like, and what purposes each fulfilled in the context within which it emerged. The French case is the most problematic, for what worked in revolutionary France seems related to nearly two centuries of postrevolutionary constitutional instability. French political patterns are often portrayed in an unfavorable light, and France's liberal credentials have frequently been questioned. The French experience will therefore be the principal object of analysis, but the overall argument embraces all three countries and aims at an understanding of the dynamics of early liberal political development. My purpose in these introductory pages is not to summarize that argument. Rather, I want to set the stage for its elaboration by explaining the typology of liberal politics it proposes and the methodological choices on which it rests.

Transaction Versus Exclusion: A Typology of Liberal Politics

Revolutions change both the organization of power and the basis of political solidarity. A central problem of politics in eighteenth-century France, as in revolutionary England and America, consisted of recasting political community around a set of increasingly compelling but radically new assumptions about the nature of political authority and obligation and about the individual. This problem was at the heart of the revolutions that occurred in each country. The emerging view was voluntarist: The state was not a divine or natural imposition, but rather an impermanent construction deliberately created by human actors for specific purposes. So conceived, the state would derive its legitimacy from the consent of the political nation. The basic unit of society was the individual, increasingly cut loose from the involuntary bonds that had previously been thought rightly to define who he or she was and what social and political roles he or she would play, and around which the ideal of a "naturally" hierarchical and harmonious community had developed. As individuals came to be seen as thinking for themselves and acting on their own, harmony seemed an improbable by-product of their interactions. Society, it now appeared, would be by nature conflictual because individuals were by nature self-interested. To bind effectively, obligations would have to be contractual, or at least consistent with some conception of self-interest. But where the state was seen as artificial, society as conflictual, and individuals as arbiters of their own commitments, social and political cohesion seemed problematic. A very old problem thus resurfaced in a new form and demanded a new organization of power compatible with the new views of conflict and community.

Like the various formulations of this problem, the solutions to it varied from country to country. Different revolutionary settlements were associated with different social configurations, ideological formulations, institutions, and patterns of political behavior. Despite such differences, however, the three future great powers of the future West made certain choices in common: They all came to share a commitment to a limited state, to personal and political freedoms, and to capitalist economic development. They all, that is, became liberal countries.

Since the problem each country faced during the revolutionary period revolved in part around the re-creation of legitimate political institutions, the solution necessarily required, in conjunction with institutional change, the elaboration of a new ideology. This ideology's enduring role, as important in the postrevolutionary period as in the revolutionary one, would be to articulate a particular conception of political power and to specify who might exercise it, by what means, and to what purposes. Representative institutions and politics captured the central role, but representative politics presupposes a community to be represented. In revolutionary times, not all people line up willingly with the new order, and the new ideology placed particular emphasis on the voluntary commitments of individuals. The composition and legitimate constitution of political society itself therefore became a visible issue, urgently soliciting an explicit response. Any response implied a policy of exclusion directed against individuals and institutions identified with the contested regime, and a politics of inclusion destined to socialize the citizenry and celebrate the new community. These elements—institutional development and community-building—were both practically and theoretically interdependent, and the logic of their interdependence appears in the particular form of liberal ideology adopted.

Where revolutionary forces and their new ideology won a clear-cut victory, exclusionary practices and discourse rapidly became obsolete or (relatively) innocuous: Their only targets were real foreigners and the occasional political maverick. For all the conflict legitimated by the triumphant ideology's individualistic emphasis, the result was what is sometimes called consensual politics.[1] Conflict did not end, but it assumed certain characteristics. The stakes of politics and the advantages of power became subject to both explicit and implicit limits. Political opposition gained acceptance because it questioned the wisdom or justice of specific policies without deliberately or directly challenging the basic rules and assumptions regulating the political game. Theory eventually incorporated the reality of diversity and competition into a new image of the ideal community and the normal pursuit of the common good. The stability of the rules, rather than substantive uniformity, became a primary index of the health of the community. Stable rules guaranteed the manageability of conflicts.

In this setting, representative politics became what I will call a politics of transaction. The politics of transaction was supported and completed by a theory of political participation, a systematic reliance on the integrative and disciplinary capacities of social institutions (which were usually independent of the state), and a permeability of politics to the changing concerns of a dynamic society.

By contrast, where revolutionary forces met with only partial success and the new ideology remained contested, the politics of inclusion and exclusion remained critical weapons in a continuing combat. The political "foreigner" lurked in the house down the street: in the French case, a Jacobin under a monarchy or a royalist in the Republic, later a Communist or a man who on his own account did indeed prefer Hitler to Blum. Since in the estimation of a significant portion of the political class, the polity was as yet improperly constituted, revolutionary politics—with its emphasis on exclusion, its preoccupation with foundational issues, and its instrumental appreciation of politi-

---

[1] English and especially American politics until recently provided the principal examples of consensual modes of political competition and (presumably related) incremental modes of political change. Scholars associated with the consensus thesis include Richard Hofstadter, Louis Hartz, and Robert Dahl. In England, the consensus thesis was related to the "Whig" interpretation of history.

From our present vantage point, the British and American political systems seem rather less consensual and less adaptable than even the more refined versions of the consensus model would lead us to expect, while French politics seems (at long last) increasingly consensual. See François Furet et al., *La République du centre: La fin de l'exception française* (Paris: Calmann-Lévy, 1988).

cal legality—continued, becoming to a certain extent a normal way of national political life. The politics of exclusion inevitably entailed a politics of identity, encouraging the elaboration of a theory of community and largely insulating the world of political discourse and cleavage from the pressures of social change. Even within the framework of representative institutions, foundational tasks often eclipsed the representation of interests; the official role of the republican deputy was the defense of the Republic.

England and America followed, by and large, the first path; France took the second. In all three countries, the process involved revolution. Considered together, the political itineraries of the three countries stand in clear contrast to the political record of almost any other country in the world. England, America, and France represent the early liberal route to modernity. In each country, revolution was the first collective response to the liberal challenge. These revolutions exemplify one form of the transition from premodern to modern society; by analyzing them, we can explore the character and limits of political change and stability within the context of that transition. Viewed separately, however, the political histories of the three countries illustrate two different types of liberal politics. This analysis attempts to keep both the similarities and the points of divergence among the three cases in focus; the argument assumes a basic similarity and seeks to explain the differences.

The revolutions in England and America successfully reassigned political authority and sovereignty, leaving the postrevolutionary community reunited around a new legitimacy. The brand of liberalism behind that legitimacy, like the institutions it upheld, had developed through an effort to construct a political world that would both provide a genuinely public realm and at the same time be consistent with a systematic protest against power in general and political power in particular. The desire to create a public arena in which citizens would participate in the elaboration of policy was tempered by the usually more urgent effort to limit the power of the state. The protest against power was proferred on behalf of the individual and of a society newly conscious of its possible autonomy. This liberalism sought to impose no common image of the ideal person (though it may have rested on such an image) and it offered no theory of community. It accepted a minimal state as necessary to prevent competition among individuals and between interests from assuming lethal forms, but it condemned the accumulation or concentration of power as an intolerable threat to security and prosperity alike. All of classical liberal theory—summarized in Locke's *Second Treatise* but elaborated and articulated in countless tracts, sermons, speeches, legal arguments, and pamphlets of the English seventeenth-century and the American Revolution—is directed at making public power truly public (that is, independent of corporate interests within society) and then at constraining it. The problem of social cohesion is either deliberately downplayed (as in Locke's *Second Treatise*) or bound over for its solution to extrapolitical mechanisms (the community of the English Saints or the sense of lonely virtue cultivated by the American revolutionaries). Thus the "tranquillity" vaunted by the Levellers, as by Locke, connotes only the successful containment of political power, not an absence of competition in civil society or a congregation of individuals unanimous in their most fundamental beliefs. Thus conceived, the liberal state does not have positive ideals or ends of its own, and it does not confer a sense of shared identity or communal purpose on its members. It is a pact to which members subscribe for primarily prudential reasons, to secure prior individual rights which might otherwise be unjustly infringed.

In this account, politics is primarily a means of settling disputes among "friends." It is the interaction between two or more actors who, although self-interested, meet in the social world neither as enemies (defending opposing rules) nor even as strangers (ignorant of each other's fundamental values), for they recognize the legitimacy of their competition and they have agreed to pursue their respective interests according to a common set of preestablished rules regulating the means as well as the stakes of the competition.[2] Representative assemblies provide the linchpin of governmental legitimacy. Their role, however, is not to reopen debate on philosophical issues (not, that is, to make foundational questions the everyday stuff of parliamentary and political life), but to sponsor the conclusion of deals between competing groups. The dominant political metaphor is that of the marketplace, but the "politics of transaction" reaffirms the presence as much as it evokes the character of the continued strife among those "huddled around the Lockeian center,"[3] and it need not obscure the violence with which those in the center occa-

[2] This formulation may remind some readers of John Rawls's description of the original position (see Rawls, *A Theory of Justice* [Cambridge, Mass.: Harvard University Press, 1971])—and therefore of the problems associated with his use of that concept. The original position is Rawls's stand-in for the more traditional concept of the state of nature. I am arguing that in an established political system organized around the politics of transaction, political actors meet as "friends."

[3] The phrase is Richard Hofstadter's. It appears in his critical reappraisal of the consensus thesis at the end of *The Progressive Historians: Turner, Beard, Parrington* (New York: Vintage Books, 1968), p. 447.

sionally turned back the claims of compatriots inclined, or supposedly inclined, toward a fundamental modification of the prevailing rules.

In this liberal world, violence and politics do not officially mix. If an issue arises on which compromise is impossible, where majority rule would "do violence" to the minority, either the issue must be buried or the established political game must be sidestepped. Such an issue challenges the assumptions around which the official political world is organized; when the assumptions no longer hold, the rules no longer apply. If important political participants consider the issue too crucial to be set aside, the result is civil war or possibly revolution—what Locke terms an "appeal to Heaven."[4] If the cause has less powerful defenders, it may be ignored; it may also be fed into a parallel, officially unrecognized but politically crucial system of intimidation, corruption, and/or violence.

The persuasiveness of such a conception of politics rested on three assumptions. It was necessary first to assume that competition, guided only by various invisible hands, would promote what the nineteenth century came to call the greatest happiness of the greatest number. Unimpeded economic competition would produce more and better goods; unsupervised intellectual competition would in its final formulations approximate the truth; religious competition would bring all men and women closer to God; and open, organized political competition would safeguard public liberty. Government could better serve the people by guaranteeing fair competition than by risking initiatives of its own.

The second assumption reinforced the notion of politics as an essentially positive-sum activity, pursued by actors whose self-interest was tempered by a certain kind of self-restraint. The assumption posited that all major public differences of opinion could in fact be reformulated as competing claims, after which trade-offs could be made and a bargain struck. Ultimately the only way of dealing with issues that could not be so reformulated, and with the groups that espoused such issues, was violence. The parallel system of coercion was unrecognized because its necessity violated the basic assumptions

---

[4] In Chapter XIX of the *Second Treatise*, Locke defends the people's right to resist and replace a government tending toward tyranny, arguing that when government oversteps its role as umpire, the political bonds and obligations associated with legitimate government are dissolved.

In *Humanisme et terreur: Essai sur le problème communiste* (Paris: Gallimard, 1947, 1980), Maurice Merleau-Ponty (after others) criticizes liberalism as predicated on the belief that the social and political status quo current at any given moment is basically satisfactory, and notes that the price is often unavowed repression at home and imperialism abroad.

on which the politics of transaction stood; at the same time, its existence was a direct consequence of the business-like atmosphere of official public life.

The third assumption was one which few people after Bentham in fact held with any confidence: It asserted that prudential considerations alone would suffice to hold together a society of self-interested individuals. By the early nineteenth century, as people reviewed the evidence of the French Revolution and meditated upon the early manifestations of secularizing trends in culture and politics, the problem of social cohesion figured with increasing prominence and frequency on the liberal agenda. Burke, with his acute if outmoded sense of political community, put the problem thus:

> On the scheme of this barbarous philosophy, which is the offspring of cold hearts and muddy understandings, . . . laws are to be supported only by their own terrors, and by the concern, which each individual may find in them, from his own private speculations, or can spare to them from his own private interests. In the groves of *their* academy, at the end of every visto, you see nothing but the gallows. Nothing is left which engages the affections on the part of the commonwealth. . . . But that sort of reason which banishes the affections is incapable of filling their place.[5]

One did not have to accept Burke's conclusions in order to share his apprehensions. Liberal revolutions, it appeared, did more than create liberal states. Along with the demystification of politics and the bridling of the state came a new form of society, characterized by an increasing equality of condition and the rapid development of a commercial middle class. In this society, political as well as social cohesion became a problem, and if the intellectual response to the problem in England and America lacked the theoretical depth attained by the French doctrinaires and their descendants,[6] it was nonetheless a problem to which nineteenth century Englishmen and Americans devoted considerable attention. They feared that rampant individualism would lead to anarchy and finally to political tyranny; they also feared that extreme privatization would result in the rule of public opinion and consequently in the abasement of the mind and mediocrity in all forms of human activity not driven by material profit.

The Anglo-American answer to these fears had two sides. The first, and perhaps sunnier, side evolved as a deliberate response to the

---

[5] Edmund Burke, *Reflections on the Revolution in France* (Harmondsworth: Penguin Books, 1969), pp. 171f. Burke's *Reflections* originally appeared in 1790.

[6] See Larry Siedentop, "Two Liberal Traditions," in Alan Ryan, ed., *The Idea of Freedom: Essays in Honor of Isaiah Berlin* (Oxford: Oxford University Press, 1979), pp. 153–74.

problem. It included an emphasis on moralism and self-improvement consonant with individualism and with liberal politics as a politics of transaction, and a certain understanding of democratic politics. Appealing for help from beyond the immediate political world, it involved the marshaling of religion and education to foster social discipline and solidarity. Writing of England, G. Kitson Clark has argued that "it might not be too extravagant to say of the nineteenth century that probably in no other century, except the seventeenth and perhaps the twelfth, did the claims of religion occupy so large a part in the nation's life, or did men speaking in the name of religion contrive to exercise so much power."[7] The New England clergyman Lyman Beecher, looking at the heterogeneous, scattered population flooding the American West, urged the necessity of "those institutions which discipline the mind, and arm the conscience and the heart." And he continued:

> Population will not wait, and commerce will not cast anchor, and manufactures will not shut off the steam nor shut down the gate, and agriculture, pushed by millions of freemen on their fertile soil, will not withhold her corrupting abundance.
>
> We must educate! We must educate! or we must perish by our own prosperity.[8]

The political aspect of this part of the answer required the gradual acceptance of political parties and the elaboration and practical realization of a theory of political participation. The most eloquent proponent of participation was the mature John Stuart Mill. Mill pleaded for participation on behalf of the individual, whereas Tocqueville (to whom Mill is often compared) was more inclined to think in terms of community. Both men extolled the beneficial effects of regular, massive citizen participation in local government; both held that such participation was the only sure antidote to the potential evils of increasingly egalitarian social conditions. In Tocqueville's mind, however, participation was the current condition of political liberty, and Tocqueville conceived of liberty as a collective good enjoyed collectively—whence his nostalgia for an idealized aristocratic France,

---

[7] G. Kitson Clark, *The Making of Victorian England* (New York: Atheneum, 1962, 1979), p. 20. See also E. P. Thompson, *The Making of the English Working Class* (New York: Knopf, 1963); Ian Bradley, *The Call to Seriousness: The Evangelical Impact on the Victorians* (New York: Macmillan, 1976); and (still) Daniel Halévy's 1906 essay, "La Naissance du Méthodisme en Angleterre," translated and introduced by Bernard Semmel, in *The Birth of Methodism in England* (Chicago: University of Chicago Press, 1971).

[8] Lyman Beecher, *A Plea for the West*, 2d ed. (Cincinnati: Truman and Smith, 1835), pp. 16, 31f.

which the centralizing monarchy had destroyed. Mill defended a form of democratic elitism, but did not share Tocqueville's aristocratic sympathies. His primary concern was for the individual, not for the community.[9] For Mill, participation, like the state itself, served the individual by affording him or her the opportunity to develop as a "progressive being."[10] Mill demanded that government provide for more than the mere physical security of its citizens, no doubt in part because he felt that persons and property were rather easily secured in nineteenth-century England. In addition to security, government was to supply the framework within which individuals might pursue self-perfection. Participation contributed directly to individual excellence by countering the stultifying effects of unabated private profit-seeking. Participation contributed indirectly to self-improvement by holding society itself together: it served as the "artificial means"[11] of inducing patriotism. In a populous, commercial society, whose members Mill described as "like the sands of the sea-shore, each very minute, and no one adhering to any other,"[12] more "natural" forms of political cement were either unavailable or undesirable.

The less attractive, and sometimes less conscious, side of the solution to the problem of community in England and America lay in those nations' responses to the outside world. In the mainstream political life of England and America, the great flourishes of "us-them" rhetoric have been reserved for the foreign foe rather than the domestic adversary. Foreigners may be seen as the source of unprovoked belligerence or simply contamination, but they are always "other" and almost invariably inferior—*politically* inferior. Neither nationalism nor imperialism is peculiar to liberal polities, let alone to England and America, but the politics of transaction did affect the form nationalism and/or imperial ambitions assumed. Through its prism, the world has alternately been viewed as a hopeless mess in which it would be imprudent and futile to become embroiled and as a fitting workplace for political missionaries bringing political reason to countries inexplicably (or unnecessarily) rent by ideological and factional strife.[13] The results for humanity may not always have been

[9] Siedentop argues persuasively that Mill echoes Tocqueville's moral concerns without embracing the underlying sociological analysis; see Siedentop, "Two Liberal Traditions," pp. 172–74.

[10] The concern for human improvement, and for the role to be played by representative government in promoting it, is present throughout Mill's work.

[11] J. S. Mill, "M. de Tocqueville on Democracy in America," in Marshall Cohen, ed., *The Philosophy of John Stuart Mill* (New York: Modern Library, 1961), p. 159.

[12] Ibid., p. 158.

[13] This argument is more obviously applicable to the United States than to Great Britain. On the connection between American liberalism and American foreign policy,

happy, but at home this type of nationalism tended to enter domestic politics primarily as a unifying force, not as a deadly weapon of party conflict. The outside world remained outside.

The system worked. Politics remained a competition among friends, though one punctuated by episodes of violence which standard histories sought to minimize. Government posed as the servant of society, the ultimate umpire of recognized disputes. Political power monopolized the legitimate use of force, but the content of politics as well as of policy changed as society changed: Since the new order was secure, political representatives could defend the particular concerns of their constituents.

In April 1641, on the eve of civil war, the Earl of Strafford stood defending his life before the House of Lords:

> Beware you do not awake these sleeping lions by the raking up of some neglected, some moth-eaten records—they may sometime tear you and your posterity to pieces. It was your ancestors' care to chain them up within the barrier of a statute; be not you ambitious to be more skilful, more curious than your fathers were in the art of killing. . . . I leave it to your lordships' consideration to foresee what may be the issue of so dangerous, so recent precedencies. These gentlemen tell me they speak in defence of the commonweal against my arbitrary laws; give me leave to say that I speak in defence of the commonweal against their arbitrary treason.[14]

Speculative predictions about a possible revolution could not have been the doomed Strafford's primary concern. His words nevertheless point to two crucial characteristics of revolutionary politics. The charge of high treason on which he stood accused, Strafford suggested, was an arbitrary one, not comprised "within the barrier" of standing laws and conventional definitions. Likewise, eight years later, Charles I would challenge the legal competence of the High Court; likewise—and equally in vain—Louis XVI in 1793 would con-

---

see Louis Hartz, *The Liberal Tradition in America: An Interpretation of American Political Thought Since the Revolution* (New York: Harcourt Brace Jovanovich, 1955), chap. 11; George F. Kennan, *American Diplomacy 1900–1950* (Chicago: University of Chicago Press, 1951); and Stanley Hoffmann, *Gulliver's Troubles or the Setting of American Foreign Policy* (New York: Council on Foreign Relations/McGraw-Hill, 1968). Britain's proclivity for balance of power politics on the Continent, though very different from American approaches, seems to me consistent with a sense of British political superiority and a desire to keep the outside world outside.

[14] Speech in J. P. Kenyon, ed., *The Stuart Constitution: Documents and Commentary* (Cambridge: Cambridge University Press, 1966), p. 213.

test the legality of the charges brought against him by the Convention. In any polity, the definition of treason is contingent upon the accepted notions of political legitimacy, power, and obligation. A political revolution occurs precisely when the political nation, previously bound together by these norms, splits over their meaning and validity. Treason then becomes a fluid, "arbitrary" concept, and a monopoly over the power to define it is part of what is at stake in a revolution. Until a new legitimacy is generally accepted and ensures its future through stable institutions, any group with a share of power may use the accusation of treason as a means of eliminating its competitors, discrediting opposing ideas, and promoting its own ideology. Revolutionary politics are, by definition, exclusionary, and were so in England and America, as in France.

Exclusion can be used by moderate revolutionaries against their various opponents; it can also be turned against the moderates by political actors to whom the initial revolutionary platform appears primarily as a springboard to a set of more sweeping changes. Thus we come to Strafford's second observation: Once the "barrier" of law is felled by the first revolutionary initiatives, the ensuing state of war may not prove so easy to control. Strategic as well as tactical superiority may fall to extremists of either camp, and the original revolutionaries may then be sidelined—torn to pieces, as Strafford graphically puts it—by the very forces they had so rashly unleashed.

The pages that follow devote particular attention to the fate of revolutionary moderates. Some definition of this group is therefore in order, and the one we will use has a substantive as well as a spatial component. Within the context of a discussion of early liberal political development, moderates are revolutionaries who accept the basic propositions of the liberal program as a fair summary of their own goals, who attach in practice as well as in theory considerable value to the integrity of procedural norms and constitutional government, and who, in general, encounter opposition both from those who find them too revolutionary and from those who find them hopelessly timid.[15] On principled as well as prudential grounds, moderates have a particularly high stake in keeping revolutionary processes under control: They will be morally, ideologically, and practically uncomfortable when forced to act openly as a revolutionary, "arbitrary" agents.

Since the seventeenth century, revolution after revolution has

[15] The spatial metaphor can be used to indicate both political and social criticism of moderate positions: the moderate would be contested from right and left, from above and below.

borne out Strafford's anxious prophecy regarding the likely fate of revolutionary moderates—revolution after revolution, but not the English Revolution, which began a year after Strafford's execution, nor the American Revolution a century and a half later. England and America represent the perhaps closed set of cases in which the original revolutionary group never lost primary leverage over the course of the revolution, even when (as in England) its primacy suffered apparent eclipse. The moderates successfully limited the scope of revolutionary demands and controlled the character and extent of exclusion. The revolutions they sponsored finished their work, and so while they wrought crucial political changes (which necessarily had long-run social implications), they resulted in ideologically complacent, constitutionally stable societies.

This was not what happened in France, where a political revolution did not finish its assigned tasks. Instead of redefining political community around a new conception of legitimacy, the Revolution intensified and diversified political divisions, vindicating all of Strafford's fears. In this significant but limited sense, the French Revolution "failed." The revolutionary disruption of political community spilled over into the postrevolutionary period, there to complicate the problem of cohesion in a liberal society. This result can be seen in, and is in part explained by, the emergence of a type of liberal argument and practice quite different from the Anglo-American model. Alongside, and often inseparable from, the liberal protest against power and the demand for a public sphere came a form of politics intended to distinguish friends from enemies: Politics became in fact what Carl Schmitt argues it in essence always is.[16] Here, the dominant political metaphor is that of the battlefield rather than the marketplace, and domestic politics may be thought of in part as the continuation of civil war by other means. If Marat preached the politics of exclusion in caricatural form, Robespierre deployed it in all its tragic grandeur.

The politics of exclusion will be examined in the chapters that follow, and this is not the place for a concluding argument. It is nonetheless crucial to place the politics of exclusion—and so also Robespierre, its most striking proponent and practitioner—within the framework of liberalism. At certain moments, some Jacobin leaders did speak of and seek to use their club as later leaders of political parties would speak of the revolutionary vanguard. As the Terror intensified, the Jacobins' tendency to treat human nature as a raw

---

[16] See Carl Schmitt, *The Concept of the Political*, trans. by George Schwab (New Brunswick, N. J.: Rutgers University Press, 1976). *Der Begriff des Politischen* was first published in 1932. Schmitt was sympathetic to the Nazi cause.

material in need of purification and careful molding did become increasingly deadly. Yet to view the Jacobins as protototalitarians both distorts the eighteenth-century record and prejudices the analyst's chances of understanding why twentieth-century France, for all its exclusionary politics, never succumbed to a native brand of real totalitarianism, of either the left-wing or the right-wing variety.[17] The supply side of the equation generally offered the option, but on the right, as on the left, demand was never sufficient.

Two underlying attitudes shaped Robespierre's politics; each built on the fundamental planks of the liberal platform. The first was his consuming hatred of the privatized world created by Old Regime politics; Robespierre held that world responsible for the humiliation and moral degradation of the individual. The second was an acute fear of power. Because each element was crucial and because they were asserted simultaneously, Jacobinism could serve as the basis for a form of liberalism. This form of liberalism established its ascendancy during the revolutionary period and subsequently shaped French political development.

The revolutionary indictment of the Old Regime,[18] common to moderates as well as to Jacobins, is summarized in a series of contrasts drawn by Robespierre in a speech on political morality and the administration of the Republic. The Old Regime cultivated personal dependence; its revolutionary opponents wanted individuals to stand as independent moral agents. If Robespierre's passion on this score sets him apart from the more measured tones of Anglo-American liberalism, the distinction is a reflection not of a disagreement over principles, but of the different world the French revolutionaries had to face. Speaking before the Convention in early 1794, Robespierre recalled the fundamental task of the Revolution:

> We want to substitute, in our country, morality for egotism, probity for honor, principles for customs, duty for propriety, the rule of reason for

[17] For recent analyses that explore the totalitarian implications of Jacobinism, see François Furet, *Penser la Révolution française* (Paris: Gallimard, 1978); and Ferenc Fehér, *The Frozen Revolution: An Essay on Jacobinism* (Cambrige: Cambridge University Press, 1987). See also Lucien Jaume, *Le Discours jacobin et la démocratie* (Paris: Fayard, 1989).

[18] Throughout the book, the reader will find "Old Regime" used to indicate specifically the prerevolutionary period in France, while "old regime" indicates the general type of prerevolutionary status quo common to England, America, and France. Similarly, "Jacobinism" refers to the revolutionary group of which Robespierre eventually became the leader, while "jacobinism" refers to an enduring political tradition. On the many meanings of Jacobinism, see Mona Ozouf, "L'Héritage jacobin: Fortune et infortunes d'un mot," in "L'Héritage jacobin," in *Le Débat*, no. 13, June 1981, pp. 28–39.

the tyranny of fashion, disdain for vice for disdain for misfortune, self-respect for insolence, spiritual grandeur for vanity, love of glory for love of money, good men for good company, merit for intrigue, genius for wit, truth for brilliance, the charm of happiness for the boredom of sensual pleasure, human greatness for the pettiness of the great, a magnanimous, powerful, happy people for an easy, frivolous, and miserable people, in sum, all the virtues and all the miracles of the Republic for all the vices and all the absurdities of the monarchy.[19]

Robespierre did not want to turn Frenchmen into regimented Spartans or indoctrinated party militants; that is not what he and the Jacobins meant when they talked about virtue, and it was not the goal of the terror they openly advocated and increasingly employed. Like the moderates to their "right," the Jacobins demanded for their countrymen the opportunity to be modern citizens in a democratic state. Whereas the moderates thought that end was within reach and could be achieved through the gradual consolidation of more discretely delineated rights, the Jacobins felt it required a frontal assault on the old order. They thus were led to attack a mode of collective life, which they could define in words but could not locate precisely in reality. Their inability to locate it only exacerbated their fears, fed their belief in conspiracy, and helped justify in their own eyes the harsh treatment of their opponents, whom they set up as symbols of all that they execrated.[20]

Persuaded that any person or group possessing any power could be safely assumed to be turning that power to private advantage, the Jacobins pushed the liberal fear of power to unprecedented lengths. They suspected *all* political power: not just that of hereditary monarchs and titled aristocrats, but that of representative assemblies, of magistrates, of anyone who had any power at all and who as a result of holding power would almost inevitably become an "aristocrat." The only individuals above suspicion were those without any power or public ambition, persons who had rights and nothing more. "The people"—the pivotal image of Jacobin discourse—therefore by definition refers to a population without a recognized public presence, incapable of true representation, since even elected deputies will not be above the treachery engendered by native self-interest.

The Jacobin world is one in which the Hobbesian account of hu-

---

[19] *Oeuvres de Maximilien Robespierre*, vol. 10 (Paris: Presses universitaires de France, 1967), p. 352.

[20] See George Armstrong Kelly, *Victims, Authority, and Terror: The Parallel Deaths of d'Orléans, Custine, Bailly, and Malesherbes* (Chapel Hill: University of North Carolina Press, 1982).

man psychology is accepted. Under such circumstances, Lockeian government is a very risky proposition. The paradox constantly encountered by the revolutionary practitioners of the politics of exclusion lay in the conflict between their desire to create a public world of responsible politics and their near-inability to supply that minimal trust without which community and thus public life are impossible.[21] The Jacobins retained representative institutions as the least menacing form of government, but instead of the politics of transaction, representative politics here was a politics based on suspicion and self-defense, very talky, very ideological, and extremely vulnerable to extraparliamentary and antiparliamentary attack.

With the Jacobin victory, political fragmentation and polarization took a quantum leap forward: While the Jacobins in fact multiplied the factions they so feared by suspecting everyone and preventing the open organization of groups around either common interests or common ideas, their ostentatious and often lethal repression of what amounted to crimes of opinion deepened ideological cleavages. Here, conspiracy theories—the common stock of political explanation in eighteenth-century England and America, as well as in France— proved comparatively impervious to the eventual advances of the social sciences. This was in part because the assumed existence of conspiracies and conspirators defined the function of the uncorrupted representative: His role was not to articulate and promote interests (for then he would inevitably slip into the exclusive pursuit of his own), but to defend revolutionary purity and unmask potential traitors. Nationalism became the sidearm of partisan political allegiances; instead of a unitary sense of national identity, the politics of exclusion engendered competing and sometimes incompatible conceptions of the "real" France.

In their efforts to secure their vision of the Revolution against its domestic and foreign foes (real or imagined), the Jacobins contributed to the construction of a centralized state and to the elaboration of an ideology in which the state assumed the task and received the credit for conceiving, guiding, and enforcing the general interest. The Jacobins thus adapted and handed down to their "jacobin" descendants institutional and mental habits they had themselves acquired from the Old Regime. That legacy nonetheless thereafter bore their mark; left to themselves, the Bourbons would obviously have constructed a rather different kind of centralized state. The

---

[21] Cf. John Dunn's examination of Locke's views on trust in " 'Trust' in the Politics of Locke," in Dunn, *Rethinking Modern Political Theory* (Cambridge: Cambridge University Press, 1985), pp. 34–53.

state the Jacobins helped build emerged as the peculiar product of men profoundly distrustful of all political power and organization. The jacobin tradition reinforced centralization, but with less partisan results than might have been expected, for in the process the Anglo-American arrangement was all but inverted. In France, it was the bureaucracy that got things done, outside of the political limelight and in spite of political turmoil: It sheltered the often secret and always essential world of bargaining and transaction that seconded the open world of intransigent ideological debate.[22]

Finally, from one end of the political spectrum to the other, the politics of exclusion sponsored an enduring nostalgia for moral unanimity and a deep-seated aversion to politics. In this account, in a well-constituted society, politics would represent a very minor activity. Politics would be a one-shot deal: After all the enemies had at last been turned out of the city, the friends would gather in a grand meeting of like-minded individuals, not to organize competition but to celebrate community. Reinforced on the right by the antipolitical prejudices of Catholic corporatism, on the left this view led revolutionaries and republicans to the elaboration of a theory of community in which diversity and competition are usually accommodated as awkward afterthoughts. A free people basks in harmony, and individual autonomy is simply asserted to be compatible with the vitality of a common identity. Here, civics rather than politics appears as the idealized mode of public behavior, with conflict constantly forced from sight. The theory's nineteenth-century apologist was not Mill or even Tocqueville, but Durkheim.[23]

Roughly summarized, this is the pattern of politics which I call the politics of exclusion, and when Robespierre was overthrown and hurriedly executed at the end of July 1794, it easily survived its first test. The Thermidorian Republic, which followed the Terror, was a deliberate attempt to recover a moderate option. It failed miserably, despite its architects' abandon of the more exacting forms of Jacobin ideology. Before Bonaparte pulled the curtain on the Revolution,[24]

[22] The classic related work remains Michel Crozier, Le Phénomène bureaucratique (Paris: Le Seuil, 1963).

[23] See Emile Durkheim, L'Education morale (Paris: Presses universitaires de France, 1974). The lectures which comprise the book were given by Durkheim at the Sorbonne in 1902–1903. For an analysis of Durkheim's effort to reconcile individualism and the need for community, see Anne Sa'adah, "Liberalism and the Republican Impulse: Learning Duty in a Liberal Society," in Murray Milgate and Cheryl B. Welch, eds., Critical Issues in Social Thought (London: Academic Press/Harcourt Brace Jovanovich, 1989), pp. 113–37.

[24] Napoleon himself preferred a different metaphor: "We have finished the novel of the Revolution: we must begin its history, looking only to what is real and possible in

post-Thermidor France staged a dress rehearsal of subsequent national experiments in representative politics. All the key features of later crises are there: pervasive, fundamental, and highly articulated ideological differences; a fragmented, poorly organized political class; strident antiparliamentarism; electoral manipulation and political violence; an active and growing bureaucracy; a parliament paralyzed before the future and preoccupied by the past; and a precarious sense of national cohesion. Bonaparte himself has his place in this pattern (and he, too, would have later counterparts): a military hero in a country where the military traditionally stays out of politics, restoring the external prestige and the authority of the state but without posing as a counterrevolutionary, heaping scorn on all forms of ideology but accommodating individualism, and ruling—or claiming to rule—above politics.

We are still in the 1790s, but we could be in the 1880s, the 1930s, or the 1950s. In France, as in England and America, the system—a different system—worked. Repeated crises, symbols on one level of chronic political instability, were on another level an integral part of a stable pattern of political life.

Methodological Choices

The events analyzed and many of the questions posed in this book are the common property of the countless men and women who have tried to understand the events since they took place. Clearly, this is not the first book about a hitherto obscure or unknown but arguably important historical event or development. Nor is it based on previously unavailable or neglected sources. If it proves useful, it will be because it approaches common sources and questions from an angle not commonly adopted. It was not written "against" any other interpretation of or approach to the developments it examines. Rather, the book is intended as a contribution to the collective and cooperative endeavor through which men and women attempt to understand their past and take charge of the present.

While the book was not written against any other book or body of literature, it does depend on the acceptance of a number of fundamental methodological choices, which other writers might wish to contest. Those choices concern the viability and validity of compara-

the application of principles and ignoring what is speculative and hypothetical. To follow any other path today would be to philosophize and not to govern." Napoleon to the Conseil d'Etat, November 1800; in Napoleon, *Vues politiques* (Americ = Edit., 1939), p. 46.

tive political studies, and the problem of causal explanations of political events. The proof of a methodological pudding is always in the eating, but a few preliminary remarks may be useful. In the process of specifying the assumed advantages and admitted limits of comparative analysis, we can bring what is being compared in the chapters that follow into sharper focus. In discussing the problem of political explanation, we can define important terms and relationships, freeing the text itself of such encumbrances.

The Liberal Route to Modernity: A Comparative Perspective

Some years ago, Oscar and Mary Handlin wrote:

> The events in the Paris of 1789 bore surface similarities to those in the Philadelphia of 1776; and participants on both sides of the Atlantic, for a time, even considered the one sequence a continuation of the other. But the characters, the courses, and the outcomes of the two revolutions have meaning only in terms of the different political and social systems in which they emerged and at which they were directed. Revolution was not a phenomenon with a generic quality of its own; it was an incident in the life of a particular society.[25]

More readily perhaps than most political scientists, this writer might be willing to entertain the appeal away from comparative study implicit in the Handlins' remarks. This book is, however, predicated on the belief that a comparative approach can respect the Handlins' basic concerns, complementing and completing the insights their more narrow focus would yield, without distorting the historical record or slipping into superficiality. While revolutions (like other forms of collective action) certainly "have meaning . . . in terms of the different political and social systems in which they [emerge] and at which they [are] directed," it is not "only" in such terms that revolutions have meaning. It need not always be useful to assume that a particular form of society coincides with and is limited to a particular country.

[25] Oscar Handlin and Mary Handlin, eds., *The Popular Sources of Political Authority: Documents on the Massachusetts Constitution of 1780* (Cambridge, Mass.: Harvard University Press, 1966), p. 2. The Handlins were presumably responding in part to the thesis developed by Crane Brinton in *The Anatomy of Revolution* (New York: Knopf, 1938, 1952, 1965), and to the approach adopted by R. R. Palmer in *The Age of the Democratic Revolution* (Princeton: Princeton University Press, 1959, 1964) and by Jacques Godechot in *La Grande Révolution: l'Expansion révolutionnaire de la France dans le monde, 1789–99* (Paris: Aubier, 1956).

History is composed of facts: France exists; the events we classify under the heading of the French Revolution occurred. Historical facts do not, however, speak straightforwardly for themselves—either to contemporaries or to later observers. Analytical historians and political scientists devise intellectual constructions, some more abstract than others, in order to sift and shuffle the facts into a story which allows the storyteller and his or her audience to assign a meaning (usually one meaning among several possible meanings) to the events under scrutiny.[26] The story then begins to make sense, either because the analyst has recovered the categories of meaning within which the events took place and the causal regularities that linked one event to another, or because he or she has used the events as a foil to explore contemporary categories of meaning.[27] In this book, intellectual constructions like "liberal politics," the "liberal state," and "liberal revolution" will be used to elucidate events and to uncover and explicate patterns that cut across events. Because it appears that some of these patterns cut across time (as well as national boundaries), we can hope that the categories of meaning we recover in examining the past will tell us something about the categories of meaning that are the currency of contemporary Western political life.

In essence, this book is about what we might call the "liberal route to modernity." The topic assumes that England, America, and France were at the time of their revolutions, and have since remained, meaningfully comparable societies, and that the revolutions themselves are usefully comparable events. At a certain point in historical time, a certain type of sociopolitical system came under concerted pressure from a similar combination of economic, intellectual, and political developments. Responses varied, with politics tending toward the mode of exclusion or transaction, but similarities of goals and outcomes outweighed variations in how the goals were conceived and the outcomes achieved, and both the similarities and the variations are best analyzed in a comparative context.

There are many ways of differentiating between the premodern world and modernity.[28] The archetypical premodern, or "tradi-

[26] The most accessible and perhaps classic account of the contrast between narrative and analytical historical writing is given by Isaiah Berlin in *The Hedgehog and the Fox: An Essay on Tolstoy's View of History* (New York: Simon and Schuster, 1953).

[27] Examples of the first sort of historical writing abound, and many will be used later in this book. Michael Walzer's introduction to *Regicide and Revolution: Speeches at the Trial of Louis XVI* (Cambridge: Cambridge University Press, 1974) represents an interesting combination of the two approaches.

[28] For a recent analysis which incorporates many of the insights of the great nineteenth-century social theorists and focuses on the question of political development, see Samuel Beer, "Modern Political Development," in Samuel Beer et al., *Patterns of*

tional," society is usually defined in reference to a set of economic, demographic, political, and cultural traits, and our view of it seems in large part shaped by our perceptions of the demographically secure world of interacting, industrializing, urbanizing nation-states that in the West replaced it. The world most of humankind has now lost[29]—in fact or (more often) in expectation—was composed of rural, agricultural, autarkic societies. The mass of the population was engaged in subsistence farming, and even the privileged classes were terribly vulnerable to the demographic catastrophes periodically provoked by bad weather and poor harvests. All authority was personal, and although its sources were diverse, it was not conferred by office or derived from the arguments of rational science. Interactions were shaped by a low level of social and political mobilization and territorial integration, all due in part to the difficulties of transportation and communication.

"Great transformations,"[30] be their focus political, socioeconomic, or cultural, do not take place overnight. It is probably impossible to knit into a tight causal explanation all the complex long- and short-term processes that brought the three countries examined here to the brink of systemic crisis. To various degrees and in different ways, prerevolutionary England, America, and France had already departed significantly from the model sketched above, while important vestiges of "premodern" forms of collective life would persist well into the postrevolutionary period. It was nonetheless within the outlines of traditional society that liberal revolution identified its primary targets. The actual shape of those targets makes the old regime a particular type of premodern society; the way the attack was conceived, considered together with the type of society contested and the type of polity proposed, defines liberal revolution as a particular type of revolution.

Two constituent elements of the old regime condemned it in the eyes of its adversaries. The first was the fusion and confusion of the social, political, and religious realms; the second was what appeared to revolutionaries as the old regime's increasingly deliberate suppression of a public world.

Our political world is secular. Our society accepts the existence of

Government: The Major Political Systems of Europe, 3d ed. (New York: Random House, 1973). See also Samuel P. Huntington, *Political Order in Changing Societies* (New Haven: Yale University Press, 1968).

[29] The reference is to Peter Laslett's book, *The World We Have Lost*, 2d ed. (New York: Charles Scribner's Sons, 1965, 1971).

[30] The reference is to Karl Polanyi's book, *The Great Transformation: The Political and Economic Origins of Our Time* (Boston: Beacon Press, 1944).

multiple hierarchies of power and influence that do not coincide, and we distinguish clearly between different types of authority and obligation. The old regime presented a radically different picture. Political authority drew upon religious sources to establish its own legitimacy, the state could of right (though not in fact) interfere in the most diverse areas of collective and private life, and the expectation was that social prestige and political power were inseparable. The first aim of liberal revolution was to untangle the different spheres of human activity and then to curtail sharply the coercive powers available to any sphere. The intended beneficiary was the individual, conceived to have inalienable—and enforceable—rights. Among the most conspicuous and immediate targets of the revolution were established religion, all shades of political absolutism, and mercantilist economic policies. The pivotal institution of the new political order was the representative assembly.

Democratic ideology, like its nationalist progeny and its totalitarian perversions, posits, channels, and exploits the political and social mobilization of an entire society. Liberal revolution does something else: It creates a public world. The old regime was a world of privilege: of private law and particularism, of private liber*ties* rather than of public liberty. What we call public affairs were considered instead to be matters of state, and information concerning them was privileged information. In the process of policy determination, men spoke when they were spoken to (and the circle of those who might be consulted was not only narrowly but also somewhat arbitrarily circumscribed); in fact, under prerevolutionary French statutes, it was held treasonous to discuss state affairs except at the invitation of the monarch.[31] The royal person had once effectively symbolized the public realm. When that symbolism cracked, the ruling circles of the old regime could only appear as they appeared to Robespierre: He saw them as decadent, intriguing, private cliques masquerading as a state and precluding by their very existence the definition and defense of the common good.[32] Only in a state governed by publicly elaborated laws can the public interest prevail, wrote Rousseau; there only, in a republic, "la chose publique est quelque chose."[33] Liberal revolution implied freedom of speech, freedom of the press, and the right of citizens peace-

---

[31] "Are considered guilty of *lèse majesté* in the second degree [punishable by death] . . . those who, without power or mandate from the prince, gather to deliberate on the affairs of the state, under the pretext of the public good, or any other pretext." Guyot, *Répertoire universel et raisonné de jurisprudence civile, criminelle, canonique et bénéficiale* (Paris: J. D. Dorez, 1775), article on "lèse-majesté," vol. 36, p. 194.

[32] See Michael Walzer's introductory essay in *Regicide and Revolution*.

[33] J. J. Rousseau, *Du contrat social*, II, 6.

ably to assemble. The new public world embraced all individuals who accepted their obligations to the state and who satisfied eighteenth-century notions of personal independence. The resulting citizenry debated issues, reviewed public policy, and held its "public servants" to account. The state, freed from corporate claims, concentrated its limited power on matters of recognized general interest.

Perhaps the most important single statement that can be made about England, America, and France is that in each country, the protection of individual rights lies at the center of the political system. In a manner to be explained in a moment, I have assumed that the English Revolution of the mid-seventeenth century and the American and French revolutions of the late eighteenth century were critical to that outcome. "Liberal revolution" is a useful concept because it points our attention toward the common political zone where rapid and radical change was taking place and because it effectively sets these three revolutions and these three countries apart from other revolutions and other countries. It will permit us to ask under what conditions, in the past and given a certain social, economic, and political setting, politics gained autonomy (that is, became disassociated from certain tasks and issues) and political power was subjected to effective limits. This question appears related to the problem of what conditions permit a finite political revolution. Both questions should allow us to understand how an "unfinished" revolution—the French one—nonetheless resulted in a state and society respectful of individual rights.

These are of course the same questions we often ask as we observe our own unsettled world. When the Shah of Iran fell and his regime disintegrated, it sometimes seemed that *Le Monde* of 1979 was telling a tale very similar to that related by *Le Moniteur* of the early 1790s. There are parallels, just as there are parallels between the French Revolution and the Russian and Chinese Revolutions. I have chosen not to draw them: in part because my primary interest is in liberal politics and the concrete political histories of England, America, and France, and in part out of the conviction that such parallels tend to be more compelling on the descriptive level than revealing on the analytical level.[34]

A great divide separates those societies which invented modernity in the eighteenth century from those grasping toward a revised version of it in the twentieth century. The disinterested study of the past cannot but serve as an aid in deciphering the present, but the aid will

[34] For another view, see Theda Skocpol, *States and Social Revolutions: A Comparative Analysis of France, Russia, and China* (Cambridge: Cambridge University Press, 1979).

more likely be methodological than substantive. Studying societies removed in time or space from our own is like learning foreign lan-
guages: The second and succeeding ones usually come more easily
than did the first. We cannot hope for more because "development"
is not, any more than is revolution, "a phenomenon with a generic
quality of its own." While economic modernization—industrialization
and increased technological sophistication—is, in its gross outlines,
unambiguously directional and probably, for all the reasons Marx
discerned, unavoidable, political modernization is a misleading concept. The only constants of political "modernization" would appear
to be those changes linked to technological and economic advances:
the social and political mobilization of the population, a vast increase
in the repressive potential of even an unorganized state (Uganda under Idi Amin would be a recent example), and—today—a high degree of vulnerability to a wide range of outside forces. Without extended reference to the particular society, little else can be
understood, let alone predicted. This, then, is not a book about revolutionary politics in general, or about how liberal outcomes were obtained in countries that got there later or by different routes, but
more modestly (all things being relative) about the shaping of liberal
politics in revolutionary England, France, and America.

Explaining Events

The adoption of a comparative approach tells us little about how we
should proceed in trying to account for specific political events. A
number of strategies are available to anyone intent on explaining why
some particular outcome obtained to the exclusion of other conceivable outcomes. Each strategy weights a different type of causal factor:
culture, legal and political arrangements, social structures and economic organization, human will, external pressures. The analyst may
bring different strategies to bear on the same event, or switch from
one strategy to another as the object of explanation shifts; he or she
may claim that the factors cited made the outcome under examination inevitable or, more cautiously, assert that they made the outcome
likely.

Viewed in the short run or over the long haul, liberal outcomes of
the sort we can observe in France, England, and America constitute
a complex political result. It should come as no surprise if their
causes turn out to be multiple, complex, and occasionally ambiguous.
The explanatory strategy adopted in this book will therefore be res-
olutely multicausal rather than monocausal, and the claim will be

that certain causes made certain outcomes very probable, but rarely inevitable.

THE ROLE OF IDEOLOGY

Although multicausal, the explanations presented will often turn on a reading of revolutionary ideology. Ideology will appear in the pages that follow as the catalyst through which other, more basic but often more diffuse causes became politically operational. Ideology, in other words, mediates between multiple "structural" causes and the actual choices made by historical actors.

Ideology is a disputed and often slippery concept, and the central role it plays in the arguments developed here invites more extended responses to three questions: What is ideology? How can we reconstitute the ideology of a given historical group? What role should references to ideology play in an explanation of some political outcome?

One way of defining ideology is by contrasting it to its cousin, political philosophy. Political philosophy addresses a series of questions about the nature of political authority, legitimacy, obligation, and action. It may fairly be judged on purely intellectual criteria—for the consistency of its propositions, the depth and breadth of its vision, and the adequacy of its epistemological foundations. The questions a political philosopher poses and the answers he or she supplies will retain meaning (the omission of the possessive article is deliberate— the meaning retained may not be the one the philosopher intended) across the boundaries of time and space because the questions considered are inherent to conscious collective life and cannot be definitively answered.

Political ideology is distinguished from political philosophy by the essential character of its relationship to political action: Political ideology is inseparable from the political project of a political actor (individual or group). Its function is to contribute to the realization of a specified political goal: It must confer on its adherents a sense of shared purpose and shared destiny; it must reassure them that their efforts have meaning; and it must provide them with a guide to action. An ideology normally fulfills these requirements through a series of propositions. An ideological construction begins with some representation of what politics is and how it relates to other human activities, positing in the process a specific view of human nature. Secondly, it offers an account of political causation and, with the account, a portrait of the world as it was, is, and should be that includes an explanation of each transition. Thirdly, it specifies key political agents (for example, "the people," the proletariat, Jews, political parties) and the political roles they play in promoting or thwarting the passage from the world-as-it-is to the world-as-it-should-be. Finally, it suggests and justifies (for example, as effective, as morally right, as both effective and right) a political strategy, together with the political means (for example, electoral competition, civil disobedience, the dictatorship of the proletariat) the strategy appears to require. To this it must be added that an ideology is never fully controlled by those who elaborate or use it, and it rarely succeeds in resisting penetration by competing ideologies. This is particularly likely to be the case in a revolutionary situation.

The distinction between ideology and philosophy is not one that normally separates one thinker or one text from another: Most thinkers and most texts do double duty. Marx offers an obvious example of a thinker whose works may be read either as philosophy or as ideology; Locke offers a similar example closer to the concerns of this book. The distinction is determined not by the intentions of the author (supposing that we could be sure of what those intentions were) or even by the intellectual quality of his or her work, but by the manner in which a given text is received. To read Locke primarily as he may have been read by his political comrades, as a harassed radical ideologist constantly on the run, trivializes his philosophical contributions, but may substantially enhance our understanding of Restoration politics; to read him as a primary philosophical exponent of liberalism may help us understand liberal political development and our own political commitments, but it distorts our vision of what was happening in England during the last third of the seventeenth century. Both readings are valid and valuable; both are of course available[35] and both will be exploited in the chapters that follow.

By acknowledging that a single text may serve as both philosophy and ideology, we improve our chances of reconstituting the contemporary meaning and impact of an ideology. In order to identify and understand the ideological currents that shape political conflict and cohesion at any given point in historical time, we must recover the "language(s)" in which men and women discussed politics.[36] We must

[35] Among the books recently published on Locke, Richard Ashcraft's (*Revolutionary Politics and Locke's "Two Treatises of Government"* [Princeton: Princeton University Press, 1986]) focuses on Restoration politics; John Colman's (*John Locke's Moral Philosophy* [Edinburgh: Edinburgh University Press, 1983]) focuses on philosophical questions; and John Dunn's (*The Political Thought of John Locke: An Historical Account of the Argument of the "Two Treatises of Government"* [Cambridge: Cambridge University Press, 1969] and *Locke* [Oxford: Oxford University Press, 1984]), try to remain sensitive to both sets of concerns.

[36] For an explanation and defense of this approach, see in particular J.G.A. Pocock, "The State of the Art," in J.G.A. Pocock, *Virtue, Commerce, and History* (Cambridge:

watch, read, and listen to our actors—Robespierre or Cromwell or
Adams—from different perspectives: contemporary and removed,
hostile and sympathetic. Only when we have carefully unpacked the
key terms of political debate—property, "the people," liberty, "aristocrats"—and explored what our actors could *not* say as well as what
they did say will we be able to evaluate their perception of their political options. Only then will we understand why they acted as they did
and why the consequences that "followed" did indeed follow.

In trying to piece together an explanation of why a series of political events occurred, I will be less concerned with the ultimate sources
of an ideology than with its political impact and its evolution in a
given sociopolitical setting. To chase after ultimate sources is in this
case to court failure: It seems unlikely today that anyone would maintain that ideological constructions hatch fully formed from the heads
of intellectuals immune to contextual factors, and we have already
rejected an understanding of ideology that would define the latter as
a simple "reflection" of some specifiable set of structural givens. I will
therefore restrict my ambitions on this score to explicating why some
emerging ideological formulations seemed more compelling to contemporaries than did other available formulations.

If the ultimate sources of an ideology are too elusive to be worth
pursuing, ideology itself can be used as an independent variable in
explaining political events. The methodological assumption here is
that ideology plays a critical role in determining what political actors
do and how effectively they manage to do it. Men and women will
not consciously adopt a strategy in open conflict with their articulated
goals, but they will also not perceive a choice if the alternatives theoretically available to them are ruled out by their beliefs about political
causation. They may therefore be "forced" to act in ways that produce consequences they never intended. Their political effectiveness
will depend on their ability to impose their vision of reality, and with
it their political agenda and their script for the political present and
future, on other relevant political actors. The more convincing their
vision of reality, the stronger the cohesion within their own camp and
the more complete the docility (or the despair) of their competitors:
Ideological hegemony confers both perceived legitimacy and a certain ability to control, and to create, events.

The explanatory usefulness of ideology presupposes that choices
made by historical actors made a difference, that if structural factors

Cambridge University Press, 1985), pp. 1–34; cf. Georges Duby, "Histoire sociale et
idéologies des sociétés," in Jacques Le Goff and Pierre Nora, eds., *Faire l'histoire*, vol. 1,
Nouveaux problèmes (Paris: Gallimard, 1974), pp. 203–30.

were in some ultimate sense responsible for outcomes, ideology was
the crucial intermediate factor: It explains why men and women
acted as they did and why the results were what they were. A sensitiv-
ity to the role of ideology allows us to assess accurately the importance of individual actors, and to differentiate between anecdotally
amusing and analytically important motivations. It can (and will) be
argued that for structural reasons, moderate French revolutionaries
never had a chance. Their defeat is played out through the political
attitudes adopted and choices made by a series of individuals and
groups: Barnave, Duport, the Feuillants, the Girondins. Those attitudes and choices, like the responses they elicited, are explained by
the ideology of the actors. What is important about Barnave is not
that he may have developed a crush on the Queen, but that he could
not understand the arguments of Mirabeau. The latter point will retain our attention; the former episode will not. The terms of the
moderates' defeat and the reading men and women made of that defeat subsequently became part of the "structure" bequeathed to subsequent political actors—part of what shaped *their* ideology, their
chances, their fate. In a chronological chain of events, a dominant
ideology appears as part of the structural situation faced by the next
set of historical actors. The more impregnable its positions, the more
critical it becomes to any explanation of events; its presence is what
turns a chronological chain of events into a political pattern.

HISTORY PAST AND PRESENT

The revolutions in England, America, and France represent finite
historical episodes; as models of liberalism, the politics of transaction
and the politics of exclusion refer to political patterns that retain
their relevance through the postrevolutionary period. The chapters
that follow attempt to illuminate later developments by elaborating
an argument about early patterns. I would not presume to "explain,"
through two models and in a few hundred pages, the richly varied
postrevolutionary experiences of England, America, and France. I
would argue, however, that the analysis I propose of revolutionary
events gives us a particularly useful handle on postrevolutionary politics in these three countries.

   We all tend intuitively to assume that the present somehow follows
from the past. We all, that is, have some inclination to behave like one
of Isaiah Berlin's hedgehogs,[37] and to look at history as though it had

[37] In *The Hedgehog and the Fox*, Berlin derives his metaphor from a fragment by the
Greek poet Archilochus: "The fox knows many things, but the hedgehog knows one
big thing." Berlin distinguishes between "those [hedgehogs] . . . who relate everything

meaning and direction. Absent some general thesis regarding what history is "about" in the teleological sense, however, there is no necessary, direct, self-evident causal link between what we can observe in the twentieth century and what we know happened in the eighteenth century. The past does not "cause" the present in any simple, mechanical way; all by itself, history does not explain history. Even if confined to the experience of a specific country or group of countries, the indiscriminate appeal to history merely invites an unending spiral of references to a prior configuration of historical events. Unaided, it cannot explain the particular weight retrospectively acquired by different historical episodes.

History is a noun that is sometimes improperly used with the singular definite article. The past is not unique; of the many pasts on record for any single country or group of countries, the historian may pick whichever he or she finds interesting. The political scientist will pick whichever he or she can prove analytically useful. The past upon which I focus in this book is that bounded by liberal revolution. The reason is not simply the fact that the revolutions were extraordinarily disruptive and dramatic moments in the life of each nation (France would have other revolutions, and America a bloody civil war), nor is the assumption that the revolutions constitute a critical "hurdle," the successful passing of which would facilitate further advances in political development.[38] The reasons for my choice add up to something far less than a teleological view of even liberal historical development.

I have suggested that there are two basic forms of liberal politics. It was during the revolutionary decade that the politics of exclusion crystalized in France; likewise it was in revolutionary England and America, where the exclusionary model was circumvented, that the foundations were laid for the politics of transaction. Thus the objects of our analysis first emerged during the period of revolutionary strife

---

to a single central vision, one system less or more coherent or articulate, in terms of which they understand, think and feel—a single, universal, organizing principle in terms of which alone all that they are and say has significance—and, on the other side, those [foxes] who pursue many ends, often unrelated and even contradictory, connected, if at all, only in some *de facto* way, for some psychological or physiological cause, related by no single moral or aesthetic principle; these last lead lives, perform acts, and entertain ideas that are centrifugal rather than centripetal, their thought is scattered or diffused, moving on many levels, seizing upon the essence of a vast variety of experiences and objects for what they are in themselves, without, consciously or unconsciously, seeking to fit them into, or exclude them from, any one unchanging, all-embracing, sometimes self-contradictory and incomplete, at times fanatical, unitary inner vision" (pp. 1f.).

[38] Cf. Samuel P. Huntington, *Political Order in Changing Societies*, p. 13.

and creativity. It is within that context that we will be able to piece together a picture of the inner logic of each form of liberal politics. The logic we uncover will be more than a relic of the political past, for despite all that has changed in the three and a half centuries since Charles I raised his standard at Nottingham, we in the West still live in the political age inaugurated by the revolutions in England, America, and France. Liberal revolution established the agenda to which we continue to refer and against which we measure ourselves as citizens. This book provides a window on that agenda, differently defined and differently fulfilled in each of our three countries.

Chapter I examines the sources and shape of revolutionary moderation in England and America. Chapter II looks at why and with what consequences the moderates lost the leadership of the French Revolution. Jacobinism—the theory and practice of the politics of exclusion—is analyzed in Chapter III. Finally, Chapter IV returns to some of the more general problems raised by the three cases studied.

I

Another Route, a Different Liberty: Initial Options in England and America

> There was, then, a revolution in 1648–9. But perhaps it was not a real revolution, just a *coup d'etat*? It is certainly true that once in power the revolutionaries were oddly half-hearted about implementing the rest of their program. It is as though the Jacobins of the French Revolution, having ousted the Girondins and set up the Committee of Public Safety, immediately begin [sic] to display the caution of the Thermidorian reaction—without an intervening Thermidor.
> —*David Underdown*[1]

[American General Charles] Lee tried to see the Revolution as a consistent whole, with every aspect in rational harmony with every other. It was a fight by free men for their natural rights. Neither the fighters nor the goals were suited to the military techniques of despotism—the linear tactics, the rigid discipline, the long enlistments, the strict separation of the army from civic life that marked Frederick's Prussia. Lee envisioned a popular war of massive resistance, a war based on military service as an obligation of citizenship. . . .

. . . But to Washington . . . this was all madness. He never seriously considered resorting to a war of guerilla bands drawn from the militia. He would have recoiled with horror from such an idea. A strategy of that kind would change the war for independence into a genuine civil war with all its grisly attendants—ambush, reprisal, counter-reprisal. It would tear the fabric of American life to pieces. It might even undermine the political process, and throw power to a junta—a committee of public safety with a Lee, not a Washington, as its military member.

Historians have often noted that the American Revolution was a "conservative" revolution, with surprising stability of institutions and continuity of leadership. But few have noticed that it was also militarily conservative, and that its conventional strategy served as a buffer for American society and politics. If Washington's strategy had

[1] David Underdown, *Pride's Purge: Politics in the Puritan Revolution* (Oxford: Oxford University Press, 1971), p. 5.

failed, as it almost did in 1776, then the Revolution would have
collapsed or turned sharply leftward.
            —*John Shy*[2]

MODERN ANALYSTS of the English and American revolutions, their expectations and the very language of their analyses shaped by the record of the French Revolution and by the recurrent spectacle of anti-
colonial revolutions in our own day, have been as impressed by the
relative lethargy of Strafford's "sleeping lions" as the Earl himself
might have been had he been permitted to observe the political up-
heavals of mid-seventeenth-century England and revolutionary
America. In England and America, triumphant revolutions, instead
of pressing relentlessly forward toward ever-receding goals, turned
"cautious" and "conservative," both ideologically and tactically. The
embarrassed use of inappropriate adjectives—it is a contradiction in
terms to label a revolution "conservative"—simply highlights the pe-
culiarity of the cases. While it is not historically unusual for a revolution to rally its first forces around a set of political demands, it is rare
indeed for a revolution to display at its conclusion that same emphasis.

The English and American revolutions began and ended as con-
tests between competing definitions of legitimate political authority
and diverging visions of political order. When compared to revolutions whose social dimensions were more directly and immediately
significant, they represent not a truncated form of revolutionary experience, but a different type of revolution. It is precisely because
they exemplify a type of revolution that they are interesting, for they
raise theoretical problems of enormous consequence to students of
revolution and political development. This chapter proposes a first
historical response to the broad set of theoretical questions discussed
in the Introduction. In England and America, revolutionary forces
triumphed in a manner that fostered the development of political stability. Why?

Seventeenth-century England and revolutionary America (1763–
1789) were, in many significant ways, quite different places, and the
revolutions they witnessed differed in aspects more obviously crucial
than the amount of time each required: The American Revolution
was also a war of independence; the English Revolution was not. It

---

[2] John Shy, "American Strategy: Charles Lee and the Radical Alternative," in John
Shy, *A People Numerous and Armed: Reflections on the Military Struggle for American Independence* (New York: Oxford University Press, 1976), pp. 161f.

might even appear that Stuart England bears a greater resemblance to eighteenth-century France (where liberal revolution did *not* produce political stability) than to eighteenth-century America, for England and France in those periods still approximated "traditional" societies, whereas America in the years preceding its revolution already did not.[3] The apparent resemblance of England and France is in part illusory, and where it is real, it proves—and is helpful precisely because it proves—irrelevant to our problem. In order to define the model of liberal politics that emerged in England and America and to explain why and how it prevailed, I will focus on patterns of ideological cleavage and competition during the revolutionary period, the structure of revolutionary opportunity as determined by the nature and distribution of power before and during the revolution, and the language of liberty that expressed the victory of the revolutionary forces. Originally articulated around a certain concept of property and dependent upon a particular reading of the Bible, that language long outlived the circumstances of its birth.

The Revolutionary Debate: The Reduction of Ideological Distance

At stake in England from the 1620s to the 1690s, and in America from the 1760s to the 1790s, was, we now realize, nothing less than the locus of political sovereignty. No issue could be more basic to the political complexion of a country; no issue, one might therefore conclude, could be more likely to sustain a bitter and unyielding struggle between clearly defined and intransigent camps, with the logic of battle favoring extremists on both sides.

The issue of sovereignty was not decided peacefully in either England or America, but in part because the issue being decided was drawn too late, the crescendo of violence did not exceed certain bounds. In their own eyes, mid-century Englishmen were fighting for the "ancient constitution," not parliamentary supremacy, and articulate Americans went to war to defend their British liberties, not to proclaim popular sovereignty. But Royalists of the 1640s also protested their reverence for the ancient constitution, while the home government of the 1760s assured its far-flung colonies that their lib-

---

[3] For a discussion of eighteenth-century social trends in American society and the hypothetical effect of the Revolution on those trends, see Rowland Berthoff and John M. Murrin, "Feudalism, Communalism, and the Yeoman Freeholder: The American Revolution Considered as a Social Accident," in Stephen G. Kurtz and James H. Hutson, eds., *Essays on the American Revolution* (Chapel Hill: University of North Carolina Press, 1973), pp. 256–88.

erties were not under attack. Thus in England and America, revolutionaries and their opponents argued—the verb is deliberate, for they did indeed argue, in public and at great length—in a common language, around a shared set of broad ideals. Before the mid-1640s in England and right up until the Declaration of Independence in America, almost everyone professed to agree on what *should* happen in a healthy polity; they disagreed deeply over what was in fact happening in their own. Their demands were ostensibly similar, their fears radically different. Only when this disagreement led to war were they forced explicitly to rethink the foundations of legitimate power, that is, to address the problem of sovereignty. Only then were they obliged to admit that their "defensive" revolutions had brought innovation upon them. Yet even then, there was a fundamental continuity of values. The purpose of government—to protect men in their property and persons—remained the same; it was the modalities of its operation that shifted. That shift signaled a profound revolution, but the oblique manner in which it was introduced also made stability at least a possible corollary of transformation. Given the social and institutional setting in which the struggles took place, the war was in effect over before the battle began. Royalists and Loyalists, competing for the same ideological ground as their adversaries, were left with nowhere to stand; in each case, their attempts to develop a viable alternative ideology failed to persuade the audiences whose allegiances were crucial to political outcomes.

This argument requires development as well as qualification. We must show that in each country, a stable group of moderates articulating stable demands existed throughout the period of revolutionary tension and strife, and that this group successfully dictated its ideological terms to would-be extremists.

Such a group did exist in England: It is the "middle group" first identified by J. H. Hexter.[4] Many of its members ended up, as David Underdown has described them, "impaled between the dictates of Providence and gentry constitutionalism."[5] Their strength, but also their ambivalence, precluded the undiminished rule of the Saints, the representative democracy of the Levellers, and the imposition of absolutist doctrine by the monarchy (both before 1640 and then again after 1660). They, or at least their political principles, were the eventual victors of England's "century of revolution."[6] They initially shied

[4] J. H. Hexter, *The Reign of King Pym* (Cambridge, Mass.: Harvard University Press, 1941).

[5] Underdown, *Pride's Purge*, p. 337.

[6] The expression is Christopher Hill's, in *The Century of Revolution, 1603–1714* (New York: Norton, 1961). I am using it to emphasize that a definitive revolutionary settlement did not intervene in England until after the Glorious Revolution of 1688. I have

away from any systemic formulation of long-range goals, but by 1640 their grievances were already well rehearsed: The pivotal group of determined, practical men so ably led by John Pym during the first years of the Long Parliament could draw on the experience of a long generation of resistance to justify its acts and actions. Their interpretation of that record was a key step in the elaboration of their ideological positions.

In June of 1604—a bare fifteen months after James VI of Scotland became James I of England—the House of Commons had prepared a "Form of Apology and Satisfaction." The document was intended to set a "misinformed" monarch straight on a number of critical points. In unequivocal language, the "Apology" identified the rights and liberties of the whole Commons of England with the privileges of the House of Commons, and insisted that those rights and privileges were not enjoyed "of grace," but "are our right and due inheritance, no less than our very lands and goods."[7]

In 1610, the Commons presented a Petition of Grievances to their king. The people, the Commons asserted, "perceive their common and ancient right and liberty to be declined and infringed in these late years."[8] James I was not making random errors of judgment; to his critics in the Commons, the king's behavior now betrayed a definite pattern. The Petition was particularly eloquent in protesting impositions laid without consent of Parliament and justified by royal prerogative. It also protested the high-handed methods of the High Commission.[9]

Charles I, who succeeded James I in 1625, promptly showed himself as "misinformed" as his late father. The Petition of Right of 1628 again asserted that the Crown could impose neither loans nor levies without parliamentary consent. Citing precedent and waving the Magna Carta, the Commons informed the king that "no freeman may be taken or imprisoned or be disseised of his freehold or liberties or his free customs or be outlawed or exiled or in any manner de-

---

focused on the earlier revolutionary period (1640–1660) both because it was then that revolutionary demands were formulated and because it was then that radical forces stood the best chance of wresting political control from the moderates.

[7] Text of the "Apology" in J. R. Tanner, ed., *Constitutional Documents of the Reign of James I* (Cambridge: Cambridge University Press, 1931), pp. 217–31. Quote appears on p. 221. For an appraisal of this document, see J. H. Hexter, *Reappraisals in History*, 2d ed. (Chicago: University of Chicago Press, 1979), pp. 195–218.

[8] Text in J. P. Kenyon, ed., *The Stuart Constitution* (Cambridge: Cambridge University Press, 1966), p. 71.

[9] The early Stuarts used the High Commission in their attempts to enforce religious conformity and Star Chamber to enforce both religious and fiscal policy. Both courts were abolished by the Long Parliament in 1641.

stroyed, but by the lawful judgement of his peers or by the law of the land."[10] The protesters were purportedly demanding only what was their due; in their own eyes, they asked for no reforms: Thus was this a petition "of right."

The battle over the interpretation of precedent and the protection of rights continued during the eleven years of Charles I's personal government, with property and religion always the issues around which conflicting claims were articulated. Future middle group positions were elaborated in the courts, as in the important Ship Money case of 1638, in Star Chamber, and before Archbishop Laud's High Commission. In each instance they gained for having been clearly and forcefully stated and repeated defeat merely heightened the sense of urgency felt by those who lost.

Thus when, in May 1641, the Commons discerned "endeavours to subvert the fundamental laws of England and Ireland, and to introduce the exercise of an arbitrary and tyrannical government by most pernicious and wicked counsels, practices, plots, and conspiracies,"[11] it was simply reiterating, in more acute form, the anxieties a broad segment of the English political class had been expressing, and to a certain extent cultivating, for nearly forty years. Since the king could do no wrong—a fiction patently false but highly useful to men still insistent on their loyalty to traditional forms and fearful of the turbulence which "remonstrating downward" might invite—the Grand Remonstrance (December 1641) supplied a list of plausible culprits and a long litany of their misdeeds. The Remonstrance reviewed the grievances cited by the Protestation (May 1641)—the "illegal taxations," "divers innovations and superstitions . . . brought into the Church," the tension between king and Parliament, and the threatening presence of an army—and attributed them to the wilfull machinations of "Jesuited Papists," "bishops, and the corrupt part of the clergy," and self-interested courtiers. To defuse the situation created by these evil men, the king needed only trust his[12] Parliament—and especially his House of Commons, for the presence of bishops and Catholic peers compromised the House of Lords.[13]

Two themes dominate pre-Restoration moderate discourse. The British subject had, the moderates claimed, an inherent, immemorial, and exclusive right to his property. Furthermore, the moderates de-

[10] Kenyon, ed., *Stuart Constitution*, p. 83.

[11] Ibid., p. 222.

[12] In its dealings with a monarch, the Commons habitually referred to itself as "your" House of Commons of "your" Parliament. The Remonstrance penned in May 1642 speaks a different language; see Kenyon, *Stuart Constitution*, pp. 242ff.

[13] Kenyon, *Stuart Constitution*, pp. 228ff.

manded that all God's Englishmen be allowed a fair shot at heaven. Both themes would resurface as key elements of mainstream Whig thought after 1660,[14] and both would be resolved to the moderates' satisfaction in the revolutionary settlement worked out in 1689. In the pre-Restoration period, moderate views on religion did not yet imply the defense of freedom of conscience even for Protestants, nor were the reformers in agreement concerning what changes should be implemented in the organization of religious life or how far such changes should go. General Puritan fervor was, however, reflected in a universal distrust of "Popery" that persisted long after Puritan zeal had dissipated. Catholicism was, to moderate eyes throughout the century, objectionable on political as well as religious grounds, for it inclined men and nations toward absolutism: The France of Louis XIV soon furnished a perfect illustration. As Shaftesbury put it in a speech to the Lords in 1679, "[P]opery and slavery, like two sisters, go hand-in-hand."[15]

Since the Stuarts spent too much, flirted with Catholicism, and talked up the royal prerogative, the moderates staked their hopes on Parliament, and more particularly on the House of Commons, where they were well represented. The moderates argued that Parliaments must be frequent and free; that Parliament alone could levy taxes; that laws could not be made without Parliament or, once made, set aside independently of Parliament; and that Parliament must exercise ultimate control over the military forces of the kingdom and be responsible for national policy in matters of religion. In the early part of the century, the House of Commons was still a parochial institution of parochial men, and so the moderates hoped it would remain: A watchdog Parliament would protect the insular, provincial world the moderates knew, and often dominated, against all hostile innovation and intervention.[16]

These positions, the moderates insisted, were consistent with the "ancient constitution." Their claims were erroneous, but in conformity with their conservative intentions. The moderates of the revolutionary period were not, as it turned out, the upholders of tradition.

---

[14] Cf. Richard Ashcraft on Whig ideology in the 1680s: "As a political movement seeking mass support, the Whigs structured their political arguments around the slogans No Popery, No Slavery and Liberty and Property" (*Revolutionary Politics and Locke's "Two Treatises of Government"* [Princeton: Princeton University Press, 1986], p. 185).

[15] Speech of March 25, 1679, quoted by Ashcraft, *Revolutionary Politics and Locke's "Two Treatises of Government,"* p. 203.

[16] A point emphasized by Alan Everitt, *The Community of Kent and the Great Rebellion, 1640–60* (Leicester: Leicester University Press, 1966).

The resistance they encountered led them to lay down the foundations of constitutional monarchy, and they became revolutionaries. They did, however, in their revolutionary careers, steer a middle course, for even within the established political class there were men to their "left" as well as to their right. John Pym's determination and legislative efforts made armed resistance to Charles I a realistic alternative to further and futile petitions, but Pym also had a fellow Member committed to the Tower when his colleague imprudently attacked monarchy from the floor of the House.[17] Oliver St. John, kinsman to Cromwell, helped spearhead the parliamentary cause after Pym's death, but declined to serve as Lord President of the High Court that presumed to try a king. Cromwell himself, whom William Haller places among the "pragmatic executive saints,"[18] stood on whatever middle ground he could find.[19]

As we shall see in the next section of this chapter, nonideological factors shaped the way the Civil War unfolded and made it highly unlikely that any group would be able to impose and maintain a constitutional settlement at odds with moderate goals. Yet the middle group's insistence on tradition and precedent lured its primary opponents onto dangerous terrain and significantly contributed to the moderation of both means and ends. A striking example of this moderating process may be found in that theoretically most radical act, the ostensibly legal execution of a reigning monarch. The middle group had disintegrated in 1648, making Army intervention possible.[20] Colonel Pride's famous Purge had placed moderates on notice that new winds were blowing.[21] The stage was set for a grand ideological confrontation. What actually happened was slightly disappointing.

[17] The colleague in question was the always feisty Henry Marten; on Marten, see C.M. Williams, "The Anatomy of a Radical Gentleman: Henry Marten," in Donald Pennington and Keith Thomas, eds., *Puritans and Revolutionaries: Essays in Seventeenth-Century History presented to Christopher Hill* (Oxford: Oxford University Press, 1978), pp. 118–38.

[18] William Haller, *Liberty and Reformation in the Puritan Revolution* (New York: Columbia University Press, 1955), p. xiv.

[19] Derek Hirst gives more space to this interpretation of Cromwell's position than does Haller; see Hirst, *Authority and Conflict: England, 1603–1658* (Cambridge, Mass.: Harvard University Press, 1986). Hirst portrays Cromwell as a moderate whose apparent ambivalence can be attributed to his equal attachment to the often contradictory imperatives of reform and stability.

[20] See Mark A. Kishlansky, *The Rise of the New Model Army* (Cambridge: Cambridge University Press, 1979).

[21] In addition to Underwood's *Pride's Purge*, see his essay " 'Honest' Radicals in the Counties, 1642–1649," in Pennington and Thomas, eds., *Puritans and Revolutionaries*, pp. 186–205.

Charles I, uninterested as he apparently was in saving his own skin, might have chosen to argue the divine right of kings. Had he so decided, he would not have been at a loss for arguments, nor would his arguments have been totally devoid of popular appeal. Charles' father, James I, in his *The Trew Law of Monarchies* and in his many impolitic speeches to his wary Parliaments, had taken such a position:

> Kings are justly called gods for that they exercise a manner or resemblance of divine power upon earth, for if you will consider the attributes to God you shall see how they agree in the person of a king. God hath the power to create or destroy, make or unmake, at his pleasure; to give life or send death, to judge all and to be judged not accountable to none; to raise low things and to make high things low at his pleasure; and to God are both soul and body due. And the like power have kings: they make and unmake their subjects; they have power of raising, and casting down; of life, and of death, judges over all their subjects, and in all causes, and yet accountable to none but God only. They have power to exalt low things, and abase high things, and make of their subjects like men at the chess—a pawn to take a bishop or a knight—and cry up or down any of their subjects, as they do their money. And to the king is due both the affection of the soul and the service of the body of his subjects.[22]

At his trial, Charles did not speak of any legitimate power to "make and unmake" his subjects; he spoke of nothing but the law and the freedom and liberty of the people of England—to whose protection his coronation oath committed him. The king was aware of the power the High Court held over him, for "there are many unlawful authorities in the world, thieves and robbers by the highways,"[23] but he steadfastly denied its legality and refused to plead until the Court's lawful authority be established to his satisfaction. Although in the practice of the day, refusal to answer a charge of treason was treated as a plea of guilty, the king's resolve could not be shaken:

> If it were only my own particular Case, I would have satisfied myself with the protestation I made the last time I was here . . . ; but it is not my case alone, it is the Freedom and Liberty of the people of England; and do you pretend what you will, I stand more for their Liberties. For if power without law may make laws, may alter the fundamental laws of the kingdom, I do not know what subject he is in England, that can be sure of his life, or any thing that he calls his own. . . .[24]

[22] Kenyon, *Stuart Constitution*, p. 13.
[23] W. Cobbett and T. B. Howell, eds., *A Complete Collection of State Trials* (London, 1908–1926), vol. IV, 995–96 (hereafter cited as *State Trials*).
[24] Ibid., p. 998.

John Bradshaw, Lord President of the Court, told Charles that the court acted "in the name of the people of England, of which you are elected King." Charles immediately and easily refuted the contention: ". . . England was never an elective kingdom, but an hereditary kingdom for these near thousand years." He would, Charles said, "stand as much for the privilege of the house of Commons, rightly understood, as any man here whatsoever," but he saw no Parliament in the court before which he had been brought: "I see no house of lords here . . . ; and the King too should have been."[25] And when Bradshaw again insisted that the judges sat "by the authority of the Commons of England, and all your predecessors and you are responsible to them," Charles shot back a familiar and unanswerable reply: "I deny that; shew me one precedent."[26] When finally Bradshaw felt that he had heard the king refer one time too many to the liberty and freedom of his subjects, the judge reprimanded his royal prisoner: "Sir, you are not to have Liberty to use this language: How great a friend you have been to the Laws and Liberties of the people, let all England and the world judge."[27]

Yet the language Bradshaw sought to deny Charles was in fact the language the king used, and he used it very skillfully indeed. It was no doubt in uncomfortable anticipation of hearing such familiar language deployed in such convincing fashion that Oliver St. John removed himself to the country rather than sit on the High Court. The persuasive quality of such language must also have motivated Lady Fairfax's two courtroom outbursts in the king's behalf. If Lady Fairfax was allowed to leave a courtroom packed with soldiers and return home unmolested, it was not because she happened to be the wife of the Lord General; his loyalties were at that moment suspect as well.[28] The Lord General and his Lady remained undisturbed because too many important people shared their opinions and because those people and indeed those opinions remained essential to the revolutionary enterprise as it continued to be understood by its leaders. Charles had been charged with treason, but the reason he had no right to invoke the freedom and liberties of Englishmen was not that such language was by definition inappropriate in the mouth of a king (as Saint-Just would later claim). Although Cromwell may have insisted on cutting the king's head off with the crown upon it,[29] Charles was

---

[25] Ibid., p. 996.

[26] Ibid., p. 999.

[27] Ibid., p. 1000.

[28] For an account of the trial, see C. V. Wedgwood, *The Trial of Charles I* (London: Collins, 1964). Lady Fairfax's outbursts are related on pp. 127f. and 154f.

[29] Cromwell is widely credited with having countered Algernon Sidney's objections

not on trial because he was king; he was on trial as "that man of blood,"[30] hopelessly duplicitous, responsible for a second civil war even more widely deplored than the first, an insurmountable obstacle to peace in a land aching for a return to tranquillity and prosperity. The court's theoretical pronouncements were sometimes weak (as when Bradshaw tried to argue the king's accountability and the preeminence of Parliament), but few men listening would have denied that Charles had, through his actions, tended toward arbitrary government and brought his kingdom to bloodshed.

Thus even the trial of the king did not destroy a certain community of political language and expectation. To advocate overtly anything other than a "return" to the system that had "always" served to guarantee what everyone knew government was supposed to guarantee—lives, liberties, and estates—was to jeopardize immediately one's support. Positions had to be backed up by precedent and grounded in established law, and people took such pains to show they had the law on their side that it is hard to believe they failed to notice that the law was on both sides.[31] Law could not decide the issue, for law was being redefined by the revolution in progress. Respect for law could nonetheless keep adversaries arguing until finally an accommodation emerged. Royalist insistence on an unbridled prerogative justified solely by divine right, or a whole-hearted and broadly based revolutionary rejection (by the Levellers or the Saints) of arguments referring to precedent and the ancient constitution, would in effect have rendered debate impossible and made all-out exclusion (through wholesale disregard for civil rights, imprisonment and execution, draconian censorship, and civil war itself) the only policy realistically open to either side. The reason all the parties to the long constitutional conflict (and a similar argument could be applied to the religious disputes among English Protestants) *could* argue at such length, instead of just, or constantly, killing one another, was that there remained enough in common among them to permit argument and even to allow for the possibility of persuasion; one of the reasons they *did* argue was that the revolutionaries knew their interpretation of the

---

to the trial of a king with the statement, "We will cut his head off with the crown upon it." See Wedgwood, *Trial*, p. 99.

[30] Phrase used recurrently, particularly in the New Model; see William Allen's account of the Windsor prayer meeting of May 1, 1648, in Kenyon, *Stuart Constitution*, pp. 318f.

[31] Cf. M. A. Judson, *The Crisis of the Constitution* (New Brunswick, N. J.: Rutgers University Press, 1949): "At times in the struggle of these years there was a direct clash between 'despotic will and law'. . . . More often, however, the clash was not between law and will, but between law and law" (p. 13).

common vocabulary could prevail only through persuasion and eventual consensus. Revolutionary vanguards can dispense with the legitimacy born of common acceptance, but there are tasks they cannot perform and goods they cannot deliver. They are best at seizing and exploiting the apparatus of the central state. Among the more zealous Saints or the less scrupulous Army officers, men willing to assume such a role and content themselves with its benefits might have been found. It is debatable whether the apparatus of the central state in mid-seventeenth-century England was worth seizing (a point to which we shall return), but such men as tried to do so in the 1650s found themselves hedged in, and usually wedged out, by their only potential allies. Those allies included the Levellers, who wanted no part of a regime based on force, and the vast and indispensable middle group in its latest incarnations. The nature of English Puritanism itself militated against the successful takeover of the state by single-minded Saints. Saints tended to double as country gentlemen or prosperous weavers; just as economic interest alone did not determine their political allegiances, so religious sentiment was not the only force that guided their public actions. Furthermore, as William Haller has argued, the historical conditions under which Puritanism developed in England—so different from those in neighboring Scotland—meant that among the Saints themselves, dissent was at a premium even though religious uniformity remained the ultimate goal.[32]

As for the middle group, it opposed the strengthening and expansion of the central government under whatever auspices. Its efforts had from the beginning been directed at preserving local autonomy and ensuring regular parliaments. The primary role of those Parliaments would be to obstruct any encroaching initiative the executive might presume to undertake. The middle group wanted a king who would be but a "lord protector." It was with General Monck in 1660, and when it came to regret the Restoration, as it had regretted the Commonwealth and the Protectorate, it was saved by similar opinions harbored by moderates on the other side. It was the Cavalier Parliament that finally decided Charles II was too cavalier for its tastes; it was the Tories who foiled the designs of James II. A united nation made William and Mary its (constitutional) sovereigns in 1689, and radical disappointment with the settlement only serves to highlight the moderates' satisfaction.[33]

[32] See Haller, *Liberty and Reformation*. The argument is essential to Haller's work and is developed throughout the book.

[33] On radical disappointment, see Richard Ashcraft, *Revolutionary Politics and Locke's "Two Treatises of Government."* Ashcraft argues that Locke spoke for the radical minority within the Whig movement, and ties Locke's positions to earlier Leveller positions. He

We noted earlier, and discounted, similarities that seemed to set prerevolutionary England and France off against colonial America. It could also be argued that the England of the Commonwealth and the Protectorate looks like, or at least something like, the France of the Thermidorian Republic and the Directory: a new regime unable to find its feet; a powerful army in a pivotal political position; a parliamentary clique prolonging itself in power; a public increasingly hostile to the government, exhausted by years of inconclusive civil strife and economic exactions, casting about for a satisfactory king. The Restoration brought no definitive solutions to England's political problems, and there is very little in the decade before the Glorious Revolution to suggest that stability and tolerance might be just around the corner. These were the years of the Popish Plot, the Exclusion Crisis, and James II's brief reign; Shaftesbury was as eager to exploit perjury and advance the Whig cause by judicial murder as his opponents were unscrupulous in their use of the same means; civil war hung in the air. It was then that Filmer's *Patriarcha* was belatedly published, then that a king sought to crush all possibility of resistance by altering charters and purging local governments. James II lost, and we remember Shaftesbury primarily as John Locke's patron, but the fact remains that it took England some sixty years to settle its constitutional problems, and that during that interval many rather ugly things happened.

The parallels between England in the 1650s and France in the later 1790s, however, can be used to expose the different realities behind the façade—although it is important to bear in mind that we are distinguishing here only between subcategories of liberal development, and that we should therefore expect to see similarities between contrasting cases. In England, prerevolutionary trends and revolutionary events had all collaborated to push people toward a common constitutional position, and the unfinished business of the Revolution proper did not leave the nation pointing politically in different directions. Discussing Restoration politics, J. R. Jones reminds us:

> It is a cliché to conclude that the Restoration failed to restore national unity, social and religious harmony and political stability. But it is less often

also allows that in the 1680s "everyone, from rabid Republicans to defenders of constitutional monarchy, could agree that a freely elected House of Commons was essential to political society as they defined it, however much their theories, taken as a whole, tended to proceed down different ideological paths. Hence the central clause of William's declaration . . ." (p. 549). Ashcraft's argument about Locke is unconventional, but what his analysis of Restoration politics and the Glorious Revolution makes clear is that moderate positions continued to operate as a revolutionary common denominator, and that they won.

appreciated that this failure did not in itself entirely discredit the concept of Restoration [defined earlier as the widely held belief "that only if the King came into his own again could the nation hope to enjoy its constitutional and legal rights, and properties, without fear of further arbitrary interference from self-constituted and oppressive military governments"]. Indeed this concept provided the main principle that underlay the ultimately successful political settlement, that which followed the Revolution of 1688.[34]

Of the latter, the same author writes:

> Briefly, but for long enough to accomplish the durable settlement that had evaded the politicians and statesmen in 1640–2 and 1660, the nation became united (as perhaps never again until 1940). The same theme of restoration is to be found in 1688–9 as in 1660, but there was one significant difference. In the latter year the restoration of the monarchy had been seen as the key-stone of the settlement, the guarantor of constitutional liberties, the prerequisite to unity, harmony and stability. But in 1688 the universal demand was for a free Parliament; only after one had been elected was the fate of the monarchy discussed. Although its reputation had been tarnished during the Restoration period by factionalism, obstructionism, corrupt practices and abuses of privilege, Parliament stood out in 1688 as the institution that embodied the interest of the nation. Symbolically as well as in practical terms the Restoration period ends with the offer of the Crown to William and Mary by the Convention Parliament in 1689.[35]

Parliament was a forum for organized conflict, and in England it was around that forum that a political consensus coalesced. In the decades following the Civil War, the English political class still stubbornly wanted—and knew it wanted—an executive limited by a representative parliament. For many years, it did indeed cast about for an appropriate king, and for an elegant formula to describe the new arrangement, but it did not vacillate between different models of authority. In France, as we shall see, the possibility of a similar consensus was preempted from the start. English political development was linear; French political development was not.

In America, the monopolization and manipulation of a common political vocabulary by revolutionary forces was even more complete

[34] J. R. Jones, Introduction to J. R. Jones, ed., *The Restored Monarchy, 1660–1688* (Totawa, N. J.: Rowman and Littlefield, 1979), p. 9. Bracketed quote appears on p. 8.
[35] Ibid., p. 29.

than in England.[36] In America, the original determination of allegiance occurred between 1763 and 1776. To the extent that it was voluntary—not dictated, as it could well be after 1774, by the proximity of British troops or the coercive activities of local "patriots"—it turned primarily on the interpretation of events, not on clashing political ideals.[37] Over and over, from the Stamp Act of 1765 through the Coercive Acts of 1774 to the Declaration of Independence's lengthy and bitter enumeration of British "abuses and usurpations, pursuing invariably the same object," the British subjects of North America asked themselves and each other whether the measures taken by the home government constituted a legitimate and innocent response to the changing needs of empire, or whether they represented the entering wedge of a deliberate design upon American freedom. The Loyalists never proposed an alternative image of polit-

[36] The analysis of revolutionary ideology that follows is based on a reading of the positions adopted by the articulate elites. Those positions seem to me to express an ideological common denominator shared by most participants in the revolutionary cause. This approach is consistent with the thesis laid out most notably by Bernard Bailyn in *The Ideological Origins of the American Revolution* (Cambridge, Mass.: Harvard University Press, 1967). Responding in part to this thesis, a later generation of historians has sought first to refute and then, more sensibly, simply to qualify Bailyn's argument by recounting the complex social tensions that characterized late colonial America and by recovering the related ideological diversity that Bailyn's deliberately general argument tended to overlook. This literature, represented, for example, by Gary Nash's *The Urban Crucible: Social Change, Political Consciousness, and the Origins of the American Revolution* (Cambridge, Mass.: Harvard University Press, 1979), has enriched our understanding of late colonial and early postrevolutionary American society and politics. As regards the Revolution, however, it seems to demonstrate that in the absence of what it hoped to find—clearly defined, intercolonial, class-based solidarities and ideologies among less privileged groups in American society—Bailyn's argument still stands. The Revolution succeeded and remained political in part because of broad interclass agreement on a number of the key elite propositions about political rule and the social order. I have therefore focused on the general formulation of the revolutionary program, as analyzed by Bailyn and by other scholars (Gordon Wood and Pauline Maier, to name but two) pursuing the same line of inquiry. This does not seem to me to preclude taking into account Joyce Appleby's emphasis on the presence of a more classically "liberal" strand of revolutionary thinking alongside the "republican" tradition; see Appleby, "The Social Origins of American Revolutionary Ideology," *Journal of American History* 64 (March 1978): 935–58; and *Capitalism and a New Social Order: The Republican Vision of the 1790's* (New York: New York Unversity Press, 1984).

[37] This point is persuasively argued by Mary Beth Norton; see Norton, "The Loyalist Critique of the Revolution," in Library of Congress Symposia on the American Revolution, *The Development of a Revolutionary Mentality* (Washington, D.C.: Library of Congress, 1972), pp. 127–48; and Pauline Maier, *The Old Revolutionaries: Political Lives in the Age of Samuel Adams* (New York: Knopf, 1980), pp. 275–79. Janice Potter argues that the different interpretations of events did add up to different ideologies; see Potter, *The Liberty We Seek: Loyalist Ideology in Colonial New York and Massachusetts* (Cambridge, Mass.: Harvard University Press, 1983).

ical life, and often they were as opposed as their patriot neighbors to the latest British measures. They tried only to convince those neighbors that men advocating resistance and finally independence were tragically (or maliciously) deluded in their evaluation of British intentions. As revolutionary passions built, their logic proved too narrow for their cause. Meanwhile, the patriots labored to promote as broad a consensus as possible around their actions, for if victory in battle was still a recognized sign of God's sympathy in Cromwell's England, in the America of the 1760s and 1770s, resistance was justified by the number of people who could be persuaded it was necessary.[38] In the 1780s, when Americans did come to rethink both the foundations and the operation of government at the state and national levels, the Loyalists were already not only out of power but out of the debate.

The changing situation that Americans had to interpret was one fraught with tension, but no one in the early 1760s had reason to expect that it would end in revolution and the birth of a new nation. Prior to the conclusion of the Seven Years War (1763), England had been content to manage its empire according to mercantilist principles. *Manage* is perhaps an inappropriate term, for England's empire, unlike Spain's, was not run by an efficient (by the standards of the day) centralized bureaucracy. England exercised her authority "from dock to dock"; for her purposes, that was sufficient.[39]

The peace required a new arrangement, for the war had bequeathed to England an unacceptably large national debt and a vast expanse of new territory. England's victory gave her title to what is now Canada and to the land between the Appalachians and the Mississippi River. These new territories, coveted by cutthroat speculators and inhabited by Catholic Frenchmen, Indians, and unscrupulous settlers, would have to be administered and policed. The job would require troops, a new conception of empire, and more money. Englishmen at home were already overtaxed; why not raise the money in America? The need for funds meant that the recasting of imperial authority was from the beginning linked to that area of English political hypersensitivity, taxation. The measures that eventually led to revolution—the Proclamation of 1763, the Revenue (Sugar) Act (1764), the Currency Act (1764), the Stamp Act (1765), the Quartering Act (1765), the Declaratory Act (1766), the Townshend Duties

[38] See Pauline Maier, *From Resistance to Revolution* (New York: Random House, 1972), for an analysis of the importance of mass support and consensus to the revolutionary movement.

[39] For a suggestive comparative analysis of British and Spanish colonization in America, see Bernard Bailyn, "Shaping the Republic," in Bernard Bailyn et al., *The Great Republic* (Lexington, Mass.: D. C. Heath, 1977), vol. I, chap. 1.

(1767), the revamping of the Admiralty Courts, the establishment of an American Board of Customs Commissioners (1767) and of a Secretary of State for the Colonies (1768)—were intended to promote peace in the West and to raise money; they also represented the groping efforts of men working toward a new theory of empire in the confused political atmosphere of the beginning of George III's reign.

The measures adopted by the British government did affect the American economy, already struggling with what we would call a recession, and some social groups (merchants in the major port towns, for example) were more hurt than others.[40] Perhaps more importantly, British measures seemed to threaten the position of an already insecure colonial elite.[41] The material impact of the British moves did not, however, cause the Revolution, and social differences were not (as we shall see in the next section) decisive in determining allegiance when revolution came. Within a shared Whig tradition, colonists squared off on how commonly held principles could best be preserved.

Americans shared the Englishman's pride in English liberties. Alone among the world's peoples (so the story went, and most of it was true), Englishmen were safe in their life, liberty, and property. Englishmen were free from arbitrary seizure and/or imprisonment and guaranteed the right to due process and a trial by a jury of their peers. They could be taxed only with the consent of their representatives in Parliament. They were secure from the tyrannical power of bishops; mixed government preserved them from a return to Stuart abuses. Finally, the people retained the right to petition for a redress of grievances—and it was assumed, at least in America, that all reasonable requests would be heard.

However, whereas the English had grown complacent in their pride, Americans perceived such confidence as both unwarranted and ill advised. The colonies were, by virtue of their social and political structure, very different from the England they ostensibly copied, and the colonists' political sensibilities were particularly vulnerable to provocation. The Americans had maintained the wariness of a "Radical Whig" or "Commonwealth" tradition now all but forgotten in England. This tradition curiously combined a Hobbesian assessment of human nature with a Lockeian account of the purpose and design of government. "The World," wrote John Trenchard and

[40] For an account of the impact of the war on American society, see Nash, *The Urban Crucible*.

[41] See Robert M. Weir, "Who Shall Rule at Home: The American Revolution as a Crisis of Legitimacy for the Colonial Elite," *Journal of Interdisciplinary History* 6 (Spring 1976): 679–700.

Thomas Gordon in *Cato's Letters*, "is governed by Men, and Men by their Passions; which, being boundless and insatiable, are always terrible when they are not controuled. Who was ever satiated with Riches, or surfeited with Power, or tired with Honours?"[42] Those words were written in England in 1721, but they were reproduced, widely circulated, and their ideas almost universally credited in the American colonies of the 1760s.[43]

Neither the Radical Whigs nor the American colonists drew Hobbesian conclusions from such impeccable Hobbesian gloom. The Americans apparently felt that social forces, geographic mobility, the abundance of New World resources, and, ultimately, the ordinary police powers of the community would suffice to moderate the universal desire for riches. Unlike Hobbes, they seem also to have made a generic distinction between wealth and power. For the Radical Whigs, riches could be pursued as a (private) end in themselves, for men enjoy comfort and are tempted by luxury. For Hobbes, private and public power were part of a single continuum: Riches had first to be wrested from the hands of another, and once obtained, they were useful primarily as a means for achieving or increasing power. Men, he said, labored under "a perpetual and restless desire of power after power."[44] To the Americans, as to their Radical Whig predecessors, public power was at least potentially distinguishable from private prosperity: By power, they meant political power, dominion, the coercive use of physical force. It is worth noting that the only consistently Hobbesian character in Locke's *Second Treatise* is the state. Men who wield political power will want more; men who do not normally exercise public power must therefore take time out from their private pursuits to check the ambitions of those who govern. In this account, private men are fully qualified to judge their public servants: "Every Ploughman knows a good Government from a bad one, from the effects of it: he knows whether the Fruits of his Labour be his own, and whether he enjoy them in Peace and Security."[45] Since the purpose of government is the people's welfare and since legitimate power can be granted only on a fiduciary basis, the continuing consent of the gov-

[42] John Trenchard and Thomas Gordon, *Cato's Letters*, no. 33, June 17, 1721, "Cautions against the natural Encroachments of Power," in David C. Jacobson, ed., *The English Libertarian Heritage* (New York: Bobbs-Merrill, 1965), p. 84.

[43] See Bernard Bailyn, *The Ideological Origins of the American Revolution*, chap. 2; Gordon S. Wood, *The Creation of the American Republic, 1776–1787* (New York: W. W. Norton, 1969).

[44] Thomas Hobbes, *Leviathan*, part I, chap. 11.

[45] Trenchard and Gordon, *Cato's Letters*, no. 38, July 22, 1721, "The Right and Capacity of the People to judge of Government," in Jacobson, *English Libertarian Heritage*, p. 94.

erned is a necessary element of the political process. If the governed decline to play their assigned role, rulers will inevitably reach for illegitimate power, and the lives, liberties, and property of all will be threatened.

Such was the importance of popular vigilance that the Radical Whig tradition furnished its adherents with a list of indicators they could use to recognize a plot against liberty in time to defeat it. First of all, they should know that the threat would indeed come in the form of a conspiracy:

> Few Men have been desperate enough to attack openly, and barefaced, the Liberties of a free People. . . . It is the Business and Policy of Traytors, so to disguise their Treason with plausible Names, and so to recommend it with popular and bewitching Colours, that they themselves shall be adored, while their Work is detested, and yet carried on by those that detest it.[46]

The conspirators would first isolate the prince from all but their own advice: Americans pointed to the disconcertingly affectionate relationship between the supposedly sinister, scheming Lord Bute and George III. The conspirators would endeavor to impoverish the people: All the revenue acts could, in American eyes, be seen in this light. The conspirators would promote faction, pervert justice, disregard merit in making appointments, encourage luxury at the expense of public virtue, coopt the legislature, and, if all else failed, alter the balance of government. Looking about them, Americans thought they saw examples of all this in the 1760s. Alongside the confused debate over representation and empire, there was therefore a more immediately determinative debate over British intentions and the nature of current trends. The latter debate soon became so urgent that the former lost its relevance:

> The colonists believed they saw emerging from the welter of events during the decade after the Stamp Act a pattern whose meaning was unmistakable. . . . They saw about them, with increasing clarity, not merely mistaken, or even evil, policies violating the principles upon which freedom rested, but what appeared to be evidence of nothing less than a deliberate assault launched surreptitiously by plotters against liberty in both England and America . . . .
>
> This belief transformed the meaning of the colonists' struggle, and it added an inner accelerator to the movement of opposition. For, once assumed, it could not be easily dispelled: denial only confirmed it, since what

---

[46] Trenchard and Gordon, *Cato's Letters*, no. 17, February 18, 1720, "What Measures are actually taken by wicked and desperate Ministers to ruin and enslave their Country," in Jacobson, *English Libertarian Heritage*, p. 52.

conspirators confess is not what they believe; the ostensible is not the real; and the real is deliberately malign.

It was this—the overwhelming evidence, as they saw it, that they were faced with conspirators against liberty determined at all costs to gain ends which their words dissembled—that was signaled to the colonists after 1763, and it was this above all else that in the end propelled them into revolution.[47]

In response to this logic, the Loyalists could only cite the real dilemmas faced by imperial administrators and the difficulties of the theoretical problem the British government faced. Loyalists could emphasize the danger of social disorder, evoke the miseries of war, which might well yield only to the harshness of defeat, and plead for timely compromise. They could also attempt to coopt their adversaries: thus Bernard Bailyn's succinct, devastating criticism of poor Thomas Hutchinson, insistently "playing the hard-headed politics of Walpole in an age of ideology."[48] What the Loyalists could not do was offer a coherent and compelling counteraccount of the events unfolding about them. Two hundred years before Albert Hirschman's quip, the Loyalists learned to their misfortune that only a paradigm—and not mere facts—can destroy a paradigm. The problem, wrote Daniel Leonard ("Massachusettensis") in a telling passage of a pamphlet written in December 1774, was that fictions had become more convincing than rational argument and obvious facts. Recounting the development of the cleavage between Whigs and Tories in Massachusetts-Bay, he explained:

> The whigs had great advantages in the unequal combat; their scheme flattered the people with the idea of independence; the tories' plan supposed a degree of subordination, which is a rather humiliating idea; besides there is a propensity in men to believe themselves injured and oppressed whenever they are told so. . . . They [the Whigs] accordingly applied themselves to work upon the imagination, and to inflame the passions; for this work they possessed great talents. . . . Effigies, paintings, and other imagery were exhibited; . . . lists of imaginary grievances were continually published; the people were told weekly that the ministry had formed a plan to enslave them; that the duty upon tea was only a prelude to a window tax, hearth tax, land tax, and poll tax; and these were only paving the way for reducing the country to lordships. . . . We were further stimulated by being told, that the people of England were depraved, the parliament venal, and

[47] Bailyn, *Ideological Origins*, pp. 94f.
[48] Bernard Bailyn, *The Ordeal of Thomas Hutchinson* (Cambridge, Mass.: Harvard University Press, 1974), p. 142.

the ministry corrupt; nor were attempts wanting to traduce Majesty itself.
The kingdom of Great Britain was depicted as an ancient structure, once
the admiration of the world, now sliding from its base, and rushing to its
fall. At the same time we were called upon to mark our own rapid growth,
and behold the certain evidence that America was on the eve of independent empire.

When we consider what effect a well written tragedy or novel has on the
human passions, though we know it to be all fictitious, what effect must all
this be supposed to have had upon those that believed these high wrought
images to be realities?[49]

At issue was not the beauty of the British constitution or the meaning of British liberty: On those points, all Americans were agreed. At
issue was the interpretation of reality. Since the men who became
Loyalists shared their opponents' basic beliefs concerning history, human nature, and political life, they could appeal only to pragmatic
caution, shared social anxieties, and the established habits of loyalty
and submission. They judged events differently and so thought resistance unjustified on Whig principles. They spoke for reason and rea-
sonableness, but they were in the wrong place at the wrong time, and
they lost. John Adams ("Novanglus"), effortlessly and effectively
turned Leonard's plea for caution on its head. He began by citing his
opponent's disparaging description of the revolutionaries' position:

"They," the popular leaders, "begin by reminding the people of the elevated rank they hold in the universe as men; that all men by nature are
equal, that kings are but the ministers of the people; that their authority is
delegated to them by the people, for their good, and they have a right to
resume it, and place it in other hands, or keep it themselves, whenever it
is made use of to oppress them. Doubtless there have been instances, when
these principles have been inculcated to obtain a redress of real grievances,
but they have been much oftener perverted to the worst of purposes."

These are what are called revolution principles. They are the principles
of Aristotle and Plato, of Livy and Cicero, and Sidney, Harrington and
Locke. The principles of nature and eternal reason. The principles on
which the whole government over us, now stands. It is therefore astonish-
ing, if any thing can be so, that writers, who call themselves friends of government, should in this age and country, be so inconsistent with themselves, so indiscreet, so immodest, as to insinuate a doubt concerning
them.[50]

[49] [Daniel Leonard], in the *Massachusetts Gazette and Boston Post-Boy*, December 19,
1774, in Merrill Jensen, ed., *Tracts of the American Revolution, 1763–1776* (New York:
Bobbs-Merrill, 1967), pp. 284f.
[50] [John Adams], in the *Boston Gazette*, January 23, 1775, in Jensen, *Tracts*, pp. 300f.

With ideological differences so narrow, every possible means—including violence—was used to bring the hesitant around to resistance. Bailyn emphasizes the role of reasonable argument;[51] John Shy prefers to emphasize the influence of "a pattern of raw power."[52] From 1776 to 1783 and even beyond, there was a proliferation of laws imposing tests, oaths, fines, confiscation, and imprisonment upon the recalcitrant; ostracism and informal coercion by local committees had begun with the 1774 Association against the importation of British goods. Loyalists who would not be persuaded and who could not at least be silenced were excluded from their communities, and many men less famous than Thomas Hutchinson were hounded out of a land they loved.[53]

Yet however ugly or painful, exclusion failed to engender ideological extremism on either side.[54] On the contrary, exclusion in revolu-

The poverty of Loyalist political thought is perhaps best illustrated by the counter-Declaration of Independence issued by *Rivington's Royal Gazette* on November 17, 1781; for the text, see Claude H. Van Tyne, *The Loyalists in the American Revolution* (Gloucester, Mass.: Peter Smith, 1959; originally published by Macmillan in 1902), pp. 309–17.

[51] Bailyn, *Ideological Origins*, pp. 16–19.

[52] Shy, "Hearts and Minds in the American Revolution," in *A People Numerous and Armed*, p. 178.

[53] See Van Tyne, *Loyalists*.

[54] Edward Countryman, who sets out to reexamine the "[c]onventional wisdom" regarding the "ease and smoothness" that accompanied the transfer of power in revolutionary America, seems to me in the end to confirm the thesis he hoped to qualify. A revolution occurred, exclusion played a necessary role in securing its victory, and new institutions rapidly emerged and proved capable of handling the demands placed on them:

"Consolidating the power of the new institutions that were set up to govern revolutionary New York was thus a process of considerable complexity. The state in which the process took place was very different from the pre-revolutionary province, for New York had, in effect, been redefined through the secession of Vermont, the temporary loss of the heavily loyalist southern district, the migrations, forced or voluntary, of many loyalists to Canada, New England, or New York City, and the civil war on the western frontier. The populace that was politically relevant for the new institutions during the war years consisted, then, of those loyalists who remained in the whig zone, of upstate whigs, and of refugees from the southern district. In a way this fragmentation of what had been New York made the task of the new institutions easier, for it saved them from having to deal with several large concentrations of people who denied the legitimacy of either the revolution or the community. The Vermonters were gone for good, and when the southern district was restored to the state at the end of 1783, large scale emigration and the unquestionability of the Revolution's triumph made its reintegration into a political community relatively easy. And ultimately, repression proved able to cope with the serious problems of loyalists who remained within the whig zone.

"The immediate problem thus lay within the whig population that neither denied the propriety of the revolutionary movement nor threatened the state's basic integrity,

tionary America seems to have contributed to moderation in both the short term and the long run, confirming our description of it as controlled and limited. Reviewing the character and relative weight of conflict and consensus during the revolutionary period, Edmund S. Morgan notes that the Revolution failed to resolve sectional conflicts. Tensions between North and South persisted, but so did differences between coastal settlers and frontiersmen; the latter often felt as unrepresented in eastern-dominated assemblies as easterners felt in the British Parliament, and they sometimes reacted in similar fashion. Sectional conflicts, however, were generally checked by a growing sense of national identity. Social conflict, on the other hand, was defused by exclusion: by Loyalism, and by the maintenance of slavery. Slavery deprived the most disinherited part of the labor force of a public voice, while Loyalism eliminated potential sources of radical discontent. Upper-class men who felt they were not getting the deference they deserved threw their support to the British, but so did lower-class men who felt their grievances were of little concern to revolutionary leaders:

> Loyalism in this way tended to absorb social groups that felt endangered or oppressed by the Revolutionary party. It operated as a safety valve to remove from the American side men who felt a high degree of social discontent. Or to change the figure, it drew off men at either end of the political spectrum, reducing the range of disagreements.[55]

Thus the problem in the American Revolution is not to define who was a moderate, but to identify someone who was not.[56] The internal

and with loyalists and neutrals whom the new system could 'reach,' one way or another. That a problem existed, that legitimizing the regime was a different matter from legitimizing the state, was recognized by the men identified in this article as 'constitutionalist patriots,' but it was the actions of the legislature rather than the arguments that John Jay wrote into the council of revision's veto messages that moved toward solving the problem. And perhaps most significant for making the new stability permanent, it was those actions that led to the development of a modern party system in the state." Countryman, "Consolidating Power in Revolutionary America: The Case of New York," *Journal of Interdisciplinary History* 6 (Spring 1976): 645–77; cited passages on pp. 645, 670.

[55] Edmund S. Morgan, "Conflict and Consensus in the American Revolution," in Kurtz and Hutson, *Essays on the American Revolution*, pp. 289–309; cited passage appears on p. 292. See also Countryman, "Consolidating Power in Revolutionary America."

[56] "Outsiders"—slaves, women, Native Americans, poorer working people—are far more easily found, and have been the object of much recent scholarly attention; see, for example, Gary Nash, *Race, Class, and Politics: Essays on American Colonial and Revolutionary Society* (Urbana: University of Illinois Press, 1986); and Alfred Young, ed., *The*

threat to the viability of the new political community did not come from extremism. It lay rather in what we may inelegantly term structurally imposed anarchy. Anarchy—the old bugbear of Loyalist propaganda—became a perceived threat when the colonists realized that their defensive, British revolution had turned into an innovative, American one, and that their enterprise was in the process of breaking all the supposedly incontrovertible rules of established political science. The "unleashing of democracy" was regrettable, and Shays's Rebellion (1786) no doubt did stir up antidemocratic sentiment, but democracy as such had never been on the revolutionary agenda, and traditional political science did indicate where acceptable antidotes might be found. The real problem was theoretically and politically of much greater moment. The colonies had won their independence as associated but separate political entities, and the Articles of Confederation conferred minimal powers on the central government. This arrangement proved unequal to the tasks and ambitions that surfaced in the 1780s. Not only was the government unable to cope with the foreign policy, fiscal, and commercial issues at hand, but the public virtue of Americans seemed to have entered a period of decline. The men who gathered in Philadelphia in 1787 faced, by the theoretical standards of the day, an impossible task: They would have to devise a republic—on paper and then in fact—on the basis of a heterogeneous mass of unvirtuous, ambitious, factious individuals spread over an immense expanse of land.

The document they produced elicited another wave of pamphleteering. The proposed Constitution was vehemently denounced—but not, as some historians have maintained, because it was seen as politically antidemocratic or socially reactionary. Rather, as Cecilia Kenyon argues,

> The objections of the Anti-Federalists were not directed toward the barriers imposed on simple majority rule by the Constitution. Advocates and opponents of ratification may have belonged to different economic classes and been motivated by different economic interests. But they shared a large body of political ideas and attitudes, together with a common heritage of political institutions. For one thing, they shared a profound distrust of man's capacity to use power wisely and well. They believed self-interest to be the dominant motive of political behavior, no matter whether the form of government be republican or monarchical, and they believed in the necessity of constructing political machinery that would restrict the operation of self-interest and prevent men entrusted with political power

American Revolution: Explorations in the History of American Radicalism (Dekalb: Northern Illinois University Press, 1976).

from abusing it. This was the fundamental assumption of the men who wrote the Constitution, and of those who opposed its adoption, as well.

The fundamental issue over which Federalists and Anti-Federalists split was the question whether republican government could be extended to embrace a nation, or whether it must be limited to the comparatively small political and geographical units which the separate American states then constituted. The Anti-Federalists took the latter view; and in a sense they were the conservatives of 1787, and their opponents the radicals.[57]

In the period prior to the Declaration of Independence, the quarrel between "different varieties of Whigs"[58] had made Loyalists of the mainstream Whigs, whereas their opponents had moved toward republicanism. In the 1780s, an analogous but less profound division occurred, between Americans who remained transfixed by traditional republican notions and those who were consciously making their peace with a liberalism that built on the assumed prevalence of passion and interest.[59]

Although revolutionaries and their opponents in England and America fought over a common vocabulary, it did, of course, matter who won. Whatever their original intentions and whatever their preferred rhetoric, English and American revolutionaries offered their respective countries a new kind of politics. They need not perhaps have won, and we will turn our attention to the material conditions of their success in the next section of this chapter. Since they did win, the content of the ideological debate and the manner in which it typically unfolded were of crucial importance. In England and America, there was nothing to be gained politically (and much to be lost) by frequent and flagrant recourse to exclusionary politics, and there was no ideology to comfort those who might have been tempted by such tactics. What came to be called revolutionary government in Terrorist France was recognized—and rejected—as rule by the sword in England. Its informal practice by local groups in revolutionary America

[57] Cecilia Kenyon, "Men of Little Faith: The Anti-Federalists on the Nature of Representative Government," in *William and Mary Quarterly*, 3d Series, 12 (January 1955): 37f. See also Maier, *The Old Revolutionaries*, pp. 280–94. Cf. arguments in Richard Beeman et al., eds., *Beyond Confederation: Origins of the Constitution and American National Identity* (Chapel Hill: University of North Carolina Press, 1987).

[58] Norton, "Loyalist Critique," p. 130.

[59] On the general problem posed here, see Albert O. Hirschman, *The Passions and the Interests: Arguments for Capitalism before Its Triumph* (Princeton: Princeton University Press, 1977).

never contaminated institutional norms, nor did it solicit theoretical justification or even acknowledgment.[60]

The Structure of Revolutionary Opportunity

Argument was possible during England's "century of revolution" and in revolutionary America because the parties to the conflicts shared many fundamental assumptions and values. Argument was not therefore inevitable, nor was it certain that political argument would engender political revolution. Had overwhelming force been the monopoly of one or the other side, there would have been no need for argument and so the type of disagreement would have made no difference. It is anybody's guess what England and America would look like today had Charles I triumphed without a fight, or the colonies lost, but neither happened. The reason argument was necessary, and therefore important in shaping the final outcome, was that power as well as law was on both sides. The prerevolutionary distribution of power, most relevantly visible in the decentralization and limited functions of the state, encouraged political strategies designed to hold the center.

Decentralization—the distribution across Stuart and colonial American societies of all forms of power, from military and political to economic and intellectual—contributed to the consolidation of liberty in other, and perhaps less morally appealing, ways than the educative ones Tocqueville often emphasizes. Since in each case the revolutionary cleavage was largely dictated by political considerations and because political allegiance was not overwhelmingly determined by any single external factor (class, status, religion), the two societies split (approximately) down the middle. That the same kinds of men were on both sides further reinforced cultural affinities; it also ensured a fair division of material resources, since each side had the means to sustain a fight.

Decentralization, however, is only half of the story—and quite possibly it is not the most important half. The often-drawn contrast between Anglo-American decentralization and French centralization assumes its full significance only if we also recall the long chain of events and decisions whereby government in prerevolutionary En-

---

[60] The Loyalists often accused Patriots of violating the values (for example, free speech) they were claiming to defend (see Potter, *The Liberty We Seek*), but Patriot moves seem more consistent with the behavior of a government at war than with that of a revolutionary vanguard in action. See Countryman, "Consolidating Power in Revolutionary America."

gland and America opted out of becoming the primary agent of social mobility and stratification or economic development. The *type* of
state intervention practiced by a prerevolutionary regime is probably
more critical in shaping the structure of opportunity for revolutionary actors than is the *extent* of state intervention, for the type of intervention determines the relationship of the political system to the social system. In England and America, revolutionary political
competition generated primarily political repercussions, even
though, in the heat of competition, political means became available
to social elements previously kept beyond the pale of political participation. It is true (as Tocqueville might have argued) that by leaving
local affairs to local elites and by tolerating representative institutions, the monarchy in England and the colonial administration in
America unwittingly sponsored the political apprenticeship of the
groups that would later challenge Stuart claims and imperial rule. It
is equally true, however, that in each case the Crown's supporters as
well as its detractors benefited from the experience. If the moderates
of the French Revolution were so rapidly overtaken by events, it was
not because a centralized regime had left them pitifully unschooled
in the practical political arts, nor was it because their political ideas
reproduced Old Regime patterns of thought or somehow prefigured
a totalitarian image of power. It was because moderate political intentions were of greatly reduced efficacy in a country where politics had
not established its autonomy. Stuart monarchs, just like their Bourbon counterparts across the Channel, might be revered as thauma-
turgical figures, but the English Crown was not, in reality, the linchpin of the social order, any more than was the colonial administration
in prerevolutionary America. That fact was of far greater consequence in shaping the chances of different political strategies in the
three countries than any isolated similarities or differences of ideology, social structure, economic development, or demographic patterns. In England and America, for structural reasons beyond both
the control and the understanding of the revolutionary actors, the
regime could be contested—successfully—as a political institution.
The relative independence of the political realm made for political
equations with limited variables. While men still made history without
fully knowing the history their history would make, political actors
were less likely to get caught in processes they could not control.

We can begin with England. Lawrence Stone places the "real water-
shed between medieval and modern England" in the short century
between 1560 and 1640.[61] The transformation Stone identifies was

---

[61] Lawrence Stone, *The Crisis of the Aristocracy, 1558–1641* (Oxford: Oxford University Press, 1965), p. 15.

the final product of incremental economic and cultural changes whose roots stretched well into the past. The passage to modernity also presupposed the submission of private armies to public authority, the extension and growing efficacy of state government, and the advance of national integration. Of these processes, state-building was the one that most obviously happened by design. State-building, however, proceeded unaccompanied by absolutism. The divine right discourse of James I, so alarming to his contemporaries, seems in retrospect somewhat pathetic: A king strapped for resources and infatuated with the likes of Buckingham might have spared himself the posthumous ridicule of posing as God's lieutenant. The great state-builders of early modern England were James's predecessors, the Tudors, and absolutist arguments might have sounded plausible enough had a Henry VIII or an Elizabeth been moved to expound them. Those monarchs might also have been able to endow the English monarchy with the institutional attributes of absolutism. Political exigencies in the sixteenth century, however, suggested a different course. It was Tudor tactics that made James's speeches sound only like the haughty mutterings of a dangerous king, for even as the Tudor state in appearance asserted the preeminence of its authority, it inscribed an ever-contracting circle of real as well as of perceived dependence around the Crown. Unable to establish its ideological hegemony,[62] promoting the relative decline of the aristocracy, and allowing the benefits of its alliance with the Commons to accrue primarily to the latter, the monarchy fostered the (re)organization and gradual mobilization of society for public, political life, but did

---

[62] For an analysis of the monarchy's efforts to do so in the 1530s, see G. R. Elton, *Policy and Police: The Enforcement of the Reformation in the Age of Thomas Cromwell* (Cambridge: Cambridge University Press, 1972). Elton's purpose is both to demonstrate the enormity of the task Henry faced and to show that Thomas Cromwell was not the terrorist villain he is sometimes made out to be. More relevant to our purposes, Elton argues that: "Cromwell's administration, faced with the big task of steering the realm through a revolution which called forth much hostility and a fair amount of resistance, rested content with the existing and traditional police machinery of the realm, a phrase which somewhat overstates the means at its disposal. The Crown relied on the activities of private individuals both for the initial discovery of offences, the passing of information to the centre, and executive action against suspects and offenders. No attempt was made to organise these methods, themselves a direct reflection of the social hierarchy of the day, into anything resembling a network of spies; . . . no plans existed for reforming or replacing these essentially informal arrangements. . . . [Cromwell] was thus compelled not only to use the locality but, up to a point, to defer to the locality; . . . he depended in the last resort on the willingness, prejudices and private ends of men over whom he had no hold except what general adjurations and general warnings could add to general loyalty and the desire to stand well with the fountain of patronage. All his actions plainly demonstrate his recognition that everything turned on the gentry" (p. 382).

not weave its own future inextricably into the fabric of political cohesion and social order.

The English Reformation rapidly compromised the prospects of the political institution that precipitated it. The Reformation ruptured the reality and finally the expectation of religious conformity, and the manner in which it was carried out ensured the degradation of the social position and moral authority of the established church. Attentive to his own immediate financial and political needs, Henry VIII quickly disposed of confiscated church property; in so doing, he deprived the Crown of land in an age where land conferred not just wealth, but power and prestige.

The Tudors subdued the querulous, quarrelsome aristocracy whose pretensions and dissensions had previously played havoc with royal authority, but while eliminating the aristocracy as a direct competitor, the Crown did not secure its mental or material subservience. The monarchy thereby alienated a natural—or at least a crucial—ally without at the same time disarming it. The absence of an English Versailles is of more than symbolic significance. The English nobility (courtiers excepted—but they were comparatively few in number and increasingly ill considered) never became mesmerized by the Court, but more importantly, the nobility did not owe, objectively or subjectively, its residual power and position to the Crown.

Against the Pope and the nobility, the Tudors cultivated and utilized the support of the Commons, but again failed to enmesh the aspirations and global socioeconomic interests of the Commons in a sociopolitical system dependent on the monarchy. Meanwhile, Puritanism extended its appeal. Unable or unwilling either to destroy Puritanism completely or to coopt it effectively in the final decades of the sixteenth century, Elizabeth greatly prejudiced the chances of a lasting accommodation emerging between Crown and Commons in the first decades of the seventeenth century.

James Harrington, looking back over these developments in his allegorical account of the sources of the Civil War, concludes:

> [Henry VIII] dissolving the abbeys brought with the declining estate of the nobility so vast a prey to the industry of the people that the balance of the commonwealth was too apparently in the popular party to be unseen by the wise counsel of Queen Parthenia [Elizabeth] who, converting her reign through the perpetual love tricks that passed between her and her people into a kind of romance, wholly neglected the nobility. And by these degrees came the House of Commons to raise that head which since has been so high and formidable to their princes that they have looked pale upon those assemblies. Nor was there anything now wanting to the destruction of the

throne but that the people, not apt to see their own strength, should be put to feel it. When a prince [Charles I], as stiff in disputes as the nerve of monarchy was grown slack, received that unhappy encouragement from his clergy which became his utter ruin, while trusting more to their logic than [to] the rough philosophy of his parliament, it came to an irreparable breach, for the house of Peers which alone had stood in this gap, now sinking down between the king and the commons, showed that Crassus was dead and Isthmus broken. But a monarchy divested of her nobility has no refuge under heaven but an army. *Wherefore the dissolution of this government caused the war, not the war the dissolution of this government.*[63]

The Tudors, struggling for (and achieving) short-term advantage, laid the foundations of a modern state, but unknowingly untied the knots which bound the political, social, and religious worlds into one. From the mystical head of the body politic, the Crown slowly descended to the role of political convenience. The immediate—and hardly trivial—result of Elizabethan political, economic, and religious policies was civil peace. The eventual result of those and previous measures was the increasing autonomy of politics, and the final beneficiaries of the Queen's policies were the increasingly restless, increasingly prosperous, and increasingly Puritan men whose representatives gathered in the House of Commons. By the early 1640s, many of these men had decided that monarchy under the Stuarts was singularly inconvenient.

Thus viewed, the decentralization and diversification of power manifest in pre–Civil War England left the monarchy vulnerable and set up a structure of revolutionary opportunity that favored moderate forces. The Stuarts came to power with no subservient bureaucracy to execute their commands, no domesticated aristocracy, no independent source of wealth, and no standing army. Had they been graced with more political perspicacity than they were, they would nonetheless probably have proven unable to assemble the material prerequisites of absolute monarchy: The moment had been lost. Late in the century, James II discovered he could supply himself out of Louis XIV's coffers; he discovered very shortly thereafter that funds alone would not solve his political problems. Facing the Stuarts were not just disgruntled individuals, but cohesive groups of men with ideas, interests, and power.

In the absence of a royal bureaucracy, Stuart England was governed by local notables. In town and countryside alike, these men

---

[63] James Harrington, *The Commonwealth of Oceana* (published in 1656), in Charles Blitzer, ed., *The Political Writings of James Harrington* (New York: Liberal Arts Press, 1955), pp. 96f.

served in various official capacities (as Justices of the Peace, for example), but often acted on their own initiative. They maintained their own power, mediated intraelite disputes without decisive intervention from the king, and sent one of their own to sit in the House of Commons. Decentralization did not imply democracy; at most, chartered towns or rural counties might be run by competing oligarchies. Decentralization did imply the emergence of a political class equipped with a Tocquevillian civic education: experienced in the use of power, confident of its legitimacy, mindful of important loyalties, and adept at political communication.

Political power was backed by military clout. Mighty lords surrounded by armed retainers were a thing of the past, but military force had devolved upon the trained bands and militia, and these were controlled by the local notables. The king had no army with which to answer their resistance; the merits of his case (or the repugnancy of the alternatives) would decide the strength of his forces.[64]

If the Stuarts were forever short of funds, it was obviously not because they presided over an impoverished nation. It was not even because their ambitions were without proportion to England's resources. It was because those resources were for the most part not at their disposal. Instead, they were in the possession of men increasingly suspicious of royal intentions and legally protected (at least "of right") by Parliament. Money followed loyalties: Parliament had little trouble finding it in the opening stages of the Civil War, much more difficulty after the eclipse of the "middle group" toward 1648.

Finally, James I and Charles I in particular were confronted with the organizational as well as the intellectual and cultural ramifications of Puritanism. In England, the Puritan clergy and the gathered churches provided a network of communication and support, which proved of considerable material importance when Parliament laid down its challenge to the king. In both England and America, religious diversity and Protestant principles helped to pry open the minds of men otherwise anchored in a traditional frame of reference and expectation. The quality of argument evident in the Putney Debates or in the lesser pamphlets of the American Revolution testifies to the political sophistication and argumentative skills of men who did not even belong to the privileged classes. For these capacities, prerevolutionary political decentralization was partially responsible: The "middling sort" in England and America had already acquired a

[64] For a related argument, see Donald Pennington, "The Making of War, 1640–1642," in Pennington and Thomas, eds., *Puritans and Revolutionaries*, pp. 161–85. Pennington examines the accommodations between supposedly royalist and parliamentary administrators at the beginning of the Civil War.

certain habit of public action and participation in the elaboration of the common good. They had a long experience of competition among, as well as of cooperation between, rival local cliques, and if they did not themselves have legal training, they lived in societies attuned to the forms of legal argument. The formal role of religious competition in paving the way for political competition was nonetheless also critical, for intellectual domestication and religious uniformity depended on each other in the seventeenth and eighteenth centuries, and in England and America, neither one obtained. The Puritan tradition and the mere fact of religious diversity pushed all individuals to test their lights on the Bible, and if Scripture could be discussed, so could anything else. The Puritans of the 1640s questioned and sought to reform the temporal world they knew, reconciling the trappings of genuine humility with the solid self-confidence of the called. As Americans moved into revolution, the audacity of their English predecessors no longer seemed so novel.

In America, a broad distribution of power is even easier to establish, and it left the colonials well armed against both the British and one another.[65] American professions of loyalty to their English sovereign were reiterated throughout the early phases of the Anglo-American crisis, but the American experience of monarchy was largely vicarious, and the experience of centralized authority, let alone absolutism, was nonexistent. The various traits of British colonization and American colonial life converged on at least one point: All militated against the efficacious imposition of an overbearing, interventionist, centralized power.[66]

Irrespective of British imperial ambitions, the conditions of social and economic life in mid-eighteenth century America effectively insulated the colonies from the kinds of manipulation that absolutism presupposes.[67] The access routes to mobility could not be fitted into

[65] Cf. Morgan, "Conflict and Consensus in the American Revolution": "American nationalism was obliged to start with the assumption that the population was armed and that no group within it, slaves excepted, could be pushed very hard in any direction it did not want to go" (p. 305).

[66] The description provided in the following paragraphs draws on many sources. See Bernard Bailyn, *The Origins of American Politics* (New York: Random House, 1968); Bailyn, "Shaping the Republic," in Bailyn et al., *The Great Republic*; Stanley Katz, ed., *Colonial America: Essays in Politics and Social Development*, 2d ed. (Boston: Little, Brown, and Co., 1971, 1976).

[67] Cf. the argument made by Berthoff and Murrin about earlier efforts to transplant some form of feudalism: "Feudal projects collapsed in the seventeenth century, not because America was too progressive to endure them, but because it was too primitive to sustain them." Berthoff and Murrin, "Feudalism, Communalism, and the Yeoman Freeholder," p. 264.

a matrix of power for the simple reason that (much to the regret of most contemporary observers) mobility—even if on the decline in the decades before the Revolution[68]—was, by European standards, endemic to the American environment and too pervasive to be controlled. With labor relatively scarce and land still relatively available, and with a burgeoning, young population, America presented a picture of unprecedented social, economic, and geographic mobility. Nowhere in America did the gap between rich and poor approach the European norm, and nowhere could those who momentarily found themselves on top of the heap—be they port town merchants or Southern planters—be assured of remaining there long. They formed only an unstable, jostling elite, born of good luck and hard work, subject to the vagaries of a vulnerable economy, and unprotected by legal sanctions.

Given such conditions, absolutism would have been a very poor bet in America; in the event, the British scarcely attempted even centralized government. In London, a multitude of governmental agencies shared responsibility for colonial affairs. Since they often worked at cross-purposes, their authority was largely ineffective, and since the decisionmaking process followed a meandering path, colonial representatives (until the reorganizing efforts of the 1760s) easily stepped in when vital interests were at stake. In America, each colony had its own administration. On paper, royally appointed governors enjoyed extensive powers, but they lacked the political and social resources to make those powers effective. Since executive officers tended to be Englishmen posted to the colonies, their power was often undermined by their status as outsiders and their reluctance to invest too heavily in a job they hoped would be temporary. Under them, there was no stable elite (in the absence of a hereditary aristocracy), no bureaucracy worth the name, and, of course, no standing army. British Americans, as we have already seen, identified standing armies with creeping despotism. Sheriffs relied on their fellow citizens for aid; magistrates could call out the militia. The catch was that the same upstanding citizens who made up the militia might on occasion come out when they had *not* been called: "Repeatedly," writes Pauline Maier, evoking the prerevolutionary role of discerning, disciplined American mobs, "insurgents defended the urgent interests of their communities when lawful authorities failed to act."[69] Finally, property qualifications were an ineffective barrier to voting rights in a so-

[68] Historians continue to debate this point.

[69] Maier, *Resistance*, p. 4; see all of chap. 1, "Popular Uprisings and Civil Authority." See also Edward Countryman, "The Problem of the Early American Crowd," *Journal of American Studies* 7 (1973): 77–90; and Dirk Hoerder, *Crowd Action in Revolutionary Massachusetts* (New York: Academic Press, 1977).

ciety where land was not hard to come by. As Thomas Hutchinson lamented, "anything with the appearance of a man" could vote.[70] Walpole would have been unable to work his stabilizing act in America: There were too few patronage slots and no rotten boroughs. The worst of it was that in a society characterized by so high a degree of mobility, the enfranchised population could not possibly have returned with the appropriate deferential regularity its "natural leaders" to office, for it was not always clear who those leaders were. Competition, made inevitable by the availability of power, and compounded and complicated by ethnic and religious diversity, which, like mobility, eluded systematic manipulation, itself in turn helped keep power accessible.

While the relative insulation of society from political manipulation made the political challenge of political institutions possible in Stuart England and eighteenth-century America, the diffusion of power made it unlikely that in the event of a politically motivated civil war, all the power and respectability would amass itself on one side. When in each case war came, there *were* social differences between the opposing camps, and the process and outcome of political revolution *did* ultimately affect the social landscape of both England and America. Thus, in England, the peerage and the greater gentry tended to side with the king, while the yeomanry, the lesser gentry, and the "middling sort" in the towns were inclined to sympathize with the parliamentary cause.[71] The exceptions, however, are innumerable; of limited descriptive validity, the generalization is moreover analytically beside the point. Social conflict did not precipitate the English Civil War; it did not supply the basis of the revolutionary program or dominate the royalist response; and it did not consolidate allegiances once the war began. As the elites split, so resources split, and both sides vied for the title to a commonly held image of respectability and responsibility. As David Underdown argues:

> Though in most counties the bulk of the established leadership was royalist, and thus excluded from power by the end of the Civil War, there always remained a significant minority of gentry of the same type who were will-

[70] Quoted in Bailyn et al., *The Great Republic*, p. 195.

[71] For more information on how England split, see Lawrence Stone, "The English Revolution," in Robert Forster and Jack Greene, eds., *Preconditions of Revolutions in Early Modern Europe* (Baltimore: Johns Hopkins Press, 1970), pp. 61–65; Underdown, *Pride's Purge*; Underdown, *Somerset in the Civil War and Interregnum* (Newton Abbot: David and Charles, 1973); Everitt, *Kent*.

ing and able to execute the commands of Parliament. The Civil War did not at first, therefore, involve any basic change in the structure of the county communities. Those who were named to Parliament's original County Committees . . . or who took over when their counties were recovered from the King's armies, might or might not have been more fervent Puritans, more ardent constitutionalists, than their Cavalier opponents, but they were men of the same class, of the same education and experience, in the long run equally anxious to heal the breach caused by the war.[72]

At certain moments during the Interregnum, in certain places (most often where revolutionary support was weakest), men of the "meaner sort," Puritan radicals, or power-hungry unprincipled individuals of indefinite convictions did briefly seize local power. Their short-lived experiments remained the exception in England because the prerevolutionary structure of power and the nature of the revolutionary cleavage precluded the type of power vacuum that would have been the necessary prelude to social revolution.

Likewise in America, such sociological distinctions as can be drawn between revolutionaries and Loyalists fail to advance our understanding of what happened and of why it happened the way it did.[73] John Adams hinted at the anxieties and expressed the ambitions of the revolutionary elite when he cited the need "to contrive some Method for the colonies to glide insensibly, from under the old Government, into a peaceable and contented submission to new ones."[74] The postwar glide was no doubt not quite so smooth as Adams would have wanted, but the revolutionary record offers few instances of public authority vanishing under the pressure of factional strife. Adams feared disorder; he did not condemn violence. The revolution he helped guide proved that there is no necessary causal link between the two. The American Revolution was a far more violent affair than is often thought,[75] but it was made possible by the crystallization, during the decade that followed the Stamp Act, of alternate institutions, which assumed legitimate authority and took over policy functions before the ink had dried on the Declaration of Independence, and

[72] Underdown, *Pride's Purge*, pp. 28f.

[73] Cf. Morgan, "Conflict and Consensus in the American Revolution": "The Revolution cut sharply across nearly all previous divisions, whether regional, ethnic, religious, or class" (p. 291). For an interesting account of the differentiation of revolutionary *role* by social class, see Shy, "Hearts and Minds in the American Revolution," in Shy, *A People Numerous and Armed*, pp. 163–79.

[74] Adams to Mercy Warren, April 16, 1776, quoted by John R. Howe, *The Changing Political Thought of John Adams* (Princeton: Princeton University Press, 1966), p. 8.

[75] See Shy, *A People Numerous and Armed*.

the Revolution did not, either by intention or misadventure,[76] alter the ground rules of American social life.

———————

In June 1643, the parliamentarian general William Waller and his army faced a royalist force under the command of Sir Ralph Hopton. Hopton, recalling his long friendship with Waller, requested a parley. In the following terms, Waller refused:

> Certainly my affections to you are so unchangeable, that hostility itself cannot violate my friendship to your person. But I must be true to the cause wherein I serve. . . . Where my conscience is interested all other obligations are swallowed up. I should most gladly wait upon you, according to your desire, but that I look upon you as engaged in that party beyond the possibility of a retreat, and consequently uncapable of being wrought upon by any persuasions. . . . That great God who is the searcher of my heart knows with what a perfect hatred I detest this war without an enemy. . . . We are both upon the stage, and must act such parts as are assigned us in this tragedy. Let us do it in a way of honour and without personal animosities.[77]

Waller's letter would move any reader; to the historian, it is also informative of the war he and his friend were fighting and of the character of the allegiances they had contracted. For this was a "war without an enemy," a detested, unnatural conflict—and yet one in which the combatants' consciences were deeply engaged, where there could be no possibility of retreat and (or so Waller wrote) no chance for persuasion.

Waller, his loyalty suspect because of his Presbyterian sympathies, would be one of the few Members of Parliament singled out for imprisonment at Pride's Purge. Could reluctant participants in an unhappy war perhaps go over to the "enemy" without feeling a need for persuasion? "I was bound by many several oaths to my king," wrote one Sir George Sondes of Lees Court in Kent,

> which I did not so readily know how to dispense with. Yet I never was so great a royalist as to forget I was a freeborn subject. Our king I was willing to have him; but not our tyrant, or we his slaves. . . . I was never against reducing of bishops to their pristine function of taking care of the

———————

[76] *Misadventure* is used in the morally neutral sense of "in unintended ways." It is obviously possible to think of many ground rules whose alteration might have been desirable.

[77] Quoted in Underdown, *Somerset*, pp. 55f.

churches, nor of the rest of the clergy, to take them off from secular employments. . . . Nor was I ever against taking away monopolies and arbitrary impositions, and imprisonment of the free subject; nor against lessening the exorbitancy of favourites, who like drones sucked and devoured all the honey which the commonwealth's bees with much toil gathered.[78]

And so Sondes supported Parliament,

so long as it was for king and parliament, and I think did them as faithful service as any. But when it came to parliament and no king, and parliament against king, then I boggled, I knew not what to do. I was contented to sit still and not do. (P. 122)

"Boggling" must have been a common malady in England between 1642 and 1660; it was the same malady, no doubt, which kept many unsecluded Members of Parliament away from London during the rough winter of 1648–1649. It played constant havoc with the apparent loyalties of ordinary men, and it profoundly influenced the course of revolution in England. Sir Edward Dering was no more inclined toward "slavery" than Sir George. He had protested Laudian policies in the church and opposed Ship Money, but he worried about social order and never lost sight of the interests and plight of his "country" (county). When Parliament took the unprecedented step of publicizing the Grand Remonstrance, Dering expressed dismay that the parliamentarians "should remonstrate downward, tell stories to the people, and talk of the king as of a third person."[79] Dering wished for a "composing third way"[80] and served first the king and then Parliament before his death in 1644. He is in many ways representative of the parliamentary "middle group" of which John Pym had been the organizer and first spokesman, the men who later execrated the brief rule of the Major Generals as "worse than the 1630s, a police state with military despots instead of Laudian bishops."[81] The steady convictions to which his apparent ambivalence testify help explain the limited scope and function of exclusion in revolutionary England. The demand for a sweeping act of oblivion was a constant feature of New Model petitions; even in the army, the thirst for retribution and the taste for scaffold symbolism extended little beyond the head of the king. After the Restoration, as before it, the efforts at reconciliation were made possible by the underlying simi-

[78] Quoted in Everitt, *Kent*, p. 122.
[79] Quoted in Everitt, *Kent*, pp. 91f.
[80] Quoted in Everitt, *Kent*, p. 120.
[81] Underwood, *Somerset*, p. 181.

larity of political expectations; they were made necessary by the persistent distribution of power.

Well over a century after Waller's letter to Hopton, in the days following the battle of Bunker Hill, Waller's anguish was relived by another man of moderate emotions trapped by the stark choices of revolution. Andrew Eliot, a Harvard graduate and since 1742 the Congregationalist pastor of New North Church in Boston, wrote: "Englishmen destroying Englishmen. . . . I cannot stand it long."[82] Eliot died in 1778, shunned by the British who considered him (with some justification) an American patriot, and slighted by his more ardent countrymen as a man who had tarried in occupied Boston. Certainly there were many men on both sides of the lines who deeply regretted that differences between England and her colonies had come to war. What traffic there was in America between the two sides, however—and among men of Waller's stature there was virtually none at all—was generally the result of coercion, not "boggling." The ideological case made on behalf of the revolutionary cause was too tight, and the transfer of authority too swift: Revolutionary moderation did not require, and could therefore afford not to allow for, permeable loyalty. There was no postrevolutionary rehabilitation of the Loyalist stance; Loyalism was not rewarded by a Restoration, and became identified with a foreign power; many of its partisans fled to England or Canada. In England's "century of revolution," revolutionary success was built on compromise; in America, it was based on effective, but finite, exclusion. In both countries, the revolutionary settlements closed the breach of political community created by revolutionary change and opened the way to a liberalism based on the politics of transaction and consistent with political stability.

Liberty and Property: The Articulation of a Political Ideal

According to the canons of political theory, the cornerstone of republicanism is virtue. In England and America, where virtue did not need to be created by the revolution itself, "property" emerged as the theoretical cornerstone of liberalism: not property as a material fact, but "property" as a moral concept and mental construct. "Property" was, of course, not the only image around which men rallied or about

[82] Quoted in Bernard Bailyn, *Religion and Revolution: Three Biographical Studies*, *Perspectives in American History*, vol. IV, 1970, pp. 107f.

which they argued,[83] but the articulation between liberty and property is both revelatory of the preconditions of the variant of liberal politics with which this chapter is concerned, and suggestive of the way the two countries would face the problem of conflict and community after a revolutionary settlement was reached.

In a text written in 1847 and published in his *Souvenirs*, Tocqueville expounds an idea of property that would have startled English and American revolutionaries of an earlier time:

> The French Revolution, which abolished all privileges and destroyed all exclusive rights, nonetheless allowed one to survive, that of property. . . . When the right of property was merely the origin and foundation of many other rights, it was easily defended, or rather, it was never attacked; it then formed the protective wall of society, of which all other rights were the outposts; no blows reached it; no serious attempt was ever made to touch it. But today, when the right of property is nothing more than the last remnant of an overthrown aristocratic world; when it alone is left intact, an isolated privilege amidst the universal levelling of society; when it is no longer shielded by other even more disputed and disliked rights, it is in great danger: alone, it must now sustain each day the direct and incessant assault of democratic opinion.[84]

To seventeenth-century Englishmen and eighteenth-century Americans, property was not a "privilege"—a liberty in the old regime sense of that word—and it never appeared as the "last remnant" of a destroyed aristocratic world. Already in seventeenth-century England, *liberty* was a noun that was used with the singular definite article. There and in America, for the vast majority of revolutionaries, as for their conservative adversaries, property was invested with a symbolic value and its security was sought as a sure and recognized index of the state's political health. Deciding *for* the king in the Ship Money case, one of the Justices of the King's Bench prefaced his opinion with a reaffirmation of common assumptions:

> I hope that none doth imagine, that it either is, or can be drawn by consequence, to be any part of the question in this case, whether the king may at all times, and upon all occasions, impose charges upon his subjects in general, without common consent in parliament? If that were made the question, it is questionless, That he may not—The people of the kingdom are subjects, not slaves, freemen, not villains, to be taxed *de alto et basso*.

[83] For another perspective, see J.G.A. Pocock, "Virtue and Commerce in the Eighteenth Century," *Journal of Interdisciplinary History* 3 (Summer 1972): 119–34; and Pocock, *The Machiavellian Moment* (Princeton: Princeton University Press, 1975).

[84] Alexis de Tocqueville, *Souvenirs*, in *Oeuvres complètes*, vol. XII (Paris: Gallimard, 1964), pp. 36f.

> Though the king of England hath a monarchical power . . . and hath an absolute trust settled in his crown and person, for the government of his subjects; yet his government is to be "secundum leges regni["]. . . . By those laws the subjects are not tenants at the king's will, of what they have. . . . They have in their goods a property, a peculiar interest, a "meum et teum." They have a birthright in the laws of the kingdom. No new laws can be put upon them; none of their laws can be altered or abrogated without common consent in parliament.[85]

It is critical to understand that property was the condition and indicator of public liberty and not just a means to or evidence of private material prosperity. Had John Hampden and John Hancock been but greedy acquisitive nascent capitalists, they would have paid out bearable taxes of however dubious legality rather than endure prison or see their goods seized.

> Liberty and property are necessarily connected together: He that deprives of the latter without our consent, deprives of the former. . . . He that assumes to himself a right to deprive me of any part of my estate (however small that part may be) on certain occasions, of which he is to be the sole judge, may with equal reason deprive me of the whole, when he thinks proper: And he that thinks he has a right to strip me of all my property, when he sees fit, may with equal justice deprive me of my life, when he thinks his own interest requires it.[86]

The writer is not John Locke,[87] but a pamphleteer of the American Revolution.

> All the main thing that I speak for, is because I would have an eye to property. I hope we do not come to contend for victory—but let every man consider with himself that he do not go that way to take away all property. For here is the case of the most fundamental part of the constitution of the kingdom, which if you take away, you take away all by that.[88]

This time the speaker is Henry Ireton, with Oliver Cromwell at his side, admonishing New Model radicals in the Putney Debates of October 1647.

The "Puritan" Revolution was a complex and multidimensional event, and covenant theology took a back seat to Radical Whig ideas

---

[85] From the argument of Sir Robert Berkley, in *State Trials*, Vol. III, 1090.

[86] [William Goddard?], "The Constitutional Courant," 1775, in Jensen, *Tracts*, p. 83.

[87] Locke makes a similar statement in the *Second Treatise*, §§ 17 and 18. For a reading of Locke's use of property that places greater emphasis on Locke's immediate political purposes, see Ashcraft, *Revolutionary Politics and Locke's "Two Treatises of Government,"* esp. pp. 246–83.

[88] The Putney Debates are reprinted in A.S.P. Woodhouse, ed., *Puritanism and Liberty* (Chicago: University of Chicago Press, 1951); Ireton's remark appears on p. 57.

in the immediate elaboration of American revolutionary ideology.[89] Yet the irreplaceable symbolic role played by property in Anglo-American liberal theory seems inconceivable outside the context of a society of Protestant believers. God—a Protestant God—was essential to the ideological edifice developed in England and employed again later in America to justify limited government. While Protestantism in no manner represents a sufficient condition for the type of revolution and revolutionary outcome that obtained in England and America, it does perhaps constitute a necessary condition. From God we receive a property in ourselves; by God we are held responsible for and constrained in the way we use ourselves and one another. Not by accident did Locke, who elsewhere struggled inconclusively with theological questions, feel compelled to assign Providence an explicit role when he came to write the political *Second Treatise*.

God was, of course, not a newcomer to political theory. Throughout the Middle Ages and right into Stuart England, theorists and statesmen used Biblical texts to preach obedience to temporal authorities, to plead the case for hierarchy and the need for order in a world dominated by sin, and to enhance the indispensable mystical underpinning of kingship. We have already heard James I compare kings to God; some years later, William Laud drew the conclusion that Puritans dissatisfied with one side of the equation would not long desist from challenging the other side:

> A parity they would have, no bishop, no governor, but a parochial consistory, and that should be lay enough too. Well, first, this parity was never left to the Church by Christ. . . .
> And one thing more I'll be bold to speak, out of a like duty to the Church of England and the House of David. They, whoever they be, that would overthrow *sedes ecclesia*, . . . will not spare (if ever they get power) to have a pluck at the Throne of David. And there is not a man that is for parity, all fellows in the Church, but he is not for [that is, but as is against] monarchy in the State.[90]

Over the course of the seventeenth century, gradually and for complex and diverse reasons, the mental universe necessary to James's metaphor collapsed, and events confirmed Archbishop Laud's apprehensions. Michael Walzer, stressing the repressive character of Puri-

[89] On England, see Stone, "The English Revolution"; and Underdown, *Pride's Purge*. On America, see Bailyn, *Religion*; and Bailyn, *Ideological Origins*. More recent scholarship on the Great Awakening would assign a more significant role to religious undercurrents.

[90] From a sermon preached to the opening session of Parliament, February 6, 1626; text in Kenyon, *Stuart Constitution*, pp. 153ff.

tan ideology and practice, argues that the links between militant Puritanism and political liberalism were inadvertent. "Calvinism," he writes, "is related . . . not with modernity but with modernization."[91] Like Jacobinism and Bolshevism, Puritanism should be understood as an "ideology of transition," a disciplinary system embraced by people caught in the threatening chaos of a changing world.[92] It was the task of the Puritan Saints to wage war upon and finally overwhelm the traditional order; it was the privilege of the liberals who came later to build a new world without compromising their construction with repression. Like Puritanism, liberalism "required . . . voluntary subjection and self-control," but liberalism benefited from the easy confidence that befalls men living in more settled times; liberalism "did not create the self-control it required."[93] Thus liberalism emerges as Puritan radicalism, its mission accomplished, wanes. The suggestion is that, as regards liberalism, the causally critical developments were taking place in society (the rise of a new class of educated men, merchants and lesser gentry) and politics (the "winning of the initiative" by the House of Commons[94]) perhaps under the protective fire of Puritanism but without its deliberate assistance.

Walzer's analysis concentrates on a certain moment in England's rendez-vous with Puritanism. If, however, one plunges Walzer's rather stiff and somewhat cerebral Saints back into the multidimensional and fast-moving world that was their own, another picture comes into focus, one in which the connection between Puritanism and liberalism, while still largely unintended, is nonetheless more direct and crucial. The Elizabethan settlement had excluded Puritans from church government but not from the ministry; at the same time, Elizabeth's policies and politics encouraged the political nation to see in the secular apparatus of the state the appropriate incarnation of national unity—promoting the autonomy of politics discussed above. Protestantism in all its forms confronted the believer with the Bible, so that each man and woman might read and accept the Word. With no resource left to them but the power of verbal persuasion exercised from the pulpit, the Puritan minority was naturally led to insist upon the right of men of diverse views to express themselves freely, the right of listeners—themselves readers and often expounders of Scripture—to arrive at their own conclusions, and the right of like-minded men and women to join voluntarily in "gathered"

---

[91] Michael Walzer, *The Revolution of the Saints* (New York: Atheneum, 1971), p. 18.
[92] Ibid., p. 312 and the entire Conclusion.
[93] Ibid., p. 302.
[94] The expression is Wallace Notestein's, in *The Winning of the Initiative by the House of Commons* (1924).

churches where they might appoint a minister of their own choosing. Dissent proliferated, eventually making the de facto neutrality of the state a practical necessity. The interminable debates of the Westminster Assembly prompted the uncomprehending Scots delegate, Robert Baillie, to write in despair: "The humour of this people is very various, and inclinable to singularities, to differ from all the world, and one from another, and shortlie from themselves. No people had so much need of a Presbyterie."[95] As the inconclusive results of the Assembly demonstrated, there would be no "Presbyterie" in England, no self-imposed but all-encompassing uniformity; the evolution of English Puritanism itself had made a Puritan establishment impossible. With the relaxation of central religious authority also came the slow erosion of the religiously inspired fear associated with Puritanism, for to many who read the Bible, the promise of redemption seemed more convincing than the threat of damnation that earlier Puritanism had left hanging over even the heads of the just.

The result of this evolution was a radical desacralization of political authority and a transformation of the view of what an individual brought to, and could expect to derive from, political society. By the time John Locke sat down to summarize and systematize the new thinking in the terse prose of the *Second Treatise* and the more eloquent pages of the *Letter concerning Toleration*, the legitimate state was conceived to have limited powers and discrete functions, and God had ceased to institute temporal authority. Now His role was simply to create men, and the individuals He created were autonomous moral agents. Having received from God both a property in themselves and the moral discernment necessary to self-government, men were entitled to the fruits of their labor, and they "owned" their thoughts and acts as well as their estates. They cooperated in political society out of interest and through exchange, and established government to serve as an umpire to their conflicts. Government kept the domestic peace and was accountable to the political nation for its performance, but the political nation was not further bound by any sense of common mission. Man and citizen alike were self-interested individuals.

Locke's argument from property in one's body to limited government by consent of the governed is too familiar to require lengthy review. What does bear emphasis is that Locke's assertions had psychological and institutional roots in the practices of his time, and that Puritanism is in large part responsible for this fact. Well before the advent of capitalist economic organization, Puritanism subverted the

[95] Quoted in Haller, *Liberty and Reformation*, p. 111.

patriarchal, authoritarian imagery which so many other aspects of seventeenth-century English life continued to reinforce.[96] Locke did more than set forth clearly what everyone already knew, but he did not invent the political language in which he spoke. In 1646, Richard Overton wrote:

> To every individual in nature is given an individual property by nature, not to be invaded or usurped by any. For every one as he is himself, so he hath a self propriety, else he could not be himself. . . . No man hath power over my rights and liberties and I over no man's. . . . For by natural birth all men are equally and alike born to like propriety, liberty and freedom, and as we are delivered by God, by the hand of nature, into this world, every one with a natural innate freedom and propriety (as it were writ in the table of every man's heart never to be obliterated) even so are we to live, everyone equally and alike to enjoy his birthright and privilege, even all whereof God by nature hath made him free.[97]

Similar arguments can be found in tracts written throughout the century. Puritan experience also credited the idea of a social contract. Writing of the Levellers' proposed "Agreement of the People," H. N. Brailsford notes that while the concept of such an agreement might seem strange to us, it came naturally to the Levellers, for it drew on "their deepest experience of social life": the gathered churches.[98] Citing the City companies and guilds as further evidence, Brailsford emphasizes: "History, for several generations round about this time, is littered with oaths, covenants and engagements which everyone, or everyone of any consequence, was expected to take. . . ."[99]

The distance traveled between the pronouncements of James I and Laud and the American Revolution can be measured by reading the famous, if by then unoriginal, sermon that Jonathan Mayhew preached in January 1750 in commemoration of the execution of Charles I. Taking Romans 13:1–8 as his text, offering another reading of those much-read verses, Mayhew stood the doctrine of passive obedience to temporal authorities on its head. Whatever the form of government is, Mayhew asserted, rulers are invested by God in an office. Insofar as they fulfill the duties of that office—to protect and

---

[96] For a different assessment of the strength of patriarchal imagery, see Gordon J. Schochet, *Patriarchalism in Political Thought* (New York: Basic Books, 1975), especially chaps. 3 and 4.

[97] Richard Overton, *An Arrow against all Tyrants and Tyranny . . .* , October 10, 1646, quoted in H. N. Brailsford, *The Levellers and the English Revolution* (London: The Cresset Press, 1961), p. 140 n. 33.

[98] Brailsford, *Levellers*, p. 259.

[99] Ibid., p. 260.

promote the common good—they deserve the obedience and support of all men. However, should a ruler abuse the power of his office and neglect the duties it imposes, he not only can but indeed must be resisted:

> If it be our duty, for example, to obey our King merely for this reason, that he rules for the public welfare (which is the only argument the Apostle makes use of), it follows by a parity of reason that when he turns tyrant and makes his subjects his prey to devour and to destroy instead of his charge to defend and cherish, we are bound to throw off our allegiance to him and to resist, and that according to the tenor of the Apostle's argument in this passage. Not to discontinue our allegiance, in this case, would be to join with the sovereign in promoting the slavery and misery of that society the welfare of which we ourselves as well as our sovereign are indispensably obliged to secure and promote as far as in us lies. It is true the Apostle puts no case of such a tyrannical prince; but by his grounding his argument for submission wholly upon the good of civil society it is plain he implicitly authorizes and even requires us to make resistance whenever this shall be necessary to the public safety and happiness.[100]

Thus there was a language of liberty—and of politics—common to England and America in the seventeenth and eighteenth centuries: a language couched in allusions to property, Scripture, and the established constitution. It is a language that was compelling only because the experienced realities of everyday life lent credence to its basic formulations, but it also shaped the way men perceived and in the end changed those realities. Its strength supplied the basis for enduring revolutionary settlements in both England and America. Part cause and part effect of the diverse historical processes that eventually assured its posterity, it is an essential element in accounting for the character of revolution in England and America.

In this chapter, an explanation has been offered of why moderation was adequate and indeed essential to the revolutionary enterprise in England and America. A sketch of a certain version of liberalism as an emerging intellectual construction has also been proposed. French liberals—Montesquieu no more than Robespierre—did not reproduce that construction. French liberalism spoke to a different historical experience, drew on a different reservoir of cultural and religious references, and developed within different constraints. It is important that from the outset we consider the prac-

---

[100] Jonathan Mayhew, "A Discourse concerning Unlimited Submission . . . ," 1750, text in Bernard Bailyn, ed., *Pamphlets of the American Revolution* (Cambridge, Mass.: Harvard University Press, 1965), vol. I, pp. 212–47; cited passage is on p. 232.

tice and theory of liberal politics in France as *different from*, rather than inferior to, the Anglo-American alternative. In many ways, French liberalism is in fact richer and more searching than its less anguished cousin. The English and American revolutionaries were concerned primarily with limiting the prerogatives of political power, and they brought to their task what might have appeared to continental eyes a shallow optimism. It remained for their French counterparts to reflect upon the fate of man in a Lockeian state. The French were explicitly concerned with the quality of life, with the personal, psychological dimensions of freedom and despotism, dependence and independence; they were sensitive to the needs of men as citizens and of citizens as men. Rarely do they pose private, bourgeois life as a morally and psychologically adequate objective, nor do they even see such life as conducive to the long-term survival of political freedom. Their critique of the narrowness and meanness of private life anticipates that of a disillusioned John Stuart Mill. In their world, the problem of community remained a constant preoccupation.

II

The First French Revolution, 1789–1792: The Sources and Significance of a Moderate Defeat

> While often the faithful partisans of truth and virtue, fearing to compromise those qualities by anything which might recall unworthy means, enemies of anything which resembles violence, confiding in the goodness of their cause, placing undue hope in men, because they know that sooner or later men return to reason, placing too much hope in the passage of time, because they know that sooner or later time will render them justice, miss the favorable moments, permit their prudence to degenerate into timidity, become discouraged, compromise with the future, and, enveloped in their conscience, finally fall asleep in an immobile good will, and a sort of lethargic innocence.
> —*André Chénier, August 1790*[1]

> Did you wish a revolution without revolution?
> —*Robespierre, November 1792*[2]

IDEOLOGICAL MOVEMENTS need not solicit revolutions, nor do they necessarily succeed in exploiting the ones they provoke. In a revolutionary situation, a group's ideological armature is nonetheless a crucial determinant of its strength. Americans often associate ideology in general and revolutionary ideology in particular with political fanaticism, escalating violence, and finally systematic terror; we contrast its supposed absence at home to its presence and deadly consequences in revolutionary France, Stalinist Russia, Nazi Germany, and certain contemporary Third World countries. Ideology itself is not, however, the culprit. Indeed, we have seen that in revolutionary England and America, the development of a coherent ideology was a condition of moderate victory.

[1] Chénier, article in the *Journal de la Société de 1789*, no. 13, August 28, 1790, p. 46. Chénier's article is dated August 24, 1790. Founded in 1790, the Société de 1789 had *fayettiste* sympathies.

[2] Robespierre, Convention, November 5, 1792; in *Oeuvres de Maximilien Robespierre* (Paris: Presses universitaires de France, 1957), vol. 9, p. 89.

That condition was not met in France. There, the moderates lost for reasons reminiscent in important ways of the Loyalist defeat in America. They lost not because they were moderates (as Strafford would have predicted and as Chénier seemed to think), but because in the absence of a common revolutionary idiom, their fears and aspirations never coalesced around a coherently motivated and systematically pursued plan of action. The moderates entered the battle in total, if for a time disguised, disarray. To suggest why is to propose a preliminary answer to the perennial question of why France was "not England."

As was true for England and America, the study of revolutionary ideology in France cannot be separated from an appraisal of the structure of revolutionary opportunity. Did the moderates sense the precariousness of their position and power? There would seem to be something curious about the political prose that André Chénier—better known to us for his poetry—penned in the summer of 1790. Chénier's impassioned plea for political toleration and the gradual incorporation of revolutionary change by reformist means was delivered during a period of relative calm. Revolutions are never wholly placid affairs; by the summer of 1790, the revolutionary coalition had already been rent by major defections, popular pressure had more than once forced the hand of king and Assembly alike, and among the crowds that gathered daily at the Palais Royal to discuss current events, Louis XVI had long since ceased to be an object of veneration. Despite the inevitable commotion, however, Chénier's political friends dominated the Constitutional Assembly, and there they worked to consolidate a "revolution without revolution." The king's abortive flight to Varennes was as yet nearly a year into the unforeseeable future; in 1790, most of the still highly circumscribed political class remained convinced that an accommodation could be reached between representative politics and a "regenerated" monarchy. Revolutionary France was still at peace with both neighboring powers and domestic dissidents. The Terror (Chénier himself would perish on the scaffold only two days before the fall of Robespierre) would not begin in earnest for another three years. Why then, in the first full summer of the Revolution, before any recognizably irreparable acts had been committed by either side, did the future seem, from Chénier's vantage point, foreclosed? Why the unmistakable accents of despair?

The moderate option for which Chénier pleaded, and of which first Mirabeau and then his sometime opponent and rival Barnave emerged as the most articulate spokesmen, arguably embodied the political preferences of a decisive majority of the delegates who sat in the first national assemblies of the Revolution. By the summer of 1792, when a popular insurrection finally toppled a monarchy discredited by months of duplicity and indecision, that option had been definitively eclipsed. Bypassed by events, it nonetheless continued to provide a sort of revolutionary common denominator, and it bequeathed both its objectives and its dilemmas to the unhappy French liberals of the nineteenth century. Before we turn to the political patterns that triumphed when the politics of transaction seemed condemned, we must therefore restore to view the moderate alternative as it took form during those first, anxious years of the Revolution, in all its apparent strength and with all its fatal ambiguities. We must probe not only its intellectual content, but also the causes and terms of its relative defeat.

Unlike Strafford, Chénier cast his lot with the Revolution. Like Strafford, however, Chénier believed that moderates—though history would eventually vindicate them—would face insuperable odds in any revolutionary situation. Strafford's fears were inspired by developments in England and proved, as we have seen, unduly pessimistic. Chénier anticipated the collapse of the moderate option in France, but wrongly held the dynamic supposedly inherent to any revolutionary situation responsible for the moderates' demise. Instead, the moderates succumbed to a political malady similar to the one that had afflicted the Loyalists. French moderates, ranging from Jean-Joseph Mounier in the early fall of 1789 to the Feuillants in the spring of 1792, shared a number of basic political convictions: All were committed to a limited political revolution requiring civil equality and resulting in a constitutional monarchy. But despite their early apparent advantage, they could never translate those common preferences into a coherent and compelling ideology. From the moment armed resistance had begun in the colonies, the American Loyalists had formed an increasingly beleaguered minority. The French moderates initially led the Revolution and commanded a political majority. With the important exception of Mirabeau, they nonetheless failed in their efforts to bring the expression of their fundamental aspirations and their theoretical understanding of the purpose and organization of government into line with a lucid reading of the evolving political situation: thus the odd ring of their tactical recommendations, which so often seem at once abstractly sensible and totally out of season.

Ultimately, the moderate majority would be easily outflanked at the center of power by former comrades who *had* developed an adequate ideological response to the political world in which they had to act. The political skill of the Jacobins prevailed over the blundering ineptitude of the moderates, but the political aspirations of the latter could not be consigned to permanent political oblivion, as had been those of the Loyalists. Decisive in tactical terms, the Jacobin victory was therefore less significant in substantive terms; Jacobinism, as we shall see in Chapter III, abandoned the path that might have led to the politics of transaction, but without at the same time developing an alternative to liberalism itself.

The first section of this chapter traces the structure of revolutionary opportunity, shaped during the two centuries that preceded the Revolution. The sociopolitical structure of the Old Regime did not preclude the formulation of liberal demands for limited government and representative institutions. It did compromise in advance the ideological underpinnings and material chances of a successful political revolution based on then-current liberal aspirations and controlled from start to finish by some French equivalent to England's "middle group." The revolutionaries' eventual recourse to the politics of exclusion appears overdetermined, but other options were articulated. What actually happened once the Revolution began turned, at least in part, on how the moderates chose to apply the doctrine of popular sovereignty, as ideology and individual actors played the roles we assigned them in the Introduction. In the second section of this chapter, we will therefore examine how the moderates understood—or failed to understand—the range of political possibilities which their unshakable adhesion to that doctrine made available. Finally, we will watch the moderates as they lost control of their Revolution, recovering the all-important political chronology of a period that unfolded before its contemporaries with breathtaking rapidity. From the summer of 1791 on, repeated declarations that "the revolution is done"[3] and that further change would lead to anarchy and then despotism rather than to the consolidation of freedom simply betray the moderates' growing sense of confusion and desperation. During the year that followed the royal family's flight to Varennes, for reasons discussed in the first two sections of this chapter, all attempts to forge a stable revolutionary coalition failed. The establishment of representative institutions—the cornerstone of liberal government—was the Revolution's great accomplishment. By the

---

[3] Adrien Duport, Constituent Assembly, May 17, 1791; *Le Moniteur*, vol. 8, p. 427. The *Gazette nationale ou le Moniteur universel* was published daily throughout the revolutionary period (and beyond). The numbers dating from the revolutionary years were reprinted in thirty volumes between 1863 and 1870. *Le Moniteur* is a standard source for speeches delivered before the national assemblies of the Revolution, and quotes from the reprinted edition are conventionally acknowledged by volume and page number. Duport's speech is discussed later in this chapter.

summer of 1792, however, the moderate leadership had lost the political initiative. It was replaced by a militant minority steeped in the politics and mentality of exclusion, and thus wedded to a different conception of how representative politics could and should work.

Liberalism Entrapped: The Old Regime and the Structure of Revolutionary Opportunity

Chronologically at least, the French Revolution capped the century of the Enlightenment. Acknowledging the importance of this legacy, Mirabeau once assured his colleagues in the Constituent Assembly, "We have ideas in the bank."[4] The remark, backed by the authority of the man who was the Revolution's first great orator and the most astute of the moderate leaders, is often cited. It is intended to remind us that the revolutionaries had been preceded by Voltaire and Diderot, Helvétius and Rousseau, the Physiocrats and Turgot, and that they stood to profit from the example already set by the American Revolution. Mirabeau implies that he and his colleagues were intellectually well-armed for the political tasks they faced. The record of the Revolution, however, suggests a different judgment. During a heated debate in late January 1791, Barnave bitterly denounced the right-wing minority in the Assembly. Addressing the majority, Barnave spoke as follows:

> Never have you rendered a great decree without hearing someone use the opportunity to abuse the name of those things most sacred among men; this word "monarchy" so dear to all Frenchmen. . . . [sic] (violent agitation on the right side of the assembly; much applause on the left); was it not invoked when you rendered your decrees against tyranny? The word "property," was it not invoked every time you rendered decrees against the confiscations which had reduced to nothing the public fortune, in order to create private fortunes on its ruins? (Applause.) Therefore do not be surprised that religion is wielded as a weapon against you when you would destroy the abuses that profane it; when, in your justice and wisdom, you have torn some from the poverty that humiliated them, and others from that opulence which made them objects of scandal. (The applause redoubles.)[5]

Barnave was not fighting to monopolize a language common to all sides in the revolutionary struggle. Rather, he was admitting that the

---

[4] Cited by François Furet in his Preface to Mirabeau's *Discours* (Paris: Gallimard, 1973), p. 15.

[5] Barnave, January 25, 1791; *Le Moniteur*, Vol. 7, p. 226.

idiom in which he would have preferred to speak had already been irretrievably corrupted by opponents with whom compromise was proving impossible and against whom exclusion seemed unrealistic.

Individuals, however, were not at fault, or at least those who were responsible had died long before the beginning of the Revolution. Historically, liberal revolutions have occurred when a broadly based group in civil society attained independent moral and material power and then employed that power to limit permanently the power of the state. The group conventionally assigned this role is the bourgeoisie, or the "rising" middle class(es) of a modernizing economy and society—a hypothesis about which we shall have more to say at the end of this book. The more independent the group, the more likely a revolutionary process dominated by moderate forces. The problem in eighteenth-century France was that no group in civil society possessed sufficient independent power to play the predicted part; instead, all were hopelessly entangled in the Old Regime. What independence they did achieve fostered a yearning for limited government and representative institutions, while their dependence on a sociopolitical system that deflected those demands precluded the development of a revolutionary ideology adequate to the situation in which the moderates had to operate.

To understand the ideological fragility of the moderate position in revolutionary France, we must consider the process of state building, which had been the major theme of sixteenth- and seventeenth-century French history. The Tudors had inadvertently contributed to an eventual structure of revolutionary opportunity that favored moderates. The political strategies adopted by French rulers from François Ier (who reigned from 1515 to 1547) through Louis XIV (1661–1715) had a very different effect. Ultimately, the sociopolitical system of the Old Regime weighed more heavily than did Diderot's *Encyclopédie* on the type of political competition that dominated the Revolution, and from the viewpoint of liberalism, the Old Regime contaminated all that it touched. The choices and patterns that determined this outcome were established by the mid-seventeenth century; the implications for a liberal political revolution received their first demonstration during the decades of parliamentary protest that preceded the crisis of the late 1780s.[6]

[6] The analysis presented in this section is based on information drawn from many sources. Most important were Keith Michael Baker, ed., *The French Revolution and the Creation of Modern Political Culture*, vol. 1; *The Political Culture of the Old Regime* (Oxford: Pergamon Press, 1987); William F. Church, *Richelieu and Reason of State* (Princeton: Princeton University Press, 1972); Robert Darnton, *The Business of the Enlightenment: A Publishing History of the Encyclopédie 1775–1800* (Cambridge, Mass.: Harvard University Press, 1979); Darnton's *Mesmerism and the End of the Enlightenment in France* (Cambridge,

The monarchs and ministers who made of France the first modern state were responding to three sets of pressures, and their task was rendered all the more urgent (and difficult) by the fact that these pressures were interrelated. The French monarchy developed both in spite and because of foreign wars, religious strife, and the activities of a rebellious nobility.

Water shielded England from attack and long shaped her foreign policy ambitions as well as her needs. France, on the other hand, from the campaigns against Charles V in the early sixteenth century to the Seven Years War in the middle of the eighteenth century, was forever fielding armies. Although, as time passed, her territorial integrity seemed increasingly assured, the wars continued. Sometimes they were the result of royal ambitions; most often they were the product of European rivalries. French security depended on a balance of power on the Continent, and that balance was frequently disrupted by marriage disputes and succession struggles, with religious differences further complicating existing interstate tensions. War placed a constant strain on state finances and put a premium on the development of national unity, a strong economy, and an efficient central administration. If taxes were to be raised or loans floated (in 1522, François Ier became the first French monarch to borrow money

Mass.: Harvard University Press, 1968); William Doyle, *Origins of the French Revolution* (Oxford: Oxford University Press, 1980); Jean Egret, *Louis XV et l'opposition parlementaire, 1715–1774* (Paris: Armand Colin, 1970); Egret's *La Pré-Révolution française (1787–1788)* (Paris: Presses universitaires de France, 1962); François Furet, *Penser la Révolution française* (Paris: Gallimard, 1978); Pierre Goubert, *L'Ancien Régime*, vol. I, *La Société* and vol. II, *Les Pouvoirs* (Paris: Armand Colin, 1969, 1973); Goubert's *Louis XIV et vingt millions de Français* (Paris: Fayard, 1966); Paul Hazard, *La Crise de la conscience européenne, 1680–1715* (Paris: Fayard, 1961); Ernest Labrousse, *La Crise de l'économie française à la fin de l'Ancien régime et au début de la Révolution* (Paris: Presses universitaires de France, 1944); Labrousse et al., *Histoire économique et sociale de la France*, vol. 2, *Des derniers temps de l'âge seigneurial aux préludes de l'âge industriel (1660–1789)* (Paris: Presses universitaires de France, 1970); Robert Mandrou, *L'Europe "absolutiste": Raison et raison d'Etat, 1649–1775* (Paris: Fayard, 1977); Mandrou's *La France aux XVIIe et XVIIIe siècles* (Paris: Presses universitaires de France, 1974); Mandrou's *Louis XIV en son temps, 1661– 1715* (Paris: Presses universitaires de France, 1973); A. Lloyd Moote, *The Revolt of the Judges: The Parlement of Paris and the Fronde, 1643–1715* (Princeton: Princeton University Press, 1971); Roland Mousnier and Ernest Labrousse, *Le XVIIIe siècle: Révolution intellectuelle, technique et politique (1715–1815)* (Paris: Presses universitaires de France, 1953); Denis Richet, *La France moderne: L'Esprit des institutions* (Paris: Flammarion, 1973); Lionel Rothkrug, *Opposition to Louis XIV: The Political and Social Origins of the French Enlightenment* (Princeton: Princeton University Press, 1965); Victor L. Tapie, *La France de Louis XIII et de Richelieu* (Paris: Flammarion, 1967); Etienne Thuau, *Raison d'état et pensée politique à l'époque de Richelieu* (Paris: Athenes, 1966); and Alexis de Tocqueville, *L'ancien régime et la Révolution* (Paris: Gallimard, 1967) (originally published in 1856).

from his subjects), some degree of governmental legitimacy had to be accepted and a rudimentary bureaucracy established; wealth was desirable both because poverty was hard (although not impossible . . .) to tax, and because it was increasingly used as an important index of national power. Domestic divisions, on the other hand, whatever their cause, could easily prove fatal, for discontented noblemen might well lend their considerable services to foreign powers, as did Turenne for a time during the Fronde.

Domestic divisions, of course, abounded, and much of modern French history prior to the personal reign of Louis XIV can be told in terms of civil war. The beginnings of the movement which would come to be called the Reformation coincided with the ascension of François Ier to the French throne, and for the next century and a half, noble resistance to and religious dissent within an increasingly unitary, centralized state often reinforced each other. From 1562 until Henri IV renounced Protestantism (1594) and promulgated the Edict of Nantes (1598), the country was ravaged by religious war. During those years, a strong monarchy looked to be a long shot indeed: as Regent, Catherine de Medici was more important than the young Charles IX (1560-1574), and she remained a major political force until her death in 1589. It was Catherine de Medici and Henri de Guise (shortly thereafter the leader of the Ligue) who engineered the famous Massacre of Saint Bartholomew in August of 1572. Their purpose was to do away with the Protestant nobility, and it is hard to believe that their motives were exclusively religious. On the other side, while the Bourbons were quite possibly convinced Protestants, their rivalry with the Guise family could only have strengthened them in their faith.

In all these apparently inconclusive struggles of the late sixteenth century, the consistent short-term loser was the state. Nor did the state seem to gain ground during the regency of Marie de Medici, which followed the assassination of Henri IV (1610). When then were the crucial moves made and a durable pattern established? If a long-term trend must, for the purposes of summary and analysis, be circumscribed by precise dates, those dates in this case would be 1624, the year in which Richelieu came to power, and 1661, the year in which Mazarin died and the personal reign of Louis XIV began. In Louis XIV's mature memories, the years of his youth would appear as years of political strife and royal humiliation. Eager to play up his own achievements, he would not readily have conceded that his accomplishments (but also the many compromises he was forced to make) had their source in the previous period. It was during the middle third of the seventeenth century, however, that the government

sacrificed or modified planned reforms in order to meet the needs of
an ambitious foreign policy; during these same years, the Fronde
(1648–1652), the nobility's last chance to do away with the ministers
it detested and remold the monarchy on its own terms, failed to generate a revolutionary movement. Most importantly, it was during this
period that the Bourbon monarchy assumed the role that the Tudor
monarchy had never taken on: that of overseeing the regulation of
the social machine and of independently elaborating and implement-
ing its own vision of the common good, without a national parliament
and in the face of a body politic that was subdued and fragmented
rather than united or organized from below. The price the monarchy
paid for what is conventionally labeled its victory is of critical importance in understanding both the monarchy's rapid demise a century
and a half later and the difficulties encountered by the moderate revolutionaries who sought to build on its ruins. The key to this story is
not the rise of the *intendants*, supervising on an increasingly permanent basis the affairs of the provinces and thereby destroying the vestiges of political autonomy and initiative. The key lies rather in the
social impact of the monarchy's financial practices, themselves in
large part the product of inflated royal ambitions. The intendants
symbolize the triumph of royal absolutism; the buying and selling of
offices suggests, among other things, that the triumph was in part an
illusion.

The sale of offices ultimately trapped both the monarchy and the
growing political class it created: The state would be reluctant to
alienate its creditors, but the men most likely to contest the Crown
would owe their social status and often their fortunes to the maintenance of the political status quo. Office brought nobility; nobility
meant privilege and prestige. Deliberately oversimplifying the evidence in order to emphasize a fundamental point, French historian
Pierre Goubert has called nobility "the ideal obstinately pursued and
the ultimate goal of the bourgeoisie."[7] Reform-minded contemporaries expressed their views more harshly. Answering in advance Sieyès's
famous question, Mably wrote: "The Third Estate is nothing in
France, because no one wishes to be considered part of it."[8] Sieyès
himself was hardly more complimentary, describing the Third Estate
in the following terms:

> This unfortunate part of the nation has reached the point of forming a
> sort of huge antechamber, where, constantly concerned with what its mas-
> ters are saying or doing, it is ever ready to sacrifice everything to the fruits
> it counts on gaining through flattery. In view of such mores, how can one

[7] Goubert, *L'Ancien Régime*, vol. 1, p. 152. Emphasized by Goubert in the text.
[8] Cited by Egret, *La Pré-Révolution*, p. 352.

not fear that the qualities best suited to the defense of the national interest will not be prostituted to those which best serve prejudices? The boldest defenders of the aristocracy will be in the order of the Third Estate and among the men who, born with much intelligence and little soul, are as eager for fortune, power, and the compliments of the great as they are incapable of appreciating the value of liberty.[9]

Dependent on the monarchy for social advancement and prestige, the bourgeois also knew where to look if he wanted to make money: In the economy of the Old Regime, the men who amassed the most impressive fortunes did so by working for the king, equipping his armies or collecting his taxes. In prerevolutionary France, then, only the very first steps of enterprising men were taken outside the bounds of state interference. Instead of a developing economy autonomously producing the new middle classes, it was the state that from the beginning manipulated the economy and shaped—both materially and mentally—the middle classes. A lively professional debate has yet to settle the question of whether or not a bourgeoisie so shaped is a bourgeoisie at all, and the differences between England's Industrial Revolution and France's more circuitous development have been analyzed at length. Goubert notes simply that at least until 1750, the French bourgeoisie's primary attitude toward its social and political surroundings was one of conformism.[10] Again, the comments of contemporaries often carry a more cutting edge. The Grenoblois parliamentarian Michel Servan remarked sarcastically in 1788:

> They [the members of the Third Estate] expect no fortune other than that won by their services, nor distinctions other than those obtained through servility before the nobility and the clergy. On the one hand, benefices in the Church, on the other, appointments in the judiciary. Their services are real; their rewards are but seductive promises and illusions. What chains in the hands of nobles and priests to overwhelm the Third Estate—chains the Third Estate receives with kisses, sometimes treating them as though they were honorable, sometimes as though they were sacred! What powerful means of separating from that part of the Third Estate as yet unaware of its own identity, the part that would be capable of recognizing its rights and defending them![11]

If the state's role as the arbiter of social mobility and prestige limited the political options of the elites, it also limited the political options available to the state itself. The two most striking traits of the

[9] Emmanuel Sieyès, *Qu'est-ce que le Tiers etat* (1789), critical edition by Roberto Zapperi (Geneva: Droz, 1970), p. 136.
[10] See Goubert, *L'Ancien Régime*, vol. 1, chap. 10.
[11] Cited by Egret, *La Pré-Révolution*, p. 351f.

French monarchy in the eighteenth century are its sustained and often successful efforts to make government more rational and efficient, and the repeated failure of all attempts to secure the financial reforms that the modernization of the regime required. Arguing, with much justification, that the real division in the Old Regime lay between the elites and the masses, Denis Richet has written that "the notion of 'orders'. . . obscures the real hierarchies."[12] What the notion of a society stratified by order—the Old Regime's self-image—does not obscure is the source of the regime's suicidal tendencies. Behind the seventeenth-century victory of the monarchy over the factions that had disputed its authority lay the broad distribution of privilege. The notion of orders conferred legitimacy on what the monarchy was doing; it also provided a respectable rallying cry for those whose material interests would have been compromised by fiscal reform. Thus the notion's appeal extended to the very forces in state and society responsible for undermining its reality. By the 1780s, the French monarchy was caught in a bind of its own creation. The Revolution—the one described in our history books—was not inevitable; a crisis was.[13] Louis XVI was a dull man constantly exposed to the reactionary impulses of his wife and the intrigues of a scheming and inconsequent court. A more exemplary character might not, however, have fared any better than Louis. Nor were his revolutionary competitors much better equipped to resolve the crisis to their satisfaction.

––––––––––

"Around 1750, without the intervention of any rupture in the political order, everything changes."[14] Denis Richet's statement refers primarily to developments in the world of ideas. The final crisis of the Old Regime had begun; in some ways, it would extend well beyond the closing date of the Revolution. We shall return shortly to what men were thinking. Other trends, beginning before 1750 but accelerating thereafter, both contributed to the shape of the crisis and conditioned the translation of ideas into behavior.

Modern economic historians, guided by the brilliant work of Ernest Labrousse, have established that the eighteenth century was, in France, a period of expansion and prosperity punctuated by an "in-

[12] Richet, *La France moderne*, p. 101.

[13] On the monarchy's role in bringing on the revolutionary crisis, see Furet, *Penser la Révolution*, pp. 139–54.

[14] Richet, *La France moderne*, p. 151.

tercycle" of economic hard times.[15] The years of economic downturn coincided, presumably not by accident, with the development of a revolutionary situation. In fact, both the expansion and the interlude of contraction posed severe problems for a regime whose survival depended on its continued capacity to derive political and economic profit from the regulation of social relations in general and of social mobility in particular.

Prosperity did not bring equal benefits to all. The gradual but sustained rise in agricultural prices benefited those whose income was based on *rente*: those, in other words, who had already reached the middle ranks of the economic, although not necessarily the social, ladder. Other economic trends—the expansion of foreign trade, the growth of production, the increased ease with which goods could be conveyed from one place to another—likewise favored those whose starting point was one of relative comfort.

Economic growth had a direct impact on demographic patterns. After remaining stagnant during the seventeenth century, the country's population grew from approximately 19 million in 1700 to 26 million in 1789, in part because the demographic catastrophes—famines and epidemics—traditionally associated with poor harvests became less common and less deadly. Average age dropped; the proportion of the population living in towns grew.[16]

Affluence combined with the increase in the density of social relations to promote what Labrousse calls "intellectual products,"[17] while the fact that all seemed to be going well buttressed liberal arguments condemning government intervention. To Labrousse, a proponent of the "social interpretation" of the French Revolution, the situation recalls the classic account of a rising bourgeoisie eventually imposing its will through a liberal revolution. "Cities-towns-bourgeoisie," he writes, "a story that explains and dominates. . . ."[18] Increasingly educated, ambitious, and restless, the bourgeoisie of Labrousse's story is already a fully developed social class: conscious of its identity, its interests, and its as yet latent force. The ambiguities suggested by Sieyès and Servan have vanished.

The economic troubles of the 1770s and 1780s, intruding upon and interrupting the habits and expectations borne of prosperity,

[15] Labrousse develops the analysis summarized here in *La Crise de l'économie* and in his contribution to *Le XVIIIe siècle*, part II, book I, "La Révolution française et les consolidations napoléoniennes."

[16] For a summary analysis of population trends, see Labrousse et al., *Histoire économique et sociale*, vol. 2, pp. 9–18.

[17] Labrousse, *La Crise de l'économie*, Introduction.

[18] Labrousse, *Le XVIIIe siècle*, p. 345.

would catapult the bourgeoisie into political action. In France as in England and America, the immediate cause of revolution lay in the central government's need to secure additional funds. The French government's financial woes were due in part to the weight of the debt accumulated during the American War of Independence. The coincidence of the economic crisis with the budgetary deficits was most unfortunate for the monarchy. Had the 1780s not been difficult years, the tax yield from existing taxes would have been higher, and the imposition of new taxes might not have seemed so unacceptable. The monarchy might have weathered the storm. Instead, it was blamed for all that had gone wrong: "An immense error of attribution produced a political crisis out of the economic crisis."[19] Pleading for money, the monarchy was resisted on the one hand by the nobility, eager to reassert its privileges under cover of liberal rhetoric about the need for representative institutions, and on the other hand by the bourgeoisie, intent on pressing its demand for civil equality— the legal precondition of bourgeois society. Forced to choose sides, the monarchy instead vacillated, and the victory eventually fell to the bourgeoisie, principal motor and primary beneficiary of the Revolution. For Labrousse, the final results of the Revolution fulfill the initial bourgeois program: "a society without orders under bourgeois management, with its crucial conquest: civil equality."[20]

Labrousse's interpretation of the Revolution minimizes the differences between the French experience and the hypothetically archetypical English one. For Labrousse, the sides are always clearly drawn, and their identities are derived as much from social theory as from the historical record. Yet the story of the French Revolution must include the story of the actual individuals who in fact made it. Their story is one of endless division and mutual exclusion. From the summer of 1789 through the Directory, all efforts to cement a stable revolutionary coalition ended in failure. To understand why, we may retain Labrousse's description of the eighteenth-century context, but we must abandon his depiction of the main protagonists.

If we return to 1750 (at which date Barnave, Robespierre, Saint-Just, Barère, and Napoleon had not yet been born; even Mirabeau was but a child of four), we will find the Enlightenment in full swing. Montesquieu published L'Esprit des lois in 1748, Rousseau wrote his Discours sur les sciences et les arts in 1750, and the first volume of the Encyclopédie appeared in 1751. The ideological challenge the Old Regime now faced was more serious even than that thrown down two

---

[19] Labrousse, La Crise de l'économie, p. xlviii.
[20] Labrousse, Le XVIIIe siècle, p. 436.

centuries earlier by the contestants in the wars of religion, for in the meantime the ideological foundations of divine right monarchy and of a political system based on institutionalized exceptions had been shattered.[21] The country's elites—"bourgeois" or "noble," but more pertinently upwardly mobile in their expectations and increasingly inclined to make public affairs their own affair—did not know how to get to the promised land, but they did have a general idea of what they would see from the mountaintop. In this sense at least, Mirabeau's reference to previously stockpiled ideas is accurate. In the last years before the Revolution, a coalition of discontent deflected all royal attempts to divide it. Its strength derived from its character; it was not, Denis Richet argues, "a merely accidental and deceptive cartel, but rested, despite divergent interests, on the common demand for limited government [*contrôle du pouvoir*]."[22] Pierre Goubert's description of the "high society" of these years, by reinforcing Richet's analysis of its political aspirations but at the same time reintroducing the problem of the elites' relations to the state, brings us back to the ambiguities and weaknesses of the developing revolutionary idiom. High society cut across the distinctions between orders; it was united "by its wealth, its power, and its glitter."[23] And its members?

> Nearly all were closely tied to the regime, which many served, and which enriched them; and nearly all nonetheless criticized its politics, its policies, or its lack of policy, dreamed of "reforms," of a "philosophical" ministry, of "enlightened" despotism, of "intermediary bodies," or of more radical transformations. Tendencies, schools, cliques were created, dissolved, and recreated at the heart of this brilliant and well-spoken society, which prepared at a distance, rather unknowingly, the only "revolution" which the most solid heads envisioned: a liberal and constitutional monarchy.[24]

A constitutional monarchy: That was the moderate demand, shared by a broad cross-section of French elites, which the Revolution would not fulfill but which Jacobinism would not discard and Bonaparte would not extinguish. Social change made its formulation plausible; the relationship between society and politics made its rapid realization unlikely, as prerevolutionary events made clear.

Before the Revolution transformed the available options, two routes were theoretically open to would-be reformers. Reform might have come from above, on the initiative of the monarchy itself. Its

---

[21] On this subject, Hazard's *La Crise de conscience* remains unsurpassed. See also Richet, *La France moderne*; and Rothkrug, *Opposition*.

[22] Richet, *La France moderne*, p. 173.

[23] Goubert, *L'Ancien Régime*, vol. 2, p. 210.

[24] Ibid.

effect would then have been to move France, perhaps definitively, in an authoritarian direction. Increasingly efficient rule by a royal bureaucracy would have led to civil equality but not to government by consent. Reform could also have come from below, and have led to the peaceful consolidation of representative institutions and a constitutional monarchy. In the latter case, the *parlements* would have been the most likely vehicle of change.[25] The two options prefigure the postrevolutionary oscillation of French politics between a Bonapartist and a liberal mode of government. In the forty years that preceded the Revolution, the partisans of each option monopolized the kingdom's political space and fought each other to a standstill. The inadvertent product of that stalemate was a revolutionary situation, and the ideas—concerning political legitimacy, sovereignty, and the modalities of political action—that then became salient were ones whose development had not been nurtured by the previous years of political controversy. In July 1788, an assembly representing the three estates of Dauphine adopted a resolution written by Jean-Joseph Mounier, who one year later would be instrumental in drafting France's first constitution. Assigning a new meaning to the events of the recent past, the assembled notables asserted: "The *Parlements*, conscious at last of their long error . . . declared that they were not the representatives of the Nation. . . . They demanded the summoning of the Estates General. . . ."[26] By condemning the "long error" of the parlements and thus renouncing the heritage of seventy years of sometimes bitter struggle between the parlements and the Crown over religious and fiscal matters, Mounier and his colleagues revealed the revolutionary nature of the enterprise on which they were embarking. Their words and actions also indicate an ideological discontinuity different in kind, not degree, from the gradual process that led from protest to revolution in England and America. It was the necessity of that discontinuity that left the French moderates ideologically disarmed as the Revolution began. Why did it happen?

By a declaration of February 1673 and by his general approach to domestic politics, Louis XIV had sharply curtailed the activities of the country's *cours souveraines*.[27] Early in the Regency, Philippe d'Orléans restored the parlements' right to remonstrate against a royal decree

[25] Since the parlements were not a parliament, I have retained the French word. I have, however, been forced to say "parliamentarians" and "parliamentary" where such words were required.

[26] Cited by Jean Egret, *La Révolution des Notables: Mounier et les Monarchiens, 1789* (Paris: Armand Colin, 1950), p. 18.

[27] The parlements were the most important of the cours souveraines. See Egret, *Louis XV et l'opposition*, pp. 9ff.

before registering it as a law. During the next seventy years, the twelve parlements, and particularly the Parlement de Paris, made ample use of the powers accorded them. Parliamentary protest in eighteenth-century France may be divided into two phases. The first extends from 1715 through the mid-1750s. This period was dominated by the dispute between the Jansenists and their opponents, a dispute that also opposed a Gallican to an Ultramontane vision of Church authority and organization. The beginning of the second period coincides (not incidentally) with the beginning of the Seven Years War, and continues up to the eve of the Revolution. The main issues here centered on questions of taxation and governmental reform, and parliamentary criticism rapidly broadened into a general attack on the political arrangements of the Old Regime. At three different times, the monarchy sought unsuccessfully to turn back the tide: with the Maupeou reforms of 1770, and with the ministries of Calonne and Loménie de Brienne in the 1780s.

At first glance, the scene seems reminiscent of England under the first two Stuarts. In France as in England, the Crown was contested for its positions on religious and fiscal questions; only after a long struggle over specific issues did the dissidents extend the scope of their protest to include some of the basic principles of the regime itself. Such similarities set the stage for the development of political liberalism in both countries. Yet given the differences between the social and political status of the parliamentary personnel in France and the status of members of the House of Commons in England, the differences in the legal and political institutions of the two countries, and their different response to the challenge of the Reformation, it is hardly surprising that similar areas of concern would give rise to different political arguments.

No national body in prerevolutionary France was charged with a legislative role; as has been noted many times, France possessed no equivalent of the English House of Commons. The most important day-to-day functions of the French parlements were judicial in character, not political. Solidarity between the several parlements (advocated toward the end of the Old Regime under the name of *l'union des classes*) was limited to moments of intense political controversy and was ephemeral even then. The parliamentary magistrates did not owe their positions to election by any constituency, however restricted; they had bought their offices and remained conscious of the social advantages their purchase bestowed. That most eighteenth-century parliamentary magistrates enjoyed noble status before acquiring their parliamentary offices is far less important than the fact that they had usually acquired their nobility in the none-too-distant past through the purchase of some lesser office.[28] The magistrates belonged, in other words, to the upwardly mobile elites whose status and advancement depended on the stability of the Old Regime. Their ultimate weapon was to declare themselves on strike, but while the ensuing disruption did create serious problems for the Crown, the magistrates risked being first isolated and then defeated by a stubborn monarch. Over time, a pattern of interaction developed. Parliamentary protest would lead to the arrest of the ringleaders. Protest against the arrests would provoke the exiling of the refractory parliamentarians. The crisis would end when the magistrates capitulated—and in exchange recovered their functions. The truce thus obtained would last for a period of time, after which discontent would resurface and the cycle would begin again.

The parlements were weak because they were scattered throughout the kingdom; they were weak because they could not draw on any institutionalized links to any organized constituency; they were weak because the country's official ideology—increasingly battered as memories of Louis XIV receded, but still unreplaced—made no room for them. In the final analysis, the magistrates needed the monarchy at least as much as the monarchy needed them. Such limitations made the parlements ineffective agents of reform, but given the broader political, social, and cultural context of the eighteenth century, these limitations could not prevent the parlements—and particularly the Parlement de Paris, whose jurisdiction extended to one-third of the kingdom's territory—from serving as forums for political discussion. Political questions sometimes arose in connection with judicial cases; on other occasions, controversy was prompted by parliamentary refusal to register measures of which it disapproved. As the demand for limited government and institutionalized political participation became increasingly current among the country's expanding elites, the political importance of the parlements grew. They were, after all, the only political body open to the concerns of the elites. At the same time, a resentful monarchy sought to exploit the parlements in its bid to gain legitimacy in the changing political atmosphere and to avoid more radical institutional experiments. That the monarchy felt it could no longer dispense with its disputatious parlements is demonstrated by Louis XVI's abandonment of the Maupeou reforms.[29]

Thus while the Enlightenment developed in Parisian salons and

---

[28] Ibid., pp. 13ff.

[29] This is one interpretation of Louis XVI's action; there are, of course, others; cf. Mandrou, L'Europe "absolutiste," pp. 31f.

provincial academies, the political battles of the eighteenth century were fought in the parlements. The first major issue to arise had been smoldering for the better part of a century. The Jansenist controversy had begun as a theological dispute born of the Reformation.[30] At the heart of the initial quarrel lay the question of predestination and its implications for the moral duties of the Christian. The Jansenists also aspired to make the Church and its rituals purer and more austere. The Jansenists' immediate enemies were the Jesuits. The latter accused the former of repeating Calvin's heretical teachings; the former accused the latter of subordinating moral consistency and spiritual rigor to their desire to gain power over the minds of men and monarchs. Rome repeatedly came down in favor of the Jesuit position, condemning Jansen's *Augustinus* (published in 1640) by papal bull (*In Eminente*) in 1643, and renewing its reprobation of the sect in 1653, 1656, and 1665. As soon as his personal reign began (1661), Louis XIV joined the attack. He probably did not pause to appreciate the theological dimensions of the dispute; as usual, his position was determined by political considerations. Louis XIV saw in Jansenism a threat to the unity and discipline of the French Church—already gravely damaged by the persistence within French borders of a vigorous Protestant community—and thus to the ideological and cultural support system on which his vision of the monarchy depended. Jansenism had in fact divided the Church, finding friends in high places as well as low, and its appeal extended to a broad, and apparently sociologically diverse, segment of the population's more educated elements.[31]

In 1688, a truce was arranged. The contending parties agreed not to discuss those issues on which they could not agree. The relative calm lasted until the end of the century. Jansenism's great men—de Sacy, Arnauld, Nicole (Pascal had died in 1662)—passed on, while its great women, forbidden from recruiting their own replacements, grew old and less numerous. The monarchy, meanwhile, turned its attention to a fierce and lengthy dispute with Rome over who should control the benefices of vacant bishoprics and, even before the formal

---

[30] For a good summary of French religious history in the seventeenth century, see Mandrou, *Louis XIV*, book I, chap. 7 and book II, chap. 3. For more detail and depth, see Jean Delumeau, *Le Catholicisme entre Luther et Voltaire* (Paris: Presses universitaires de France, 1971). On Jansenism, see Antoine Adam, *Du Mysticisme à la révolte: Les jansénistes du XVIIe siècle* (Paris, 1968); Louis Cognet, *Le Jansénisme* (Paris: Presses universitaires de France, 1961); Lucien Goldman, *Le Dieu caché: Etude sur la vision tragique dans les Pensées de Pascal et dans le théâtre de Racine* (Paris: Gallimard, 1955).

[31] In *Le Dieu caché*, Goldman makes the case for tying Jansenism to the social interests and milieu of the parliamentary class. The sociology of Jansenism raises questions similar to those raised by the sociology of English Puritanism.

revocation of the Edict of Nantes in 1685, to the renewed wholesale persecution of the "so-called reformed religion." It was during these years that Bossuet composed his *Politique tirée de l'Ecriture sainte.*

Jansenism during this first period would appear to bear some resemblance to English Puritanism. The debate between the Jansenists and their adversaries reopened at the turn of the century, and assumed a political character for both sides when Clement XI's anti-Jansenist bull Unigenitus (1713) was followed by Louis XIV's death (1715) and the resurgence of the parlements. The Jansenist controversy, however, did not do to French politics what the Puritan controversy had done to English politics. The reasons are multiple, but they are not limited to the institutional and sociological considerations discussed earlier with regard to the parlements. Jansenism never became a militant body after the manner of the English Saints. The Jansenists' reluctance, and perhaps their inability, to assume any such role was in large part the product of past French religious history. In France, the Reformation and the ensuing civil wars had both split the national community and left the Catholic majority under the continued authority of Rome. The Jansenists of the first period therefore labored flanked on their "left" by a Calvinist reformed Church with which they did not want to be confused. Instead, the dissidents reaffirmed their theological and hierarchical loyalty to Rome. While the Calvinist presence served as a strong brake on the Jansenists' theological and organizational audacities, it also drained away potential support. Port-Royal was a meeting place and a symbol; it in no way approximated the Puritan network already in place as James I ascended the throne. Nor would Louis XIV have permitted such a network to develop, given his concern for ideological conformity. Even pamphlet warfare, so prevalent in Stuart England and so important to the evolution of seventeenth-century English politics, was severely restricted in Louis XIV's France. Indeed, the most powerful and popular pamphlet generated by the controversy, Pascal's *Lettres écrites à un provincial* (1656–1657), antedates Louis's personal reign. When cultural life broke free after 1715, it was too late. The eighteenth century paid the price of Louis XIV's and Bossuet's momentary victory, as militancy fell to the skeptics and atheists who, thanks to Louis's policies, identified religion with divine right kingship and intolerance. Finally, as state building proceeded under Louis XIV and his successors, Roman control over the French Church was a constant thorn in the monarchy's side. That issue, decisively addressed if not entirely resolved by Henry VIII in the 1530s, provided the central point of contact between religion and politics in eighteenth-century France, both before and during the Revolution.

It forced the sidelining or the reformulation in its own terms of other concerns, including those of second-generation Jansenists, themselves more attentive to the quality of religious life than to considerations of state.

As a result, Jansenism failed to sponsor any trend toward a political translation of individual accountability. Instead, even as the quiet diffusion of a "religious sensibility," a sensibility still alive in the twentieth century, proceeded,[32] the Jansenist controversy entered parliamentary politics transmuted into a dispute between Gallicans and Ultramontanes. With varying degrees of fervor, the parlements adopted the Jansenist/Gallican cause, offering arguments the king himself might have made, and leaving everyone caught in a web of contradictions. The interplay of grace and good works was no longer the central issue; the issue was whether important decisions binding on French Catholics could be made and imposed unilaterally by the Pope, without deliberation by a general council and without passing through the customary institutional channels in France. As the Parisian parliamentarian René Pucelle put it in 1730: "I am too loyal a subject of the king to consent that he should be stripped of his rights and declared a vassal of the Pope."[33] The Crown meanwhile looked to Rome for assistance in settling, or at least silencing, a controversy that still split the Church and that was sustaining an uncomfortably high level of parliamentary agitation. Royal measures were colored by the politically motivated anti-Jansenism of the Cardinal de Fleury (Louis XV's principal minister from 1726 to 1743) and by Jesuit influence at the court, and were ultimately shaped by the assumption articulated in 1753 by the Dauphin:[34] "We can make do without the *Parlement*, but we cannot make do without Bishops."[35]

After a lull, the struggle between the Crown and the parlements over the questions raised by Jansenism climaxed in the mid-1750s. Louis-Adrien Lepaige's *Lettres historiques* (1753–1754)[36] came closer than any other pamphlet to elaborating a radical argument for the rights and unity of France's parlements. To support his contentions, however, Lepaige turned to the historical record, not to religious terminology or concepts. The appeal to history had been made without great effect by other writers earlier in the century; as it necessarily

---

[32] "*Sensibilité religieuse*"; the expression is Mandrou's, *Louis XIV*, p. 203.

[33] Cited by Egret, *Louis XV et l'opposition*, p. 27.

[34] Louis (1729–1765), then first in line to the throne, was Louis XV's son and Louis XVI's father.

[35] Cited by Egret, *Louis XV et l'opposition*, p. 59.

[36] Louis-Adrien Lepaige, *Lettres historiques, sur les fonctions essentielles du Parlement; sur le droit des Pairs, et sur les loix fondamentales du Royaume* (Amsterdam, 1753–1754).

justified the privileges of the nobility,[37] it was unlikely to provide a
compelling platform when those privileges themselves came under
attack.

As the Jansenist controversy subsided, religion was replaced by another familiar subject of political contention: taxes. Once again,
France was at war: in 1754 in North America and in 1756 in Europe.
The expenses Britain incurred during the French and Indian and the
Seven Years Wars were, as we have seen, largely responsible for the
fiscal measures that so alarmed the American colonists. The hard-
pressed French monarchy, too, was soon casting about for additional
revenues. The imposition of new taxes, combined with the prolon-
gation and more rigorous enforcement of existing levies, soon
sparked renewed conflict between the Crown and the parlements.
Exasperated by parliamentary criticism, Louis XV answered with the
Maupeou reforms. The reforms reorganized the parlements, redefined their functions, abolished the sale of parliamentary offices, and
excluded many current magistrates from further service. Louis XVI
dismantled the reforms, but the threat that their memory left hanging over the magistrates' heads secured for the monarchy a decade of
parliamentary docility. The relative calm ended when another war—
French involvement in the War for American Independence—
helped plunge French finances into crisis again. The monarchy was
eventually forced to summon an Estates General, the first to meet
since 1614.

The Jansenist quarrel seemed initially to suggest issues raised earlier by Puritanism in England; as outlined above, the subsequent parliamentary battles would seem to recall the fight over taxation that
had been critical to the maturation of revolutionary aspirations and
ideology in England and America. Yet just as the first parallel has its
limits, so does the second. The continuing dependence of the political
class on the regime still prevented the emergence of a revolutionary
ideology; it also precluded the consolidation of parliamentary solidarity through the union des classes.

Jean Egret has described and documented the parliamentary "trial
of the administrative monarchy" and the "revolt against the authoritarian monarchy," which he argues characterize the last fifteen years

[37] See for example part II, letter 8, pp. 16–25; Lepaige explains at some length why
the nobility of the sword's scorn for the nobility of the robe was misplaced. For summary statements of Lepaige's view of the relationship between the Crown and the
parlement, and his assessment of the sources of the latter's legitimacy and the extent
of its power, see part I, letter 4, pp. 150–54 and the later note ("b"), beginning part II,
letter 8, p. 15, regarding this passage.

of Louis XV's reign.[38] The story he tells is one dominated by parliamentary attacks on individuals and royal officials—principally the *fermiers généraux* and the intendants—who were responsible for the distribution of the tax burden and the collection of revenues. The parliamentary proceedings amounted to a catalogue of abusive practices, and conveyed to the monarch the portrait of a suffering population. Their plaintive tone, however, dulled whatever revolutionary impulses their content might have inspired. Almost invariably included was an appeal to the goodness and mercy of the king: Surely the monarch could and would alleviate the misfortune caused by unscrupulous or inadequately informed lower officials. "*Si le roi savait!*" was hardly a radical cry, but it would be the cry still sounded, repeatedly, naively and confidently, in the *Cahiers de doléances* of 1789.[39] There was no transition in prerevolutionary France, as there had been in prerevolutionary America, from the condemnation of evil officials to the indictment of a malicious monarch and the rejection of a fundamentally flawed political system. Even after Varennes, the moderates of the Revolution would continue to burden themselves with the singularly cumbersome person of Louis XVI. Despite the increasingly widespread sense that the regime was becoming despotic, the dissent of the parlements remained couched in fundamentally traditional terms.[40] In England and America, it had been possible to suffuse traditional language with revolutionary meaning. The realization of that possibility had proved crucial to the triumph of the moderates. The language of privilege, however, did not lend itself to the same manipulations as had the language of property.

In England and America, liberty and "property" had marched hand in hand. The reference to property first provided a decisive argument in favor of limited, representative government. It then informed a debate on the nature of representation, leading to a reflection on the representation of interests and eventually to an acceptance of the inevitability of conflict, facilitating in England and America the consolidation of the politics of transaction. In France, a different legal and political history, as well as the country's Catholic heritage, prevented eighteenth-century dissidents from making a similar moral investment in the imagery of property. We earlier cited Tocqueville's statement identifying property with Old Regime privilege. Since under the Old Regime, privileges were indeed properties

---

[38] See Egret, *Louis XV et l'opposition*, chaps. 3 and 4.

[39] See Pierre Goubert and Michel Denis, eds., *1789: Les Francais ont la parole: Cahiers de doléances des Etats généraux* (Paris: Julliard, 1964).

[40] Richet makes a different argument: see *La France moderne*, book III, chaps. 3 and 4.

(and property sometimes a privilege), revolutionaries hoping to transform the political system while avoiding social disruption in fact had an interest in skirting the reference to property—as a frustrated Barnave understood. Prerevolutionary malcontents did not notice the problem. They regularly based their case on the legitimate defense of long-established privileges—the only "liberties" of which they had any experience. In this light, the Parlement de Paris's untimely insistence in 1763 on its superiority over the provincial parlements is more revealing than the sporadic talk about the union des classes.

As revolution approached in England and America, the self-assurance of the men who became revolutionary leaders seemed to harden. In France, on the other hand, as the century wore on and discontent deepened, the parlements became increasingly skeptical about their own capacity to represent the nation. Since the nation—a word whose more frequent use in the 1770s and 1780s is in itself significant—had in no way selected the parliamentarians, they would have to prove their legitimacy. For the parlements to assert a representative function and "win the initiative" away from the Crown, as had the House of Commons before them, the union des classes would first have to become a reality. Writing after the Revolution, a former parliamentarian would explain why this had been impossible.

> The idea [of the union des classes] was a great one, but one might say that it was too great. For such an idea did not correspond to the origin of the *parlements*, which was purely royal, or to their organization, which provided for neither common deliberations nor the expression of a common will. Indeed, they were constituted as different bodies, distinct by virtue of the successive dates of their establishment, separated geographically and even more by the opposing customs, privileges, and interests of the Provinces in which they were established to administer justice. The new doctrine was but an ingenious dream. . . .[41]

The Crown itself was not blind to the interest it had in maintaining the parlements, thus reinforcing the doubts of dissenters. To the Crown, the parlements were a nuisance, but if properly exploited, they might prove both harmless and useful. Already in 1753, the Marquis d'Argenson, always an acute if partial observer, had drawn a number of conclusions from his reading of Lepaige's *Lettres historiques*:

> All things considered, the king has great claims to universal and absolute power, and if his authority is well advised, it will cling to the small *parle-*

[41] Portalis, cited in Egret, *Louis XV et l'opposition*, p. 180.

ments of today, subdivided by Province, composed of bourgeois, of clerks, . . . and of venal placemen in long robes. For if ever the Nation were to recover its will and its rights, it would not fail to establish a universal National Assembly of much greater danger to royal authority. This Assembly would be made necessary and ever-present; it would be composed of great lords, of deputies from each Province and from the cities. The Parliament of England would be imitated in every regard. The Nation would reserve to itself the task of legislating and leave to the King only a provisional right of execution.[42]

As a pamphleteer protesting the Maupeou reforms ruefully acknowledged, the ultimately compliant parliaments gave the king "at once the desirable image of limited power, and the strength of an absolute power."[43] D'Argenson's political sarcasm should not be mistaken for social snobbery, although the latter no doubt contributed to the expression of the former. The Marquess's nobility was obviously not to be confused with that of the "bourgeois" who peopled the parlements (however Lepaige might define and defend them), but d'Argenson's political scorn was prompted by the very factor which made the rebellious parliamentarians politically useful—their dependency on the Crown. Thus the "venal placemen in long robes" were politically harmless (as well as socially ridiculous), whereas deputies—whether "from the cities" (that is, real bourgeois) or "great lords"—with a legitimate claim to represent the nation commanded d'Argenson's respect: Their arrival would signify a revolution.

D'Argenson was right, but the event was still years away. In the meantime, if the parliamentary personnel—whose ranks included most members of the Old Regime's highly exclusive political class who were neither Court figures nor government officials—remained trapped by the sociopolitical arrangements to which they owed their power and position and were thereby prevented from contributing to the elaboration of a revolutionary ideology adapted to moderate needs, what of the century's great thinkers? Attack the regime the *philosophes* certainly did, with ridicule and satire (Voltaire; the Montesquieu of the *Lettres persanes*), invective (Helvétius), and rational inquiry (the Encyclopedists), but they were rather less forthcoming, and above all far from united, when it came to proposing guidelines for reform. Rousseau addressed the critical issue of sovereignty, but his slashing attack on bourgeois society and his repudiation of representative government made him politically marginal; his day would come after the Revolution had begun and the moderates had lost.

[42] Cited in Egret, *Louis XV et l'opposition*, pp. 91f.
[43] Elie de Beaumont, cited in Egret, *Louis XV et l'opposition*, p. 217.

Not even Montesquieu—the apologist of intermediary bodies and the advocate of the separation of powers, himself a parliamentarian (from Bordeaux), and a man widely read by his contemporaries— could provide the moderates with the ideological armor they needed. The *Lettres persanes* (1721) is, in addition to being humorous, a book about despotism and its dismal consequences. It is, however, quite unlike the seventeenth-century English and eighteenth-century American tracts, which denounced despotism—and which, generally speaking, were not funny. The English and American pamphleteers sought to insure the integrity of the individual against external threats; in the *Lettres persanes*, Montesquieu is concerned instead with the individual's own psychological propensity toward despotism. Despotism is perceived first as a relation of man to himself; at its origin, Montesquieu sees either persistent self-delusion or the sin of pride. Anyone can be a despot, and that is precisely the point. The Spanish inquisitor and the Oriental prince (not to mention Bossuet and Louis XIV), so immoderate in their tyrannical practices and so easily ridiculed, appear in the book as passing celebrities. It is not they who retain the focus of Montesquieu's analytic attention, but rather the familiar Usbek, morally alert, intelligent, doubting, and pathetically caught between his own purported values and the despotic habits of his private life. Despotism is his personal tragedy. Montesquieu's analysis certainly tells us more about our private selves than does Locke's *Second Treatise*, but it could hardly help those inclined toward militant public action. Public freedom is little discussed in the *Lettres persanes*. One would expect to find it at the opposite end of the scale from despotism; instead, that place is filled by happiness, and the examples Montesquieu gives of this condition are the Guebres, who pursue a happy, just existence in a despotic state (Turkey), and Rica, Usbek's untormented, compassionate comrade, who soon adjusts to life under a European divine right monarchy.

Political freedom is a more explicit concern in Montesquieu's *Esprit des lois* (1748), but the author's assertion of his work's political neutrality is only partly disingenuous.[44] Montesquieu's primary goal is to understand, not to recommend. The result is a work of social theory, not political theory, and certainly not a manual for revolutionaries. Montesquieu was probably more useful to those who tried retrospectively to explain why the Revolution had gone awry than he was to the men who through their actions sought to shape its course.

The "high" Enlightenment thus provided little help to moderates seeking to develop a revolutionary praxis. The intellectual currency

[44] See Montesquieu, *De l'esprit des lois*, Preface.

of the "low" Enlightenment was of even less use.[45] Pornography, mesmerism, and Freemasonry may well have been or become expressions of frustrated political discontent, but such forms of dissent were unlikely to have the same political effects as dissent informed by Puritanism and the defense of property.

The English and American revolutionaries and their opponents argued in a shared political idiom. At the same time, the decentralization of power in England and America allowed the revolutionaries to slip into power first and justify themselves through a new doctrine of sovereignty second. In France, the net of social interdependence trapped all the parties to a dispute that seemed to have no solution. The point is not that the French elites failed to embrace the ideological framework that had led the English and American revolutionaries to success. The point is that until very late in the game, they did not—and could not—develop any ideology likely to take them where they wanted to go. The parlements could not have supplied what the situation required and what the danger of a power vacuum once a revolution started made all the more urgent: a reflection on sovereignty. Sieyès' pamphlet, *What Is the Third Estate?* (written in 1788 and published in January 1789) spoke to this need, whence its impact and importance.[46]

Political Crossroads

Strictly speaking, the Estates General called by the king for the late spring of 1789 never met. The king's summons had left undecided the crucial issue of whether votes would be tallied by order (in which case the Third Estate would be powerless) or by head (in which case the Third Estate would be in a position to muster the same number of votes as the two privileged orders combined). By mid-June, with negotiations between the delegations at an impasse, the deputies of the Third Estate ran out of patience. On June 17, seconded by a handful of priests, they declared themselves a National Assembly, leaving the door open to deputies of the nobility and the clergy who might wish to join them. Three weeks later (on July 9), the National Assembly became the National Constituent Assembly. To the more intransigent deputies of the Third Estate, the Old Regime, with its three orders and its all-embracing system of privileges, was no longer

---

[45] On the relationship between low Enlightenment activities and politics, see Darnton, *Mesmerism*.

[46] On the reception accorded to Sieyès's pamphlet, see Zapperi's Introduction, pp. 84–93.

acceptable. The transition from an Estates General meeting at the behest of the monarch to a National Assembly meeting by right symbolizes a political revolution similar in its underlying ambitions to the revolutions that had previously reshaped politics in England and America.

We have seen how the Old Regime created an unfavorable structure of opportunity and thereby compromised the chances of a liberal revolution controlled by moderates. The prerevolutionary structure of opportunity left the moderate revolutionaries ill-equipped to turn the pressure of circumstances and events to their advantage. As the National Assembly began its deliberations, the people lacked bread, the government wanted cash, popular disorders (in town and countryside alike) were a source of constant concern, and rumors that the king might attempt a *coup de force* and peremptorily send the delegates all packing appeared entirely plausible. The nagging suspicion that Louis's professed acceptance of the new order was insincere was born with the Revolution itself, and seemed increasingly justified. Since the Constituent Assembly's actions often came in response to situations it would have preferred to avoid entirely—and since there was so much to do in so little time—it is sometimes difficult to deduce precisely what policies the majority would have pursued had it enjoyed greater freedom of action. It is nonetheless the task of this section to sort out what the moderate revolutionaries—and in 1789–1790 and on into 1791, anybody who was somebody in the Revolution was a moderate—wanted, and then to suggest why they did not get it. How did they envision the "regenerated" monarchy of their dreams, before they were overtaken by events they helped create and by the Jacobins with whom they could not compete? How far were they willing to see change go? Sieyès's *What Is the Third Estate?* may be read as a summary theoretical statement of the revolutionaries' minimum position, and used to introduce the fundamental political choice that faced the leaders of the Constituent Assembly. At least one man among them, Mirabeau, understood the full implications of the available options. "Any attitude can be defended, gentlemen," he warned his colleagues, "except a disregard for consequences [*l'inconséquence*]."[47] Frequently confusing the middle position with a moderate position, suspicious of an individual who was known to be venal and was reliably rumored to have slept with his sister,[48] unsure of one another, and overawed by the risks inherent to their enterprise, the

[47] Mirabeau, May 18, 1789; *Discours*, p. 32.
[48] For a brief and perceptive portrait of Mirabeau, see Furet's Preface to the *Discours*. Furet repeats the rumor about Mirabeau's relations with his sister on p. 9.

moderates unconsciously chose a "disregard for consequences." As Chénier's words indicate, they never understood what happened to them; they never realized that moderates do not always, necessarily, lose.

Sieyès: Stating the Case for Popular Sovereignty

On the evening of June 15, 1789, as his colleagues earnestly debated their own title and the name to be given to their assembly, Malouet intervened in the proceedings. As usual, the future *monarchien*[49] used his talents to counsel caution. In the course of arguing against the radicalism embodied equally in the competing motions presented by Sieyès and Mirabeau, Malouet posed in clear terms the fundamental question facing the gathered delegates:

> What is . . . the constitution of any assembly? It is the declaration of its legal existence, made in accordance with an already established law, or in accordance with a law which one has the power to make on the spot.
>
> If I ask now what a law is, I find that it is a just and useful intention expressed by a sovereign will. . . .
>
> According to these principles which are, I believe, indisputable, I ask what the manner of constitution of the representatives of the nation [proposed by Sieyès] means? What is the law which authorizes it? Where is the sovereign will which has expressed this just and useful intention? Are we by ourselves the legislative power? Can we substitute ourselves for it? Has the general will so authorized you?[50]

Under the Old Regime, as Malouet and his listeners all knew, sovereignty was vested in the king. In theory at least, the king exercised it (as Louis XV had informed the Parlement de Paris in 1766) "without dependence and without partners."[51] Two years after the debate in which Malouet had raised the question, the Constitution of 1791 would announce a new understanding of sovereignty. Title III ("Public Powers") contained the following provisions:

> Art. 1 — Sovereignty is one, indivisible, inalienable, and imprescriptible. It belongs to the Nation; no section of the people, nor any individual, can attribute to itself the exercise of sovereignty.

[49] Led by Malouet and Mounier, this group argued in 1789 for a constitutional monarchy with a bicameral legislature. Mounier resigned from the Assembly after the October Days and emigrated in May 1790.

[50] Malouet; *Le Moniteur*, vol. 1, p. 77.

[51] Louis XV, March 3, 1766; Jules Flammermont, ed., *Remontrances du Parlement de Paris au XVIIIᵉ siècle*, vol. 2 (1755–1768) (Paris: Imprimerie Nationale, 1895), p. 557.

Art. 2 — The nation, from which alone all powers emanate, can only exercise its powers by delegating them. — The French Constitution is representative: the representatives are the legislative branch and the king.[52]

In the Revolution's new world, sovereignty was the inalienable property of the nation; its exercise was the delegated responsibility of the elected legislature and the king. Both statements were basic to the revolutionaries' position, and would remain critically important even after the demise of their moderate expounders. The first in particular captured Sieyès's attention in *What Is the Third Estate?*

There is rather more to Sieyès's pamphlet than the summary answers to the three questions—about the identity, current status, and legitimate demands of the Third Estate—with which the book begins. The positions articulated by Sieyès are revolutionary in scope and character, and the tract offers a first statement of revolutionary ideology. Sieyès sounds a vigorous and consistent call to battle against the Old Regime in both its general and its specifically French manifestations; he offers an account of the origins and purposes of political life and uses that account to elaborate a new conception of political legitimacy; and he outlines a program of immediate action.

For the Old Regime in all its various historical phases, Sieyès professed nothing but scorn. Thus there was no point in searching France's past for political models. France, Sieyès argued, had rarely been a monarchy, let alone a limited one.

> One need but read history to be convinced that it is a great error to believe that France has been ruled by a monarchical regime. Strike from our annals the few years of Louis XI, of Richelieu, and the few moments of Louis XIV, when one sees only pure despotism, and you will think you are reading the history of a *court* aristocracy. It is the court which has reigned, and not the king. . . . And what is the court, if not the head of this immense aristocracy which covers every part of France, which through its members reaches everything and exercises everywhere all that is essential in every aspect of public affairs? . . . Is it not enough . . . to open one's eyes to what is going on right now [November–December 1788] around us? What do we see? The aristocracy alone fighting all at once reason, justice, the people, the minister, and the king. The outcome of this terrible struggle is as yet uncertain; now tell us that the aristocracy is a chimera![53]

That the government was bankrupt was for Sieyès beside the point. On his political agenda, the need for a constitution that would pro-

---

[52] Text of the Constitution in Jacques Godechot, comp., *Les Constitutions de la France depuis 1789* (Paris: Garnier-Flammarion, 1970); cited articles on pp. 38f.

[53] Sieyès, *Tiers Etat*, pp. 132f.

vide the basis for legitimate rule took precedence over the question of taxes.

The foundation of aristocratic rule was privilege, and it was against privilege that Sieyès directed his attack. Privilege encouraged social fragmentation and set one group against another. A society based on privilege could be held together only by oppression and ignorance. Sieyès proposed a different kind of community, one based on rights, and he explicitly rejected the Old Regime equation of privileges with "liberties": "One is not made free by privileges, but by the rights of the citizen, rights which belong to all."[54] Sieyès did not invent the word "nation," nor did he even introduce it into political discourse. He did, however, assign a new meaning and importance to the term. For Sieyès, the nation—"a body of associates living under a *common* law and represented by the same *legislature*, etc."[55]—is a deliberate political creation of men as they leave the state of nature:

> In the first [period in the formation of a political society], one imagines a greater or lesser number of isolated individuals who wish to come together. By this fact alone they already form a nation: they have all the rights of one; all that remains is for them to exercise those rights.[56]

During a second period, the nation will rule itself by direct democracy. Then, when the size and population of the country make direct democracy impracticable, representative government will be established. This will usually be achieved by means of a constitution. The nation, however, can never be bound by past constitutional commitments: "The nation antedates all else; it is the origin of everything.[57] Its will is always legal, it itself is the law. Prior to it and above it there is only *natural* right."[58]

The Third Estate, Sieyès argued, could supply everything any society could need. Alone, it was "a complete nation."[59] The nobility, on the other hand, because of its "iniquitous and antisocial privileges, . . . abominable fruits of abominable feudalism,"[60] formed "a people apart in the great nation,"[61]

[54] Ibid., p. 127.
[55] Ibid., p. 126.
[56] Ibid., p. 178.
[57] Lepaige, however reluctantly, still assigned this role to the king. See passages noted above, n. 37.
[58] Sieyès, *Tiers Etat*, p. 180.
[59] Ibid., p. 124.
[60] Ibid., p. 195.
[61] Ibid., p. 124.

but a false people who, unable for lack of useful organs to exist independently, attaches itself to a real nation as do vegetable tumors which can only live on the sap of plants which they dry out and exhaust.[62]

The description is not particularly endearing, nor was it intended to be. Reforms would be in vain, Sieyès insisted, if they left the privileged orders intact:

[I]t is no longer the moment to work for the reconciliation of the concerned parties. . . . They [the privileged orders] have dared to utter the word *scission*. With it they have threatened the king and the people. Eh! By God! how happy it would be for the nation if it were consummated for all time, this infinitely desirable scission! How easy it would be to do without those marked by privilege! How hard it will be to bring them to become citizens![63]

Extensive exclusion would be the necessary corollary of liberal revolution in France, Sieyès maintained, and he knew success would not come easily:

I realize that these truths, however certain they may be, become bothersome in a state which was not established under the auspices of reason and political equity. What can I say? Your house remains standing only through artifice, with the help of a forest of ill-formed supports erected without taste and without design, unless it be that of shoring up the parts that were threatening to collapse; it must be rebuilt, or else you must resign yourselves to living, from one day to the next, uncomfortably and with the anxiety of being in the end crushed beneath its debris. Everything is of a piece in the social order. If you neglect one part of it, it will not be without effect on the other parts. If you start with disorder, you will necessarily see its results in what follows. This chain of events is necessary. Eh! If one could derive from injustice and absurdity the same fruits as from reason and equity, where would be the advantages of the latter?[64]

Sieyès's reconstructed house would have been one in which Locke might have felt quite comfortable. The goals that the French pamphleteer assigned to political society were the familiar goals of liberalism: "common security, common liberty, the public good [*la chose publique*]."[65] The powers of representative government were to be sharply curtailed not only by the nation's right to rescind its mandate,

---

[62] Ibid., p. 125, n. 1.
[63] Ibid., p. 194.
[64] Ibid., p. 199.
[65] Ibid., p. 205.

but also by the limited function of the law: "The law grants nothing; it protects what exists until such time as what exists begins to hurt the common interest."[66]

> All that belongs to citizens— . . . common advantages, particular advantages (provided that these latter do not contravene the law)—is entitled to protection; but the social union having been made possible only by the existence of common points, it is only the common quality that is entitled to legislation.[67]

The purpose of this demonstration, however, was again to promote the exclusion in fact of those whose status already excluded them in theory from the right to sit in a national representative assembly:

> A privileged class is . . . harmful, not only because of its *esprit de corps*, but by its mere existence. The more it has obtained favors necessarily contrary to the common liberty, the more essential it is to keep it away from the National Assembly. The privileged person would be *représentable* only in his general quality as a citizen; but in such a person, this quality has been destroyed. He is outside the civic sphere, he is the enemy of common rights. To give him a right to representation would introduce an obvious contradiction into the law; the nation could only have submitted to it through an act of servitude, and that cannot be imagined.[68]

Sieyès's pamphlet was widely read and widely applauded in the months immediately preceding the Estates General. His vehement prose, directed against human as well as institutional enemies, neatly summarizes the fears and aspirations of his revolutionary colleagues. Their most difficult and most important mission would be to extirpate every last trace of "feudal barbarism"—a process of national purification whose hypothetical result would be a homogeneity of basic interests among those individuals who remained. In America, revolution required the definitive repudiation of certain political positions and the exclusion of anyone who found such a repudiation unacceptable. In France, a revolution professing a similar view of the ultimate shape of political society required the destruction of an entire way of social and political intercourse. When privileges were abolished and the nation restored to its rights, the revolutionaries believed, limited government through representative institutions would follow almost naturally.

[66] Ibid., pp. 208f.
[67] Ibid., p. 210.
[68] Ibid., p. 211.

The Politics of Popular Sovereignty: Initial Options

With the Tennis Court Oath (June 20, 1789), the deputies rejected Malouet's earlier caution, affirmed the rights of the nation, and asserted the duties of its first representatives:

> The National Assembly, considering that as it was called upon to determine the constitution of the kingdom, to effect the regeneration of public order, and to maintain the true principles of the monarchy, nothing can prevent that it should continue its deliberations in whatever place it is forced to establish itself, and finally that wherever its members are gathered, there sits the National Assembly;
>
> Decides that all the members of this Assembly will immediately swear a solemn oath never to separate, and to meet anywhere where circumstances may require, until such time as the constitution of the kingdom is established and strengthened on solid foundations.[69]

During the night of August 4–5, 1789, the deputies would begin the delicate task of dismantling the Old Regime's system of privileges. In the meantime, the most urgent political problem posed by the Revolution—a problem the Revolution would fail to resolve decisively—was already before them. The country had a monarch; now it also had a National Assembly, and that Assembly had declared the people sovereign. How would the new constitution, based on popular sovereignty, define the relationship between the executive and the legislature? "The National Assembly labored under a terrible disadvantage," Rabaut Saint-Etienne would later write, "and one which hurt it for a long time: that of having to constitute a monarchy with the monarch already there."[70] Could Louis XVI be induced to preside over the new order? If not, was his person (as opposed to his office) expendable?

Sieyès was better at providing abstract formulations than political leadership. Mirabeau had a gift for both, and although his recommendations were often shunned by an uncomprehending Assembly and an unwilling Court, he alone, among all the leaders of the Revolution, proposed a coherent political strategy constructed around the moderate demands. Writing to the Court, Mirabeau summarized those demands as follows. He argued that no event—not even civil war or France's defeat by foreign powers—could now succeed in removing the demands from the nation's agenda, and presented

---

[69] Resolution quoted immediately precedes oath; *Le Moniteur*, vol. 1, p. 89.

[70] Cited by Egret, *La Révolution des Notables*, p. 156.

his strategy as the way to "reconcile public liberty and energetic authority":

> What does the French nation want? It wants to profit from the advantages of the Revolution, and I defend them all; it wants a constitution, and I seek to improve the one we have; it wants above all to preserve the fundamental principles of this constitution, and I want precisely to guarantee that those principles remain unaltered.[71]

Mirabeau alone seems to have understood the political possibilities as well as the political dangers opened up by the doctrine of popular sovereignty. The positions he adopted bear comparison to the propositions formulated just a short time earlier by the authors of the *Federalist Papers*.[72]

Mirabeau, like Sieyès, emphasized that taxes were a minor matter when compared with the need for a constitution. With all his colleagues, Mirabeau argued that sovereignty was vested in the people, that it could not normally be exercised directly, and that the purpose of government was to guarantee security and to ensure civil and political equality through the rule of established laws passed by the people's representatives and applied equally to all citizens. From these shared assumptions, however, Mirabeau derived an unconventional argument. If the people were sovereign, then they were free to delegate authority as they wished.[73] Clearly, they would wish to do so in such a way as to check effectively the pretensions of any single part of the government to absolute power. Like Madison, Hamilton, and Jay, Mirabeau placed little stock in public virtue. He feared Paris in general and its populace in particular, he distrusted the existing Court if not the king, and he worried that even after the demise of the old nobility, oligarchic domination would reemerge in a new form, most probably in the usurpation of authority by an elected assembly. On the tactical level, Mirabeau's disabused assessment of human nature justified political means that were cynical, complicated, and ultimately ineffective.[74] His overall strategic recommendations

[71] Mirabeau, "Note terminée le 23 décembre 1790," in Guy Chaussinand-Nogaret, ed., *Mirabeau entre le roi et la Révolution* (Paris: Hachette, 1986), pp. 184, 185. This book includes the full texts of all known correspondence from Mirabeau to the Court, as well as a number of Mirabeau's speeches. Hereafter cited as *Mirabeau*.

[72] There is some evidence to suggest that Mirabeau was aware of the American debate over the Federal Constitution; see "Note terminée le 23 décembre 1790," in *Mirabeau*, p. 195.

[73] Mirabeau defended this idea regardless of audience; for the version addressed to the Court, see ibid., pp. 183f.

[74] The convoluted and often cynical character of Mirabeau's tactical recommendations is clearly evident in his notes to the Court. But a careful reading of those notes

were nonetheless lucid, and in the French context, original. The solution to the problem created by the democratic "new order," Mirabeau argued, was to set up a system of checks within the government. Mirabeau might well have made his own the classic terms in which Madison had stated the case for the "inventions of prudence":

> The great security against a gradual concentration of the several powers in the same department, consists in giving to those who administer each department the necessary constitutional means and personal motives to resist encroachments of the others. . . .
>
> Ambition must be made to counteract ambition. The interest of the man must be connected with the constitutional rights of the place. It may be a reflection on human nature, that such devices should be necessary to control the abuses of government. But what is government itself, but the greatest of all reflections on human nature? If men were angels, no government would be necessary. If angels were to govern men, neither external nor internal controls on government would be necessary. In framing a government which is to be administered by men over men, the great difficulty lies in this: you must first enable the government to control the governed; and in the next place oblige it to control itself. A dependence on the people is, no doubt, the primary control on the government; but experience has taught mankind the necessity of auxiliary precautions.
>
> This policy of supplying, by opposite and rival interests, the defect of better motives, might be traced through the whole system of human affairs, private as well as public. We see it particularly displayed in all the subordinate distributions of power, where the constant aim is to divide and arrange the several offices in such a manner as that each may be a check on the other—that the private interest of every individual may be a sentinel over the public rights.[75]

Since France was of course not America, Mirabeau's institutional recommendations differed from those advocated by the Federalists. His own proposals, as well as his perception of what the consequences of their rejection would be, suggest the positions a successful moder-

---

and Mirabeau's speeches only confirms the contemporary judgment of Mirabeau's Court interlocutor, Count La Marck, who said that Mirabeau "gets paid for holding the views that he holds" (quoted by Furet in *Discours*, p. 19). Mirabeau began his correspondence with the Court with a "profession of faith" in which he called counterrevolutionary goals "dangerous and criminal" as well as "chimerical"; see "Note" of May 10, 1790, in *Mirabeau*, p. 37.

[75] James Madison, Federalist 51, February 8, 1788. The reference to the "inventions of prudence" directly follows the quoted passage. Cited passage appears on p. 337 of the Modern Library Edition (New York: Random House, n.d.).

ate strategy might have embraced, and are therefore worth reviewing in some detail.

Like Sieyès before him and Robespierre after, Mirabeau took as his point of departure a blistering attack on "old prejudices, the gothic oppressions of barbarous times":

> That at the end of the eighteenth century a group of citizens should unveil and pursue the project of replunging us [into the barbarous times], that this group should demand the right to stop everything when everything must march onwards, in other words that it should demand to govern everything according to its whims, and should speak of this truly delirious pretension as of its *property*, that a few *individuals*, a few *persons* from the three estates, because in the modern idiom they have been called *orders*, oppose without modesty to the general interest the magic of this word empty of meaning, without deigning to dissimulate that their private interests are in open contradiction with the general interest; that they should wish to return the people of France to these forms which sorted the nation into two types of men, oppressors and oppressed; that they should strive to perpetuate a purported constitution according to which a single word pronounced by one hundred fifty-one individuals could stop the king and twenty-four million men; a constitution according to which two orders which are neither the people, nor the prince, will exploit the latter to bring pressure on the former, and the former to inspire fear in the latter, and circumstances to reduce all that is outside their orbit to nothingness . . . is undoubtedly the height of arrogant absurdity; and I have no need to color in this faint sketch to show that the division between the orders, that the *veto* of the orders, that deliberation and the expression of opinion by order would be a truly sublime invention intended to establish constitutionally egoism in the priesthood, arrogance in the nobility, baseness in the people, strife amongst all the interests, corruption in every class which makes up the great family, cupidity in every soul, the frivolity of the nation, dependence on the prince, and ministerial despotism.[76]

Mirabeau would reiterate his condemnation of the old order in unequivocal terms whenever political backsliding seemed a possibility and every time the king seemed inclined to resort to menacing gestures, but he was also acutely conscious of the Revolution's vulnerability. Sieyès's proposed remedy to the weakness of the Third Estate had been to issue what amounted to a declaration of war against those who constituted "a people apart in the great nation." Robespierre would develop Sieyès's argument and translate its suggestions

---

[76] Mirabeau, to the deputies of the Third Estate (who had not yet become the National Assembly), June 15, 1789; *Discours*, pp. 43f.

into action; Mirabeau consistently denounced it, preferring to speak of a "great family." In his view, the Revolution could succeed only if everyone who had counted under the Old Regime could somehow be accommodated in the new regime. Exclusion was impracticable and inherently dangerous. Instead, without ever compromising, either verbally or materially, on the fundamental issues of sovereignty and political rights, Mirabeau sought either to coopt the Revolution's many adversaries, or to turn each, be it against his will, into a "sentinel over the public rights." Sieyès had likened the nation's task to that of a carpenter reconstructing a house. Mirabeau, who sometimes paid ironical tribute to his colleague's theoretical thoroughness,[77] knew that political action and construction work obey different rules. Even as he argued that the measures adopted during the night of August 4–5, 1789, were constitutional in nature and therefore not subject to the king's approval, he repeated the case for cooptation:

> We are an old nation, and undoubtedly too old for our times. We already have a government, a king, and entrenched prejudices. We must, insofar as possible, match all these things with the Revolution, and weather the passage. We must persist in this path until such tolerance results in a practical violation of the principles of national liberty, in an absolute dissonance in the social order.[78]

From the time he arrived in Versailles until his death on April 2, 1791, Mirabeau tirelessly pushed his strategy, arguing openly before the Assembly and maneuvering secretly (after March 1790) at the Court. He offered rhetorical enticements to potential opponents, appealing to the Christian virtues of the clergy and referring to "the sacred person of the king."[79] He constantly endeavored to augment the Revolution's chances by using what strength it had to create situations where influential individuals—always self-interested, often power-hungry, and for the foreseeable future of dubious loyalty—would be forced to do its bidding:

> If the minister is weak, support him against his weaknesses, lend him your strength, because you need his strength. A king as good as ours does not wish what he does not have the right to wish.[80]

Mirabeau's constitutional recommendations were entirely consistent with his willingness to accept men as he found them and his de-

[77] For example, in the Constituent Assembly on August 18, 1789; *Discours*, pp. 98f.

[78] Mirabeau, Constituent Assembly, September 18, 1789; *Discours*, p. 121.

[79] Mirabeau, Estates General, May 27, 1789: "the ministers of a God of peace"; *Discours*, p. 39; and June 15, 1789; *Discours*, p. 52. See also parliamentary interventions of July 8, 9, and 11, 1789; *Discours*, pp. 67–80.

[80] Mirabeau, Estates General, May 18, 1789; *Discours*, p. 33.

termination to manipulate them into accepting the new order. He first expressed his ideas during the debate over the royal veto (late August to mid-September 1789). He developed them most fully several months later, in what was perhaps the most significant debate of the Constituent Assembly: In May 1790, the Assembly tackled the problem of who should have the right to declare war. In each case, Mirabeau's allies were not the ones he might have preferred, for they were often men in the process of becoming émigrés. Mounier abandoned the Revolution in November 1789; d'Antraigues became a counterrevolutionary leader; Maury would walk out of the Assembly in January 1791—during a speech by Mirabeau—to protest the requirement that clergymen swear an oath of loyalty to the Civil Constitution of the Clergy. The men on whom the success of Mirabeau's strategy ultimately depended were those who, like Barnave, Duport, and the Lameth brothers, heckled Mirabeau from his "left." These men—"those who are frightened by great power, because the only way they know how to judge it is by its abuse," as Mirabeau described them[81]—were consumed by their fear of the king and his ministers. They seem never to have grasped the political logic of Mirabeau's proposals.

To Mirabeau, the need for a strong executive at the head of any French government appeared self-evident. He based his contention on three sorts of arguments. France, he knew, was geographically large and politically fragmented. Her borders, unlike England's and America's, were not shielded by water. Only a strong executive could preserve such a country against the twin threats of external attack and internal sedition. Conscious of the paltry political education of his compatriots, Mirabeau also believed that only a monarch could fix the affections (as Burke might have put it) and command the respect of the general population. To a people as yet unable to understand their rights, the king would stand as a symbol of legitimacy and community. Finally, and most importantly, only a strong executive would be able to hold in check an elected assembly:

> The nature of things not necessarily placing in the role of representative those most worthy, but those whose position, fortune, and personal circumstances designate as most easily able to sacrifice their time to the public cause, there will always result a sort of de facto aristocracy, which, ever inclined to acquire a legal consistency, will become equally hostile to the monarch, whose power it will rival, and to the people, whom it will constantly seek to abase.[82]

[81] Mirabeau, Constituent Assembly, September 1, 1789; *Discours*, p. 114.
[82] Ibid., p. 107.

As early as June 16, 1789, Mirabeau had spoken in favor of confiding a veto power in the king:

> I believe the royal *veto* so necessary that I would rather live in Constantinople than in France were the king not to have it; I can imagine nothing more terrible than a sovereign aristocracy of six hundred people who tomorrow could grant themselves tenure for life, then make their seats hereditary, and who would, in the end, like aristocracies all over the world, invade everything.[83]

Against the common and constant threat of a new aristocracy, Mirabeau emphasized a "natural and necessary alliance between the prince and the people"

> Based on the fact that having the same interests, the same fears, they must have an identical goal, and therefore identical wills. . . .
>
> It is therefore not at all in the defense of his particular advantage that the monarch intervenes in the legislative process, but in the interest of the people; and it is in this sense that one can and must say that the royal sanction is not at all the prerogative of the Crown, but the property, the domain of the nation.[84]

The king would be able to play his appointed role, Mirabeau argued, only if the powers granted to him by the constitution were real, for regardless of constitutional provisions, the power of the elected assembly will be real enough. Give the king an absolute veto over legislation, Mirabeau insisted, and allow him to declare war in the name of the people; in return, he would check aristocratic rumblings, ensure security and order, and be content to remain within the bounds set on his power.

Given the natural competition between the executive and the legislature, constitutional arrangements should seek to promote cooperation rather than conflict between the two branches. Thus Mirabeau defended the king's right to declare war in the following terms:

> Without doubt the king is not at all the mouthpiece of the public will, but nor is he completely external to the expression of that will. Thus when I limit myself to demanding the cooperation of the two branches delegated by the nation, I am in perfect harmony with constitutional principles.
>
> . . . In examining whether we should accord the right of sovereignty to one branch rather than to another, to the delegate called *king*, or to the delegate . . . which will be called the *legislative body*, one must discard all

[83] Mirabeau, Estates General; *Discours*, p. 55.
[84] Mirabeau, Constituent Assembly, September 1, 1789; *Discours*, pp. 107f.

vulgar notions of incompatibility; it is up to the nation to determine, for the exercise of a given act of its will, which branch it wishes to see act. . . .

. . . People speak of an exclusive right, and I speak only of a necessary cooperation.[85]

Can one not, for one of the functions of government, one which involves both action and will, both execution and deliberation, require cooperation toward the same end, without excluding one or the other, on the part of the two powers, one of which constitutes the force of the nation, and the other of which represents its wisdom? Can one not restrain the rights, or rather the abuses, of the old monarchy, without paralyzing public power? Can one not, on the other side, hear the nation's wishes regarding war and peace through the supreme organ of a representative assembly, without transporting into our midst the disadvantages that we find in this part of the public law of the ancient republics and of a few states of Europe?[86]

Mirabeau was by no means blind to the dangers attendant upon the enhancement of the king's position. With images that, from our vantage point evoke a famous product of the constitutional and political difficulties of the Directory more than any past French monarch, Mirabeau acknowledged the risks:

I have imagined to myself that martial and conquering king, winning the hearts of his soldiers through corruption and victory, tempted to become again a despot upon re-entering his country, fomenting faction within the empire, and overturning the laws with the very arm that the laws alone had armed.[87]

Such risks were fewer and less plausible than the risks to be incurred if the king were to be stripped of any real power, and they could be minimized by institutional and political remedies. Mirabeau reminded his colleagues that the Assembly would meet annually, that it would be free to disapprove of what the king had done, that it alone had the power to levy taxes and appropriate funds, and that a permanent National Guard could be placed under its control. To facilitate communication between the two branches, and to shield the king from the political consequences of any errors he might commit, Mirabeau advocated not only ministerial responsibility, but also frequent and easy contact between members of the Assembly and ministers (who might themselves be parliamentarians). Finally, Mirabeau seems to have been more certain than his colleagues regarding the

[85] Mirabeau, Constituent Assembly, May 20, 1790; *Discours*, p. 211.
[86] Ibid., pp. 200f.
[87] Ibid., p. 210.

distinction between the office and the person of the king. Reconstructing a hypothetical conversation between an "exalted royalist" and a "friend to the throne and to liberty," Mirabeau took the part of the second, arguing:

> Who denies that France needs a king, and wants a king? But Louis XVII will be king just as is Louis XVI; and if one succeeds in persuading the nation that Louis XVI is the instigator and accomplice of the excesses which have taxed the nation's patience, the nation will summon a Louis XVII.[88]

This sort of reasoning allowed Mirabeau to counsel the Assembly to "construct the office of the king as it should be, and do not fear that a rebellious king, abdicating by his own choice his throne, will expose himself to the risk of running from victory to the scaffold."[89] Responding to protests from the right that the person of the king had been declared inviolable, Mirabeau continued:

> I will of course refrain from responding to the charge made against me in bad faith; you all hear my supposition of a despotic and rebellious king, who would come with an army of Frenchmen to conquer the place of tyrants: but a king, in such a case, is no longer a king.[90]

It is of course impossible to know what position Mirabeau would have adopted during the critical weeks of crisis that followed the king's flight to Varennes on June 20–21, 1791, but the observations cited above offer some indication.[91]

Should the Assembly refuse his recommendations and reject the principles on which they were based, Mirabeau predicted that political instability and the destruction of freedom would inevitably result. He cited three possible causes. Deprived of power to which he could conceive a legitimate claim, impotent against legislative measures of which he disapproved, the king would eventually be tempted to resort to "illegal and violent forms of resistance."[92] Similarly, the people's only weapon against an Assembly that had overstepped its authority would be insurrection. Finally, Mirabeau argued, if the legislature replaced the executive as the principal war-making power, sections of the population might be incited to impetuous political acts,

---

[88] Mirabeau, Constituent Assembly, October 2, 1790; *Discours*, p. 281.

[89] Mirabeau, May 20, 1790; *Discours*, p. 222.

[90] Ibid., pp. 222f.

[91] In his final "Note" to the Court (February 3, 1791), Mirabeau did comment on the "strange departure" (p. 241) of the king's aunts; see text of Note in *Mirabeau*, pp. 240–43.

[92] Mirabeau, Constituent Assembly, September 1, 1789; *Discours*, p. 117.

destroying the authority of the Assembly in the name of popular sovereignty, but in a country where direct action could only mean the
tyranny of an activist minority, not direct democracy. "Do you think
so lightly of the danger of superimposing republican forms on a government which is simultaneously representative and monarchical?"
he asked.[93]

> Do you not fear that the people, knowing that its representatives declare
> war directly in its name, will not thereby be pushed dangerously in the
> direction of democracy, or rather of oligarchy; that the call for war and
> peace will rise from the provinces, will soon be the subject of petitions, and
> will agitate a great mass of men as only a matter of such importance can
> excite them?[94]

From the beginning, Mirabeau sensed that the doctrine of popular
sovereignty placed the *constituants* before a political choice, and that
the success of the moderate Revolution would depend in large part
on the wisdom of their moves. If his conception of executive-legisla-
tive relations was rejected and if the king and the Assembly failed to
work out a viable system of mutual accommodation, then the ensuing
confusion, suspicion, and indecisiveness would credit another interpretation of popular sovereignty. That interpretation would soon be
known as Jacobinism, but already in the fall of 1789, its plausibility
was established and its adepts could be heard: The first issue of Marat's virulent leaflet *L'Ami du peuple* was published in mid-September
1789. On the night of October 5–6, 1789, street demonstrations had
ended in bloodshed and had forced the return of Louis XVI from
Versailles to Paris. The National Assembly had followed. During the
days of tension, Lafayette and Jean-Sylvain Bailly (the mayor of Paris)
were instrumental in maintaining public order. On October 19, Mirabeau moved a vote of thanks to the two men, and used the opportunity to blast the competing interpretation of popular sovereignty,
under which political stability would be impossible:

> Let us set an example for a certain number of men who, filled with decep-
> tively republican ideas, become jealous of authority the second they dele-
> gate it, and despite the fact that they will recover it after a fixed term; who
> are never reassured either by the precautions established by law, or by the
> virtue of individuals; who are constantly frightened by the phantoms of

[93] Mirabeau, Constituent Assembly, May 20, 1790; *Discours*, p. 215.

[94] Ibid., p. 214. Mirabeau had a well-developed fear of the effects of popular pressure on government. See, for example, the passage from the "Note terminée le 23
décembre 1790," in which he evokes "this kind of exercise of sovereignty by the whole
body of the nation, the most noticeable effect of which is that the legislator himself is
nothing but a slave . . ." (in *Mirabeau*, pp. 192f.).

their imagination; who do not seem to know that men do honor to themselves by respecting the leaders they have chosen; who do not realize that
the zeal for liberty must not resemble the coveting of places and personal
jealousy; who make room too easily for all rumors, all calumnies, all re-
proaches. But this is how the most legitimate authority is exasperated, de-
graded, and debased; how a thousand obstacles are raised to hinder the
execution of the law; how suspicion spreads its poisons everywhere; how
instead of presenting the spectacle of a society of citizens who together are
erecting the edifice of liberty, we would bear greater resemblance to muti-
nous slaves who had just broken their chains and were now using those
chains to fight and destroy each other.[95]

Mirabeau unquestionably had more allies in the Constituent Assembly than did Marat. The ambient culture, however, was more
likely to amplify the hallucinations of the latter than to reinforce the
rigorous institutional arguments of the former. In the Western world
of the eighteenth century, everyone everywhere believed in the ubiq-
uity of conspiracies—"designs," as Thomas Jefferson, or any number
of other American revolutionaries, might have said. Eighteenth-century Frenchmen, like their English and American counterparts, still
belonged mentally to that preindustrial, predemocratic world we
have now lost. Theirs was a world in which power tended to be concentrated conspicuously in the hands of a very few people. Individuals, it was therefore thought, made history, and knew the history they
made; any discrepancy between stated intentions and actual results
could only be explained by the existence of deliberate deception. The
eighteenth-century belief in conspiracy cut across lines of political
cleavage, social distinction, and nationality. It was based, as historian
Georges Lefebvre understood, in part on an exaggeration of real
causal factors, in part on a conceptual inability to assess impersonal
historical trends and forces. Lefebvre's description of the "revolutionary mentality" recaptures the logic of common revolutionary reflexes as they first emerged in July 1789, and it deserves to be quoted
at length:

The Third Estate was immediately persuaded that the nobles would obstinately defend their privileges, and from this expectation, which the opposition first to doubling the voting power of the Third Estate, then to
voting by person, confirmed, a thousand suspicions were born and easily
transformed into certitudes. The nobles would stop at nothing in their efforts to "crush" the bourgeois. They would get around a well-intentioned
king and obtain the dissolution of the Estates General. They would take up

[95] Mirabeau; *Discours*, p. 126.

arms, withdraw into their castles, and would, to sustain civil war, recruit their troops from amongst the "brigands," just as the recruiting agents of the kings enrolled the miserable poor; the prisons and the dungeons would each provide regiments. Since they were already withholding their grain in the hope of starving out the Third Estate, the nobles would look kindly on any move to pillage the harvest. Between the fear they inspired and the fear of brigands, the link rapidly became general, thus compounding the consequences of the summoning of the Estates General and those of the economic crisis. In addition, foreign powers would be called in to help; the fear of foreign intervention, which weighed so heavily on the history of the Revolution, was a factor right from the start, and in July, many feared an invasion. The Third Estate in its entirety subscribed to the theory of an "aristocratic plot."

The weight of monarchical centralization and the conflict between the orders dominated the image of the crisis which the Third Estate con-structed; neglecting to incriminate nature and incapable of analyzing the economic situation, the Third Estate assigned responsibility for the crisis to the monarchy and the aristocracy. While incomplete, this perception was nonetheless not completely inexact.[96]

Yet Mirabeau's colleagues were not the peasants of the "great fear," nor were they hungry Parisian artisans. From the distinguished As-sembly—and it was distinguished—Mirabeau demanded intellectual effort and political courage. Toward the end of his second long speech during the debate on the power to declare war, Mirabeau again put the fundamental choice before his colleagues:

> Any attitude can be defended, except the disregard for consequences: tell us that we do not need a king, but do not tell us that we need only an impotent, useless king.[97]

"L'Inconséquence"

Mirabeau never indulged the illusion that success would come easily. The Court ("What a grotesque mixture of old ideas and new projects, of petty aversions and childish desires, of willfulness and lack of will, of aborted love and sterile hatred!"[98]) was at best undecided, the for-mer privileged orders were inclined to hostility, the people would be

[96] Georges Lefebvre, *La Révolution française*, 3d ed. (Paris: Presses universitaires de France, 1963), pp. 138f.

[97] Mirabeau, May 22, 1790; *Discours*, p. 238.

[98] Cited by Furet in his Preface to the *Discours*, p. 20. Furet gives the date of Mira-beau's remark as January 20, 1791.

too ready to "sell the Constitution for bread,"[99] and the Assembly was almost as often the butt of Mirabeau's irony as it was the object of his advice. Mirabeau's own tactics invited the very disaster he foresaw, for the only effective way to bring pressure to bear upon the king was to invoke the possibility of unruly street demonstrations and popular activism. Certainly the man to whom Mirabeau referred (in between threats or admonitions) as "the best of kings" and "a legitimate and cherished king"[100] did nothing to facilitate his would-be advocate's task. Indeed, the first major blow to Mirabeau's proposed strategy was delivered by the king in his speech to the three orders on June 23, 1789.[101] In what was perhaps his last uncoerced, comprehensive political statement, Louis made clear what was acceptable to him and what was not. He was willing to grant—constitutionally, forever—certain political reforms and rights. He invited the Estates General to propose measures tending toward greater personal freedom and liberty of expression. He gave assurances that taxes would henceforth not be imposed without the prior advice and consent of the "representatives of the nation,"[102] and he abolished the immunity from taxation previously enjoyed by the nobility and the clergy. He agreed to drop all internal customs barriers. He proposed the establishment of provincial bodies where delegates from each of the three estates would deliberate on local matters. On the fundamental issues, however, Louis refused to renounce the Old Regime:

> Art. I [of the King's declaration concerning the Estates General then meeting]. The King desires that the former distinction between the three orders of the state be conserved in its entirety, as fundamentally linked to the constitution of his kingdom; [and] that the deputies, freely elected by each of the three orders, forming three houses, deliberate by order, and able, with the approval of the sovereign, to agree to deliberate together, can alone be considered to form the body of the representatives of the nation. . . .
>
> VII. His Majesty having exhorted, for the salvation of the state, the three orders to come together, during this meeting of the Estates only, to deliberate together about matters of general utility, wishes to make known his intentions on the manner the proceedings should follow.
>
> VIII. Shall be expressly omitted from those matters to be discussed in

[99] Mirabeau, Estates General, June 15, 1789; *Discours*, p. 45.
[100] Mirabeau, Constituent Assembly, July 8, 1789; *Discours*, p. 70 and p. 69, respectively.
[101] For the text of the king's speech, see *Le Moniteur*, vol. 1, pp. 92–95.
[102] Louis XVI, *Le Moniteur*, vol. 1, p. 93.

common session, those which concern the ancient and constitutional rights and honorific prerogatives of the first and second orders.[103]

Louis concluded his speech with an all but explicit threat:

> Gentlemen, you have just heard the result of my disposition and of my views; they are in harmony with my lively desire to promote the public good; and if, by an unwanted turn of events which I do not even wish to imagine, you abandon me in such a fine enterprise, I will provide for the good of my peoples alone; alone, I will consider myself to be their true representative. . . .[104]

In compliance with the king's wishes, the nobility and most of the clergy withdrew from the hall as soon as the king's address was finished. The Third Estate and a number of clergymen remained. According to *Le Moniteur*, "a desolate silence reigned in the Assembly."[105] Mirabeau immediately rose to reaffirm the position symbolized by the Tennis Court Oath, which all had sworn three days earlier. Sovereignty, he made clear, lay with the people and in the Assembly, not in the king.

> I confess that what you have just heard could be the salvation of the country if the gifts offered by despotism were not always dangerous. What is this insulting dictatorship? The display of arms, the sullying of the national temple, to command you to be happy? Who gives you this command? Your delegate. Who gives you these imperious laws? Your delegate, he who should receive them from you, from us, gentlemen, who are clothed in an inviolable and political ministry; from us, from whom alone, twenty-five million men await certain happiness, because that happiness must be agreed to, given, and received by all.[106]

Still, Mirabeau sought to extricate the king from the debacle toward which Louis's announced intentions could only lead. Rather than attack the king directly, Mirabeau denounced the intentions that "had been suggested to the king"—adding for the benefit of his colleagues as well as for the master of ceremonies that the deputies would not be forced from their places except "by the force of bayonettes."[107]

Louis's initial intransigence and the increasingly obvious dissem-

---

[103] Ibid., pp. 93f.
[104] Ibid., p. 95.
[105] Ibid.
[106] Mirabeau, June 23, 1789; *Discours*, pp. 64f. Mirabeau later told the king what he might have said; see "Note terminée le 23 décembre 1790," in *Mirabeau*, p. 190.
[107] Mirabeau, *Discours*, p. 65.

bling that went on at Court would clearly have complicated the implementation of Mirabeau's constitutional scheme. Yet we have seen that Mirabeau himself seemed willing to detach his loyalties from the person of an uncooperative monarch. Everyone was familiar with the precedent provided by England's Glorious Revolution. Louis XVI's position and tactics were therefore unhelpful, but they were not decisive. The destabilization of representative institutions in the early years of the Revolution was rather the immediate responsibility of André Chénier's influential political friends, among whom Antoine-Pierre Barnave, the Lameth brothers (Alexandre and Charles), and Adrien Duport figure prominently. The actions of these men—conditioned by the structure of opportunity discussed earlier—were instrumental in bringing about the political outcome the moderates most feared. Often enough, Barnave and his associates ended up on the same side of a question as did Mirabeau; all were, after all, revolutionary leaders, and all rejected the intransigence and panic fear that moved Mounier, their early ally, to desert the Revolution. On several important occasions, however (the king's veto and the question of who would declare war are two examples), their positions diverged. Their differences turned out to be more significant than the many instances where they agreed, for their differences reflected the lack of a common underlying political understanding: Mirabeau's theoretical insights and practical recommendations fell on deaf ears. Immediate causes as well as long-term factors contributed to the moderate leaders' hearing difficulties.

If our eighteenth-century forebears tended to exaggerate the role played by individuals in history, current scholarship tends to underestimate it. Personal factors were very important in the Constituent Assembly, and they did not work in favor of Mirabeau's proposed constitutional arrangements or political strategy.

Personal factors counted because political parties did not exist. Political parties in the modern sense of the term did not exist anywhere in the early 1790s, but in France they did not exist even in the loose sense we use when we discuss "parties" in pre-nineteenth century England. For this lack of prior political traditions and organization, the revolutionaries had the Old Regime to thank. During the early months of the Revolution, deputies often met to discuss public affairs with other deputies from the same part of the country—thus the Jacobins were originally simply the "Club breton." The like-minded gradually learned to seek one another out, but their meetings served as forums for discussion and debate rather than as effective strategy sessions. The revolutionary elite also gathered in Parisian *salons*, mixing social pleasures and political affinities. At the same time, as Paris offered renewed examples of its impatience and the king answered with repeated demonstrations of his ill will, the deputies grew increasingly conscious of the enormous uncertainty and terrible risks attendant upon their enterprise.

Given the lack of formal political organization and the dangers of the hour, it is hardly surprising that personal feelings and trust (or the absence thereof) should have played such a considerable role in consolidating or undermining political alignments. Unfortunately for constitutional government, no matter how similar their political aspirations, Mirabeau and a man like Barnave did not share the same moral universe. Mirabeau was an older man, a noble and a *déclassé*, irreverent, provocative, of dubious personal morality, a politician profoundly attached to certain principles, but always ready to maneuver and willing to manipulate. Barnave was younger, more provincial, a Protestant, earnest and austere.[108] To him as earlier to his even stiffer *dauphinois* colleague Mounier, Mirabeau must have seemed devious and dissolute.[109] Barnave's speeches were almost always serious and somewhat self-conscious efforts; Mirabeau, for all his rigor, was easily ironical.

Personal distrust, compounded by conflicting personal ambitions, readily engendered political distrust. The "triumvirate" (as the dominating trio of Barnave, Duport and Alexandre de Lameth were known in 1790) concentrated their distrust on the king, his ministers, and their accomplices in the Assembly. As we have seen, their suspicions were well founded. Already in October 1789, before the storm over the reorganization of the Church broke, Barnave could assert privately:

> The ministry, not excepting M. Necker and majority of our Assembly, has never wanted a Constitution. . . . They have never enjoyed a moment of superiority without attempting to overturn, with incredible bad faith, all that they had seemed to accept. . . . Their contacts throughout the kingdom embrace almost everyone who exercises any authority. . . . Since the decrees of August 4, almost the whole governing part of the Nation has become our enemy and the enemy of liberty. . . . To give, under such circumstances, great energy to the old order, would almost certainly mean its re-establishment, offering it the means to destroy us almost without a fight, since it would have had on its side the Government and the majority of our

[108] No one has attempted a major biography since Jean-Jacques Chevallier, *Barnave ou les deux faces de la Révolution* (Paris: Payot, 1936).

[109] Jean Egret speaks of Mounier's relations with Mirabeau as being colored by an "invincible suspicion," Egret, *La Révolution des Notables*, p. 85.

Assembly ready to declare itself, as soon as it found itself unconstrained by fear and the strongly expressed will of the Nation.[110]

If the king and his partisans were deemed hostile on ideological grounds, Mirabeau was thought to be corrupt; he was, in fact, receiving money from the Court. Mirabeau's revolutionary colleagues suspected that he would do anything for money and a ministerial post. Once again, their fears, while in this case mistaken, were plausible, and it was fear, rather than political lucidity, that determined the positions they adopted on constitutional and institutional issues. Thus during the first discussion of ministerial responsibility, provoked by the king's sudden dismissal of Necker in July 1789, Mirabeau responded sharply to comments made by both Mounier and Barnave. Mounier did not want to diminish the powers of the king; Barnave did not want to abandon a mechanical application of the separation of powers. Mirabeau answered:

> If there is an impious and detestable maxim, it must be that which would forbid the National Assembly from declaring to the monarch that his people have no confidence in his ministers. This view contradicts the nature of things, the essential rights of the people, and the law of ministerial responsibility, a law that we have been asked to formulate, a law that is even more important, if that is possible, to the king than to his people, a law that will never be freely exercised if the representatives of the people cannot initiate an accusation. . . .
>
> But, some will say, you would mix [confondre] the branches of government . . . [sic].
>
> We will soon have occasion to examine this theory of the three branches, which correctly analyzed will perhaps show the facility with which the human mind mistakes words for things, formulae for arguments, the facility with which it falls into the routine of a certain order of ideas, without ever going back to examine the intelligible definition which it took as an axiom.
>
> The valiant champions of the *three branches* will then try to make us understand what they mean by this grand expression, the *three branches*. . . .
>
> For now, it is enough for me to say to them: you forget that this people, on whom you impose the limits of the three branches, is the source of all power, and that the people alone can delegate that power. . . . You forget that we do not in the slightest pretend to place or displace ministers by virtue of our decrees, but only to express the opinion of our constituents as regards one or the other minister.
>
> And how would you refuse us this simple right of declaration, you who grant us the right to accuse them, to try them, to create a tribunal that

[110] Private letter, October 4, 1789; cited by Egret, *La Révolution des Notables*, p. 168.

would punish these artisans of inequity, while, by a palpable contradiction, you propose that we contemplate their works in respectful silence? Do you not see how I prepare a kinder fate for our leaders than you do, how I am more moderate than you? You admit of no interval between a desolate silence and a bloody denunciation. . . . And I, I warn before I denounce, I denounce before I punish, I offer a path of retreat to ill-advised action or incompetence before I treat them as crimes.[111]

Several months later, the Assembly would reconsider the question. Mirabeau insisted not only on a degree of ministerial responsibility, but also on the right of the king to choose his ministers from among the ranks of the National Assembly, and on the duty of ministers to participate in parliamentary deliberations. Holding England up as an example, Mirabeau bolstered his earlier position with new arguments: The king's choice would fall on men in whom the people had already expressed confidence; ministerial evasion and duplicity would become more difficult; and the Assembly would be guaranteed easy access to vital information. The ensuing debate included a bitterly sarcastic speech by Mirabeau, who proposed that the left act on its fears and exclude him alone, by name, from ministerial office.[112] The discussion ended with a resolution barring any member of the National Assembly from accepting a ministerial appointment. Personal distrust and immediate fears weighed more heavily, and were more easily perceived, than the broader issues and long-term considerations on which Mirabeau based his case.

Conscious that the king must have some power over the legislative acts of the Assembly but unwilling to grant the logic of Mirabeau's argument, Barnave and Alexandre de Lameth looked for middle ground. They defended a limited veto, and the Assembly adopted their position. In the debate over who should have the right to declare war, Barnave engaged Mirabeau in a verbal duel. "Never has a more important subject occupied the attention of this Assembly," Barnave admitted;[13] what he then went on to say amply demonstrated both his inability to comprehend Mirabeau's constitutional proposals and his acute distrust of the executive and its agents. As regards the former, Barnave insisted unequivocally:

It is impossible for the power to declare war to be exercised by both the king and the representatives of the people. Such an arrangement would be nothing but a confusion of political powers and a *constitutional anarchy*.[114]

[111] Mirabeau, Constituent Assembly, July 16, 1789; *Le Moniteur*, vol. 1, p. 167.
[112] Mirabeau, November 7, 1789; *Le Moniteur*, vol. 1, p. 167.
[113] Barnave, May 21, 1790; *Le Moniteur*, vol. 4, p. 422.
[114] Ibid., p. 134.

As regards the likely actions of the executive, Barnave seemed swayed more by a nightmare vision than by a reasoned argument:

> It will perhaps happen that the legislature will be misguided; but it will come to its senses, because its opinion will be that of the nation, whereas the minister will almost always be misguided, because his interests are not the same as those of the nation. The government whose agent he is advocates war . . . : it is in the interest of a minister that war be declared, because then his authority will grow without measure. . . .
> . . . If the ministers alone make war, do not count on being consulted. The ministers calculate coldly in their cabinet; it is the massacre of your brothers, your children, that they order. They see only the interest of their agents, of those who nourish their glory; their fortune is everything; the misfortune of nations is nothing: such is a ministerial war.[115]

Barnave and his friends regularly defended positions on specific questions which were fundamentally inconsistent with their deep-seated longing for constitutional government and political stability. Their mistakes were understandable, but also eventually fatal. The inconsistency of their positions perpetuated the initial lack of organizational cohesion from which moderate forces suffered, while political measures motivated by fear further alienated an already unfriendly king. Peasant unrest, food shortages, fiscal problems (soon compounded by inflation), and the uproar over the Civil Constitution of the Clergy contributed their share to the process of destabilization. The heightened sense of insecurity that resulted tended both to credit the interpretation of popular sovereignty that Mirabeau had condemned and to invite the popular mobilization he had feared. Unable to discern the connections between their own tactics and the worsening situation, the moderates around Barnave could do little more than voice their alarm. In May 1791 (a month after Mirabeau's death), a protracted debate over colonial matters sharpened the moderates' sense that the Revolution was getting out of hand. On May 16, on a motion presented by Robespierre, the members of the Constituent Assembly voted overwhelmingly to exclude themselves from eligibility to serve in the Legislative Assembly soon to be elected. On May 17, provoked by what he had heard during the colonial debates and by what he had seen the day before, Adrien Duport rose to decry the course events seemed to be taking. The eloquence of his lengthy speech reflects the depth of his anguish.

"That which we call the revolution is complete," Duport insisted;[116]

---

[115] Ibid., pp. 428f.
[116] Duport, May 17, 1791; *Le Moniteur*, vol. 8, p. 427.

again and again, he returned to the need for "a wise and free constitution, a loyal, just, and firm government,"[117] "a just and solid government," "a solid and durable government."[118] Instead, he said, "you
have been led to a true and complete disorganization of society."

> I know not what mania for simplistic principles men have, for a certain
> time now, attempted to impart to you. Their effect, well calculated by those
> who are their prime proponents, is to relax all the sinews of government,
> and to destroy, not governmental abuses—that you have already gloriously
> done—but the salutary and preserving capacity of government; or, to put
> it better, [their effect is] to lead to a complete change in the form of the
> government; for, despite all protest to the contrary, one must be very ig
> norant of how the world works to doubt that grand plans exist in this re
> gard.[119]

The dangerous "simplistic principles" were none other than liberty
and equality, coupled with the constant rhetorical recourse to arguments based on natural right:

> Do not believe that the ideas of liberty and equality ever retreat; on the
> contrary, they tend by nature to extend, and to spread more and more
> broadly. One can, as I have said, and this is the great secret, this is what
> must be done, one can enmesh them in felicitous nets that restrain and
> constrain them. . . . Otherwise they continue to crumble; they ceaselessly
> level, ceaselessly dissolve. . . .[120]

At the end of this road lay not just the destruction of freedom, but
also the dissolution of political society. Duport maintained that history was a cyclical process, and warned that if unchecked, revolutionary trends would precipitate a return to the state of nature.[121]

In addition to dangerous principles, Duport warned, there were
also dangerous men: men who secretly hoped to alter the form of the
government and who had excited public opinion, "shallow minds
which harbor a completely mystical and fantastic idea of liberty."
"Why," he asked,

> has it occurred to no one that stability too is a principle of government? Do
> we think that the normal condition of a country is revolution, and do we
> wish to expose France, whose inhabitants already have such a mobile and
> ardent character, to witness a revolution every two years as regards opin-

---

[117] Ibid., p. 427.
[118] Ibid., p. 428.
[119] Ibid., p. 427.
[120] Ibid., p. 428.
[121] Ibid., p. 427.

ions, principles of administration, commerce, finance, taxation, and in political and commercial treaties? In all honesty, I think I must be dreaming
when I see that we are forced to respond to such miserable arguments.[122]

Duport had no doubt that he and his colleagues stood at a critical
juncture:

> The National Assembly as a whole, and emerging public opinion, are mov-
> ing in opposite directions. The Assembly is trying—or so I suppose—to
> rally all around a common point, which is the Constitution; and public
> opinion, in a contrary movement, is moving away from the Constitution.[123]

Failure, Duport knew, would mean the destruction of everything
the Revolution—his revolution, the moderate revolution—had endeavored to establish:

> Everything, including our weary indifference, indicates that we must finish
> the constitution, and leave after us an order of things which cannot be
> changed except by the express will of the nation, expressed in a pre-deter-
> mined manner. . . . Would you wait until events have credited the view,
> common both to our enemies and to purported patriots, that your consti-
> tution . . . cannot survive? . . . What will the situation be then? The defend-
> ers of your work, simultaneously fighting both our eternal enemies and the
> new patriots, pathetically attached to royal authority [*tristement serrés contre
> l'autorité royale*] and to the other powers which it will be fashionable to at-
> tack, caught in the pose in which you saw the *impartiaux*, the *monarchistes*,
> and others, will have no other resource than the resort to force, to that
> detestable and perilous instrument, martial law.[124]

Duport then reviewed popular misconceptions of the ideas of liberty and equality and again attacked men who stood ready to exploit
public opinion:

> They dare not flatter these ideas directly, but they spread the idea that at
> least these two principles . . . would be more religiously observed and more
> solidly united under a different form of government. This is not a chimera
> or a supposition that I present to you. . . . In vain will one say that such a
> plan is ridiculous; is it because things are unreasonable that they are im-
> possible? It will also be said that those who spread such ideas are noticeable
> only because of their profound incompetence. . . . All that means nothing
> when measured against the tendency of public opinion. . . .
>
> The first efforts toward such a system would be accompanied by incal-
> culable misfortunes. First it would be necessary to drown in blood the last

122 Ibid., p. 429.
123 Ibid., p. 428.
124 Ibid., pp. 427f.

defenders of the throne; the intrigues which at present agitate and divide society would become real and nefarious factions which would tear the empire apart. . . . He who today devotes himself to the noble calling . . . of systematizing calumny, would suddenly become the terror and tyrant of his fellow citizens. Finally, after long and unsuccessful attempts, despotism would arrive, presenting itself as an agreeable asylum to all the washed out, exhausted souls who would then envision happiness only in rest.[125]

Duport's vision of the future was more accurate than his analysis of the past, for he still failed to see why moderate institutional preferences had not been consolidated and why the "shallow minds" had won such a following. In his description, the Revolution was trapped in a vicious circle: the "inflation of public ideas" was itself the inevitable consequence of feeble institutions, of the "lack of a common center, of a national interest which draws and unites [men]."[126] In his account, there was no beginning and no exit; his analysis suggested no specific plan of action. In fact, the moderates, having rejected Mirabeau's coherence, were still paying the price exacted by the Old Regime's structure of revolutionary opportunity. It was the resulting absence of a viable revolutionary ideology that had precluded the development of a "common center."

One month after Duport's speech, Louis XVI attempted to flee the country. Unfortunately for the Revolution, he never made it to the border. The moderates' reactions to the king's move would leave them, as Duport had predicted, "pathetically attached to royal authority," and after being the creators of events they did not want, they would become the victim of events they could not control.

Toward the Politics of Exclusion

On April 20, 1792, after months of tension and debate and over the (different) objections of both Barnave and Robespierre, France declared war on the "king of Hungary and Bohemia."[127] Two months later, a mob invaded the grounds of the Tuileries in implicit defiance of constituted authorities. The Parisians who participated in the demonstration of June 20, 1792, were alarmed by military setbacks and reports of treasonous plots in high places, exasperated by a series of royal vetoes, and pushed into action by Louis's dismissal of his Girondin ministers. No prominent member of the Legislative Assembly (in

[125] Ibid., p. 428.
[126] Ibid., p. 427.
[127] For the text of the declaration of war, see *Le Moniteur*, vol. 12, pp. 174–76.

office since October 1, 1791) marched with the crowd; on the contrary, parliamentary leaders were dispatched to plead for calm. On July 11, the Assembly formally articulated revolutionary fears by declaring in an address to the country that "the nation is in danger."[128] On August 10, an insurrectionary riot brought down the monarchy, and with it, the constitutional order established by the Constituent Assembly. On September 21, a new constituent body, the Convention, met for the first time. The Convention drafted a republican constitution to replace the document hammered out by the Constituent Assembly, but the Constitution of 1793 was never implemented. Instead, on October 10, 1793, the Convention made official what political developments had already demonstrated: "The provisional government of France is revolutionary until peace comes."[129] As peace proved a long time in coming, so too did nonprovisional, nonrevolutionary government.

The declaration of war and the final collapse of constitutional government are inextricably linked. Despite the menacing tones of the ill-advised Declaration of Pillnitz (August 27, 1791), however, no invading foreign army imposed war on the Revolution. To those who advocated its declaration in the winter and spring of 1792, war had become a matter of domestic political necessity. The Revolution appeared betrayed from within as well as besieged from without; war, its partisans argued, would tear away the masks of the key political players and reveal the true loyalties of everyone from king to foot soldier. Public spirit would be galvanized and given that "common center" and "national interest" whose absence Duport had deplored; enemies and traitors, on the other hand, would be eliminated. Then political community and stability—still primary revolutionary goals— would be possible, for with the obliteration of counterrevolutionary forces, the Revolution's work would be complete.

The explicit recourse to revolutionary government and the adoption of the politics of exclusion were closely associated. To Brissot and his "Girondin" comrades—the great sorcerer's apprentices of the Revolution—the politics of exclusion appeared to be the Revolution's only option. Thus the politics of exclusion, at least in nascent form, *precedes* and in fact explains (in part) the declaration of war, and its first practitioners were the Girondins. The Girondins dominated the Legislative Assembly, signaling the final discrediting of the moderate ex-leadership of the Constituent Assembly. The moderate leaders, all

---

[128] Text of Assembly's declaration in *Le Moniteur*, vol. 13, p. 108.

[129] Text of decree in Saint-Just, *Oeuvres choisies* . . . , edited by Jean Gratien (Paris: Gallimard, 1968), pp. 184f.

deputies, were excluded from membership in the Legislative Assembly by the self-denying law of May 1791. In Paris, they stood little chance of mobilizing extraparliamentary forces sympathetic to their positions, and they rapidly demonstrated themselves incapable of organizing provincial support. They had, at any rate, already been overtaken by events. Had their chief spokesmen been present in the new legislature, the subsequent history of the Revolution would probably not have been substantially different. The Girondins' own lack of political cohesion and the form of politics they adopted minimized the chances of survival of a broadly based revolutionary coalition, even one defensive in character. That the Girondins' views prevailed was the immediate consequence of decisions made during the summer of 1791.

On the night of June 20, 1791, the royal family slipped out of the Tuileries and headed for Montmédy. Their probable intention was to leave the country. The party was recognized the next evening in the small town of Sainte-Ménehould (where it was noticed that one of the travelers resembled the figure on a fifty-pound *assignat* note) and in the neighboring town of Varennes, a hastily summoned local detachment of the National Guard blocked the king's passage. Barnave, Jérôme Pétion, and Latour-Maubourg were dispatched to escort the royal family back to the capital. As declarations of support flooded in from town halls and revolutionary organizations in the provinces, the Constituent Assembly met in permanent session. Its first efforts were directed at guaranteeing public order and the security of the borders, and at ensuring that government operations continued normally despite the absence of the chief executive. The deputies soon turned, however, to the critical constitutional and political question raised by the king's departure and by his now declared hostility to the Revolution. In a speech before the Jacobins on June 27, Girey Dupré bluntly summarized the deputies' dilemma: "Do we want to preserve our constitution and no longer have Louis XVI as king, or else, do we want to keep Louis XVI as king, and no longer have our constitution[?]"[130] After considering the risks, the moderate leadership of the Assembly refused Girey Dupré's formulation of the alternatives and concluded that the Constitution could not be preserved unless Louis XVI remained on the throne. The moderates consciously rejected the English precedent of 1688—not to mention that of 1649. Greater audacity on their part might not have been rewarded—particularly given the unprincipled Duc d'Orléans' eagerness to take advantage

[130] Girey Dupré, *Journal des Jacobins*, no. 17, p. 3.

of the situation—but in the end they were poorly served by their caution.

That the king was hostile to the Revolution and habituated to deceit, there could no longer be any doubt. Two months before Varennes, a letter written in the name of the king by the Minister of Foreign Affairs (Montmorin) had been publicly addressed to foreign governments. The text is useful as another statement of what the moderates wished the king could be made to think of the Revolution and of what they hoped the Revolution's final shape would be. The Revolution, the letter claimed, had profited king and people alike by destroying the "real force of the abuses of a few aristocratic bodies" and by precluding, "by a glorious revolution, the revolution that the abuses of the former government would soon have provoked." The king's adhesion to the new order, the letter insisted, had come without hesitation and remained without regret; his rumored unhappiness was a counterrevolutionary invention.[131]

The royal proclamation left behind on the night of June 20, 1791, told a different story. In it, Louis reaffirmed his acceptance of the "sacrifices" he had enumerated on June 23, 1789. Further he would not go, and he bitterly denounced the course political events had taken since that date. The proclamation piled petty personal complaints on top of constitutional objections. Forced to reside in an ill-furnished palace in Paris and to entrust his security to the National Guard, prevented (in April 1791) from taking a trip to Saint-Cloud, the king had felt himself a "prisoner in his own lands [Etats]." And as Mirabeau had predicted, the king had found his emasculated powers an insult to his status: "let the different areas of administration be examined, and it will be seen that the king is excluded from them all. . . ."[132]

Such illusions concerning the king's pliability as had been possible before June 21, 1791, thus became untenable after that date. The deputies who spoke of the king's "abduction" during the debates of June and July were consciously creating a political fiction. Their refusal to dethrone Louis was based neither on misplaced trust in his person or convictions nor on an inability to make the crucial distinction between the man and his office, and while all were conscious of Orléans's ambitions, they were also able to focus on more fundamental matters. Pétion, although he opposed the king's reinstatement, articulated a common understanding when he spoke to the question on July 13:

[131] Text of the letter in Le Moniteur, vol. 8, p. 213. Letter is dated April 23, 1791.
[132] Text of the king's proclamation in Le Moniteur, vol. 8, pp. 721f.

Will the king himself be made an issue? . . . What is immunity [granted to the monarch by the constitutional clauses adopted prior to Varennes]? . . . The real perspective in which it should be viewed, is that in all functions of the royalty, the king cannot be held responsible. In all civil suits, he can be called before the tribunals. The case of criminal actions remains to be considered.

. . . Is the king a citizen? Yes. Is the king a public functionary? Yes, you have declared him one. As a citizen, as a public functionary, is he subject to the law? If he is not subject to the law, he is above it, and if he is above the law, he is a despot. . . .

The king, people argue, is an office [*pouvoir*], and one cannot punish an office. What grovelling subtlety! The king exercises a great office, but he is not an abstract being: a judge is not justice; a king is not the monarchy.[133]

Prugnon retorted the next day that "judges are not the whole system of justice, whereas the king is the whole of the royalty,"[134] but to Alexandre de Lameth, Duport, and Barnave, that argument was not convincing. Their decision, supported by the five major legislative committees charged with examining the question and eventually approved by the Assembly as a whole, was based on practical, not theoretical, considerations. If Louis were to be dethroned, Alexandre de Lameth reminded his colleagues, either he would have to be replaced (and Orléans foiled) or constitutional monarchy would have to be abandoned:

The question which demands our attention is not the examination of the facts; it is a great political question, a constitutional question, and one of the utmost importance. We must examine from every angle the principle of the King's immunity . . . ; we must weigh the political considerations which, coming to the aid of abstract principles, will make you appreciate all the ills which will befall our country if, giving ourselves up to extreme opinions, we do not perceive the dangers, either of a regency during a long minority, or of the establishment of an executive council. (Several voices: That is not the issue.)

I beg your pardon, but that is the issue, for you cannot separate your decision from its inevitable consequences.[135]

Duport and Barnave excluded the republican alternative by rehearsing familiar arguments about the necessity of maintaining a monarchical form of government in France. If a regent were to be chosen from among those suggested by the rules of heredity, his loyalties

[133] Pétion, Constituent Assembly, July 13, 1791; *Le Moniteur*, vol. 9, pp. 120f.
[134] Prugnon Constituent Assembly, July 14, 1791; *Le Moniteur*, vol. 9, p. 125.
[135] A. de Lameth, July 13, 1791; *Le Moniteur*, vol. 9, p. 120.

would be no more certain than those of Louis. Stepping outside the
normal line of succession, or appointing a committee, would only excite the factious behavior the moderates wished to calm. Thus weakened, the executive would be unable to fulfill its assigned political and
constitutional functions; the chances of foreign attack and domestic
subversion would be enhanced, and the executive would not have the
strength needed to check and balance the Assembly. Less convinc-
ingly, Barnave added that if the drafted constitution were a good
one, it would function regardless of the personal qualities of the man
who was king—and that otherwise a great king would be far more
dangerous than an incompetent or ill-intentioned one. Here Barnave
spoke as if the constitution were long established, whereas the problem was precisely that it was not. Barnave concluded by returning to
the themes Duport had articulated three months earlier:

> Any change in the Constitution will be fatal, any prolongation of the rev-
> olution will be disastrous. Here is [where] I would locate the real issue: Are
> we going to end the revolution, or are we going to begin it anew? (Ap-
> plause in all parts of the chamber.) If you distrust the Constitution once,
> where will you stop? What will you leave to your successors? What will they
> do? I have said that I did not fear foreigners, but that I fear the distur-
> bances of a crisis which would know no limits. No one can harm us from
> without, but great ill can be done to us from within, by perpetuating a
> revolutionary movement that has destroyed everything that needed to be
> destroyed, and that can only be stopped by a peaceful and common rally-
> ing of all the components of the nation.[136]

The Old Regime was gone forever, Barnave insisted, and his account of the Revolution's accomplishments summarized the programmatic goals of the Constituent Assembly and its moderate leadership:

> You have made all men equal before the law; you have consecrated civil
> and political equality; you have recaptured all that had been confiscated of
> the sovereignty of the people; one step further would be a fateful and cul-
> pable act, one step further in the direction of liberty would be the destruc-
> tion of the monarchy; in the direction of equality, the destruction of prop-
> erty. . . . It is therefore true that it is time to end the revolution; . . . it must
> stop when it is done; . . . to wish more, is to wish to begin to stop being free
> and become guilty. (The chamber echoed for a few minutes with unani-
> mous and sustained applause.)[137]

[136] Barnave, July 15, 1791; *Le Moniteur*, vol. 9. p. 144.
[137] Ibid.

Barnave's opinion prevailed. Louis's royal powers remained suspended through the summer while the Assembly worked to revise the Constitution. On September 14, 1791, Louis took an oath of loyalty to the final text and recovered his powers as constitutional monarch. Before we can understand the political patterns which emerged as a consequence of his reinstatement, however, we must return to July and to events unfolding outside of the Assembly.

In the months preceding the king's flight, extraparliamentary agitation had gained in organization and assumed increasingly radical tones. Even before the commotion of late June, 1791 had not been a placid year. In addition to constant uncertainty regarding the intentions of the king, the period had been marked by growing resistance to the Civil Constitution of the Clergy, counterrevolutionary unrest in the provinces, and a steady emigration, symbolically important because it included the king's aunts and materially important because it depleted the officer corps of the regular army. Georges Lefebvre and Albert Soboul have both stressed the defensive and punitive emphasis of popular agitation.[138] By the summer of 1791, it appeared to many activists that defending the Revolution meant preserving it not only against the concealed scheming of the king and his counterrevolutionary allies, but also against the pusillanimity of the Assembly. Thus Marat—influential and surely one of the most repellent figures of the revolutionary era—predictably vilified the king ("that crowned brigand, perjuror, traitor, and conspirator"[139]), but then extended his invective to the "traitors of the National Assembly,"[140] whose motives he supposed base. He even attacked the "babbling and stupid people,"[141] long on words and short on action. The Revolution had purposefully exploded most of the Old Regime's limits on political space, but the Revolution's key institution, the representative assembly, failed to monopolize the space the Revolution created. Already by 1791, extraparliamentary political activity tended to foster a particular sort of antiparliamentary sentiment. Representative assemblies, it seemed, were indispensable in theory but inevitably corrupt in practice. Support was therefore to be tempered with suspicion.

On July 14, 1791, the Assembly received a petition sponsored by the radical Cordeliers Club. The text was brief, menacing, and to the point.[142] The Cordeliers opposed the reinstatement of the king and

---

[138] See Georges Lefebvre, *La Révolution Française* and *La Grande Peur de 1789* (Paris: Armand Colin, 1970); Albert Soboul, *Les Sans-Culottes*.

[139] Marat, *L'Ami du peuple*, no. 503, June 27, 1791.

[140] Marat, *L'Ami du peuple*, no. 497, June 22, 1791.

[141] Marat, *L'Ami du peuple*, no. 522, July 18, 1791.

[142] For the text of the petition, see *Le Moniteur*, vol. 9, p. 131.

demanded that the constitutional issue be decided through direct consultation of the sovereign people. On July 16, the Jacobin Club, which had previously provided a common forum for all revolutionary views represented in the Assembly, split. The club's moderate majority installed itself in another empty convent and became known as the Feuillants. The Feuillants' political and numerical strength would gradually dwindle, while the Jacobins reconstituted their forces and acquired a definite political orientation. On July 17, a demonstration on the Champ-de-Mars in support of the Cordeliers' petition was met with a declaration of martial law and dispersed by gunfire from Lafayette's National Guard.

The summer of 1791 thus witnessed a significant increase in the extent and impact of extraparliamentary political activity, a fissuring of the revolutionary leadership in Paris, and finally the reinstatement of a king who was widely viewed as a traitor. Two weeks after Louis took his oath, the deputies who had presided over the first two years of the Revolution stepped down. The institutional order they had with such difficulty devised was under attack not only from the right but also from the left; its defenders would be few and ineffectual. Barred by law from reelection, the Feuillants failed to rally the centrist majority of the Legislative Assembly. Barnave, exhausted and discouraged, left Paris in January 1792. Prominent Feuillant figures who remained in the capital chose to act as advisors to the king rather than as tutors to the new Assembly. Outside the Assembly, they were unable, and probably also unwilling, to duplicate the emerging Jacobin organization. Deprived by their own actions of political resources and "pathetically attached to royal authority," they no longer spoke for the Revolution.

During the many months that separated the demise of the Feuillants from the consolidation of Jacobin rule, the Girondins—Brissot, Vergniaud, Gensonné, Guadet, Isnard—dominated, in their own rather disorganized fashion, the political stage.[143] The Girondins—or Brissotins, or Rolandins, as they were variously called by contemporaries sensitive to the importance of personal relations—were linked by common social connections and political ambitions rather than by a shared political program. Their supposed preference for decentralized government, like Mirabeau's views on the same matter, was based on opportunistic and shifting calculation rather than deepseated conviction (see Chapter III). Interested in power, capable of

---

[143] The basic work on the Girondins remains M. J. Sydenham's *The Girondins* (London: Athlone Press, 1961). See also Gary Kates, *The Cercle Social, the Girondins, and the French Revolution* (Princeton: Princeton University Press, 1985).

brilliant oratory, the Girondins were politically out of their depth and appear pathetically shallow in comparison to either the Feuillants or the later Jacobins. The Jacobins of 1793–1794 made explicit the motivations of their political conduct; the Girondins of 1792 practiced the politics of exclusion without system and without reflection. Their primary contribution, if it can be so termed, to the Revolution was the war which began in April 1792.

During the period that followed the reinstatement of Louis XVI, a pattern of political interaction developed among the primary revolutionary actors: the Assembly, the executive, and the extraparliamentary activists. Against a backdrop of deteriorating economic, political and international circumstances, the Legislative Assembly repeatedly underwrote ostensibly defensive measures: Required oaths multiplied; freedom of movement was restricted; military preparedness was enhanced; and legislation was passed penalizing nonjuring priests and émigrés. These moves were resisted by the king and supported by mounting popular pressure. An intolerable air of siege seemed to hang over the Revolution; as early as December 1791, it appeared to many that the only way to lift the cloud of suspicion and uncertainty was for the Revolution to break out of its defensive posture. By harboring émigrés, Austria offered a ready target. The advocates of war argued that open hostilities, rapidly and successfully executed, would bring about the elusive political stability everyone professed to desire. Unlike the moderates of the Constituent Assembly, however, the Girondins seemed to have lost all sense of what political life might look like once stability was achieved.[144]

The most persistent and vociferous advocate of war was Jacques-Pierre Brissot, whose several speeches in the Assembly and before the Jacobins were broadly disseminated by his journal, *Le Patriote français*. It was Pierre-Louis Roederer, however, who most succinctly stated the political case for war. In so doing, he also described a country succumbing to the politics of exclusion:

> As I see it, gentlemen, it is a mistake to see things in terms of the question: shall we attack or shall we not attack. Shall we make war, or shall we remain at peace? But, gentlemen, we are not at peace at all. . . . We are under attack; will we defend ourselves? We are engaged in a hidden war [*guerre sourde*], a ruinous and debasing war; shall we prolong this war, or shall we make it an overt one in order to have peace? That is really the issue: we are at war, because the rebels beyond our borders have come together, . . . they have known commanders who are French princes . . . we

---

[144] Two years later, the Girondins denied—genuinely, it would seem—that they had ever favored any version of the "aristocratic" constitution of 1791.

are at war, because all Frenchmen are insulted by foreign courts, where the rebels gather and gain approval. We are at war against our seditious priests who support domestic rebellion. In truth, this war is as yet hidden and silent, but why? Because men wish to undermine us, to exhaust us. . . .

Is this a foreign war, between kings, between peoples? No: this is a war between Frenchmen, between individuals; combined with conspiratorial princes; civil war combined with foreign war. . . . It is the war of the nobility against the people; of all tyrannies against the liberty and security of individuals. . . . To attack is to defend ourselves.

Finish with Coblentz, and fanaticism and speculation will end. Let Coblentz insult you openly, and all is lost. . . . Our enemies are the enemies of the constitution and the most dangerous of our enemies are among us; they are masked and disguised: patriots can distinguish them only by virtue of certain forms, certain words, but the law mingles them all: they detest the constitution and they share in all its benefits, they enjoy liberty. . . . and in their hands the constitution is truly the great weapon of counterrevolution. No one has clamored as noisily as they for the constitution, they who want to overturn it. . . . The longer the period which is termed peace lasts, the longer this ill will last and spread. You will never be able, given this state of affairs, to identify the real friends of the constitution, by unequivocal signs. The way to recognize the real friends of the constitution is to make people act; sound the attack, let everyone fall in, let the ranks form up. . . . As soon as we are in a state of open war, as soon as this war absorbs all interests, petty quarrels will evaporate before the common war, every word, every movement, even silence, will be sure indicators of the sentiments of each individual, and will classify each individual as an enemy or friend of the constitution. . . . War therefore, let us have war, if we do not want the constitution itself to be the downfall of the constitution. . . .[145]

Robespierre vigorously opposed the declaration of war, but only because his reading of the domestic political situation was even more extreme than Roederer's. To Brissot's "Destroy Coblentz!" Robespierre retorted, "[T]he real Coblentz is in France, . . . that of the bishop of Trèves is only one of the threads of a deep conspiracy laid against liberty, a conspiracy whose hearth, whose center, whose commanders, are in our midst."[146] Historically, wars had always tended to strengthen the executive: In the case at hand, the executive had already been proven untrustworthy. Robespierre concluded that the temptation of war must be a trap, and those who favored it either fools or traitors (in Robespierre's view, most probably the latter). In

[145] Roederer, Jacobins, December 18, 1791; *Journal des Jacobins*, no. 113, pp. 3f.

[146] Robespierre, Jacobins, January 2, 1792; *Oeuvres*, vol. 8, p. 86. Brissot delivered his "Détruisez Coblence" speech at the Club on December 16, 1791; see *Journal des Jacobins*, no. 112, and *Le Patriote français*, No. 862.

opposing the declaration of war, Robespierre was therefore not pleading for peace or political trust, but for a different sort of war than the one the Girondins proposed. His position at least enjoyed the virtue of being consistent.

French arms did not fare well in the war's initial battles, and by early June, Paris was rife with accusations. Extraparliamentary activists were not alone in casting aspersions on the competence and intentions of constituted authority. In mid-May, Isnard had spoken to the political problems afflicting the country, denouncing "a secret committee which works without interruption for the success of a well-spun counter-revolutionary plot."[147] This secret committee, Isnard charged, was promoting anarchy by manipulating the king into an uncooperative posture, exploiting fanatical priests, and provoking the revolutionary clubs to immoderate and divisive actions. Isnard's "secret committee" soon came to be called the "Austrian committee," and revolutionaries both in and out of the Assembly fancied its conspirators to be ubiquitous. Popular petitions, presented in person to the Assembly by representatives of the petitioning body, urged vigilance. Responding to an atmosphere of growing panic, the Legislative Assembly adopted three measures in late May and early June: The first made non-juring priests liable to deportation; the second disbanded the king's personal guard (suspected of cultivating counter-revolutionary sentiments); and the last mandated the creation of a military camp in Paris, to be composed of revolutionary "*fédérés*" recruited from around the country. The king vetoed the first and last measures and fired the cabinet, precipitating the demonstrations of June 20.

The demonstration of June 20 was directed against the king, but its real casualty was the political independence of the Legislative Assembly. During the weeks that followed the demonstration, as the Girondins in their turn sought an accommodation with the king and as accusations and petitions circulated with increasing vehemence, there were frequent calls for the Assembly to reassert its authority and insulate itself from outside pressures. Those calls were uttered in vain, as the insurrection of August 10 would prove. The fracturing of revolutionary unity and the declaration of war had fundamentally altered the structure of revolutionary opportunity—none too promis-

[147] Isnard, Legislative Assembly, May 15, 1792; *Le Moniteur*, vol. 12, p. 393. Cf. similar speech given by Isnard at the Jacobins on March 25, 1792; *Journal des Jacobins*, no. 166.

ing from the outset for moderate forces. As the Assembly slipped
from its position of preeminence, the Feuillant dream of a form of
representative politics based on limited political goals, controlled conflict, and timely compromise faded. Representative institutions survived the summer of 1792; as a plausible political option, the politics
of transaction did not. Once Mirabeau's preferred interpretation of
popular sovereignty had been rejected, the interpretation he had
hoped to preclude became increasingly current.

The events of 1791–1792 did not afford contemporaries much opportunity for leisurely, let alone dispassionate, political analysis. On
several occasions, key revolutionary actors did nevertheless attempt
to understand and to explain what was happening. We shall examine
the Jacobin explanation in Chapter III. Girondins and Feuillants
agreed that a new revolution was beginning; their respective analyses
of its origins and probable course were colored by the increasingly
urgent requirements of political self-defense. Neither account could
compete with the inventions of Jacobin ideology, but each tells us
something about the politics and political understanding of the men
and groups who lost to the Jacobins. Barnave, in his *Introduction à la
Révolution française* (summer 1792), probes both personal responsibilities and underlying circumstances in an effort to comprehend why
English political development, leading to "free and limited monarchy, the happiest, the most beautiful type of government ever to
reign on earth,"[148] had not been possible in France. The blind spots
in his otherwise intellectually respectable work are revealing. Isnard's
verbal assault on the Constituent Assembly is an example of the Girondins' haphazard use of the politics of exclusion. It attests to their
unwitting role as a bridge between the moderate and the Jacobin
phases of the Revolution.

In the same speech in which he denounced the "secret committee,"
Isnard condemned the record of the Constituent Assembly. Isnard
accused the constituants of fiscal irresponsibility and political naiveté,
and of falling for "the illusions of credulous hope" in their dealings
with the king. His most fundamental criticism, however, was that the
Assembly, "with unlimited possibilities, dared go only half way."[149]
Under the Constituent Assembly's leadership, the Revolution had
failed to establish a new legitimacy:

> [The Assembly] did not grant any appearance, any attribute of grandeur
> to the new conception of sovereignty; instead it endowed the old despotism
> with all the human pomp, without realizing that a great number of citizens

---

[148] Barnave, *Introduction à la Révolution française*, in *Oeuvres de Barnave* (Paris: Jules
Chapelle et Guiller, 1843), vol. 1, p. 60.
[149] Isnard, Legislative Assembly, May 15, 1792; *Le Moniteur*, vol. 12, p. 392.

hear and think only through their eyes, and admire and respect only that which dazzles them. . . .[150]

Having failed here, the Constituent Assembly had failed in its primary political task. Isnard attributed the failure to cowardice, and the cowardice to an inappropriate fear of unavoidable unrest. Both revolutionary politics and the politics of exclusion, Isnard implied, had their place, and he indicted the Constituent Assembly for its stubborn attachment to legal formalities and for the restrictions it had placed on the Legislative Assembly:

> This famous Assembly [the Constituent Assembly], while clearing the land on which the ancient forest of abuses had grown, left in the field of liberty, mingled with the roots of the young tree of the constitution, the old roots of despotism and aristocracy, and . . . instead of enabling us to extirpate those roots, should they begin again to grow, the Assembly bound us to the constitutional tree like impotent victims consecrated to the rage of enemies whom the Assembly believed already annihilated, and whom in fact it had by no means destroyed.[151]

Isnard ridiculed the moderate leadership of the Constituent Assembly as "petty intriguers, talkers, . . . who circled round a seductive court."[152] That he and his friends had always been had by the more radical forces they coddled escaped Isnard's notice.[153]

Barnave's description of the Legislative Assembly was scarcely more flattering than Isnard's, but it was not the centerpiece of his analysis. Drawing on Montesquieu and employing such tools of the modern social sciences as were available to him, Barnave argued in the first part of the *Introduction à la Révolution française* that the "nature of things" and not the "will of men" determines the general form of political outcomes.[154] After acknowledging the critical role played by geography, Barnave assigned primary causal status to prevailing social conditions: the nature of a country's economy, the size, distribution, and organization of its population, the level and content of cultural attainment. Modern European political history had been shaped by the ongoing struggle between three forces: the landed aristocracy, the Crown (whose strength lay in its command of "public force"), and the bourgeoisie. At any given time, political dominance depended on evolving social conditions, but at moments when the

---

[150] Ibid.

[151] Ibid., p. 393.

[152] Ibid., p. 394.

[153] This pattern first appears in the interactions between the Cercle Social group and other groups to its left (for example, the Cordeliers). See Kates, *The Cercle Social.*

[154] See Barnave, *Introduction*, part I, particularly chaps. 1 and 2, in *Oeuvres*, vol. 1, pp. 1–4.

contending parties found themselves more or less equally matched, "accidental" causes, such as human decisions, could be decisive. To Barnave, the years 1789–1792 represented such a moment. Circumstances had not favored France to the same degree as they had England, but they had made the Revolution possible; once the Revolution had begun, human actions had compromised its success. Barnave spared no one. He criticized the king, not for his later duplicity, but for his indecision during the early weeks of the Revolution. He criticized the Constituent Assembly for disbanding at the worst possible moment:

> The Assembly precipitated its end: believing it could end the revolution with a wave of its wand, it did in a few days the work of several months, and fleeing, so to speak, at the moment when its experience was most necessary, it left its enemies fully armed, and its own work without defense, without protection, and so to speak, without roots.[155]

Finally, Barnave heaped scorn on the Legislative Assembly, initially well intentioned, but totally lacking in political preparation and soon the easy target of the radical propaganda disseminated by a near-unanimous Parisian press:

> There was little to be expected of such an assembly; its incertitudes, its weakness, its hesitations, would have sufficed to strengthen all that would destroy it; but the assembly was destined to become the instrument of a few men who had laid their plans in advance; who were preparing the fall of the constitution even before it was finished, and who, finding themselves on favorable terrain with all their weapons ready, alone with prepared plans and a fixed goal, easily led into their traps those deputies who had arrived from all the departments of the kingdom, without a guide, without experience, without knowledge of the factions that they would have to fight. The agitators, in contrast, had what was needed to disrupt everything; knowing how to profit from the remains of the fermentation they had provoked and from the ideas their writings had disseminated, they maintained, on the domestic front, the revolutionary movement, and prepared, on the foreign front, the events the reaction to which would favor their domestic projects. While they pushed minds toward war, they had the skill to distract public attention from their own manuevers, by occupying it with a thousand phantoms.[156]

The Legislative Assembly's conduct during the summer of 1792 was deplorable, but predictable:

[155] Ibid., p. 157. The Ideologues would later subscribe to this criticism, overestimating the significance of the self-denying law of May 1791.

[156] Ibid., pp. 208f.

The impotent legislature, always at the mercy of anyone who could impress it, without a plan, without resolve . . . , by its base weakness finally imparted to a handful of men the audacity to undertake to subjugate it and to accomplish a great revolution in the state, by means of a popular riot.[157]

Barnave's analysis is not wrong, but it is incomplete, and it never refutes Isnard's primary charge. Even as he wrote the *Introduction à la Révolution française*, Barnave still saw no way out of constitutional inconsistencies and improvisation. Preoccupied (as Isnard rightly perceived) with pragmatic, short-term considerations of public order, he did not understand that the Constituent Assembly's improvisations had left the Revolution without a convincing image of its own legitimacy. In the end, he attributed the destabilization of the Revolution to the effects of battle fatigue among moderates and to the demonically determined actions of the radical minority. There is, in Barnave's book, no intermediate analytical ground between the broad social causation emphasized in the first part and the human factor stressed in the second: thus the pervasive use of the conditional tense throughout the last chapters of the work. The Constituent Assembly could have prolonged its tenure by six months, Barnave argues, and consolidated the new order. Even after the convening of the Legislative Assembly, the situation could have been saved had responsible action been taken. The first step would have been to "complete the reestablishment of order," and it could have been achieved: "a legislature earnestly desirous of it, and which knew how to command respect, could have accomplished it in three months."[158] Barnave's account of why the Feuillants failed to maintain their initial advantage over the Jacobins indicates that his understanding of why the moderates had lost control of the Revolution as a whole was not fundamentally different from that of Chénier:

> During the first two weeks, the *Feuillants* received the adhesion of four hundred departmental sections, while the Jacobins received not even a dozen. If this beginning had been followed up with some care, if proper publicity had been given to these first successes, if the correspondence of the *Feuillants* had been active and instructive, if they had elaborated on their conduct and principles in good writings, it is conceivable that they might have become the center of the revolutionary party, that they might have lent, during the first months, great support to the constitution, and

[157] Ibid., pp. 217f.
[158] Ibid., p. 201.

that they might have been one of the greatest obstacles in the path of a second revolution.

But things were not to turn out that way. The Jacobin Club had remained composed of a great number of ardent spirits, for the most part journalists or pamphleteers, who staked all their glory and their entire existence on preserving the credit of their club and on assuring its victory; they made incredible efforts to sustain themselves, and brought into play two great weapons: the fear of pikes and the fear of slanderous pamphlets.[159]

There was more behind the moderate defeat than "the stupid spite of the right, the manuevers of the republicans, the exhaustion of the majority, and all the secret passions which it is so easy to awaken for a moment in the heart of men."[160] Similarly, there was more to the Jacobin victory than personal ambition supported by "the fear of pikes and the fear of slanderous pamphlets." In this chapter, I have argued that the sociopolitical structure of the Old Regime made an easy transition to the politics of transaction unlikely, since the monarchy's chosen role as social arbiter made all but impossible the prerevolutionary development of a type of liberal ideology that could have sustained the necessary views of conflict and community. Shunning Mirabeau's formulations, the moderates of the Constituent Assembly tried to respond to events in a pragmatic manner, and lost because ultimately their primary political motivation seemed to be the fear of public disorder. They proposed no new political imagery to replace the Old Regime symbols they had pushed aside. Despite their courage and intelligence, they thought it was possible to accomplish a revolution simply by writing new laws and devising new institutions, and to end one with "a wave of the wand." Combined with their fear of disorder, their ideological insensitivity led them to make unfortunate decisions. Those decisions in turn reinforced a rival view of politics within the revolutionary camp—amongst Frenchmen, that is, who, like the moderates, cleaved to the liberal ideals of individual rights, limited government, and representative institutions. The politics of exclusion was not a response to the national emergency generated by the war, for the war was largely its creation; it was rather a response to the ideological vacuum the moderates could not fill and to the political blunders that vacuum had greatly facilitated.

[159] Ibid., pp. 137f.
[160] Ibid., p. 207.

III

The Jacobin Alternative: Toward a Second Model of Liberal Politics

Suspicion, you [Brissot] say, *is a dreadful condition*! Much less dreadful, no doubt, than the stupid confidence that has caused all our troubles and all our ills, and that has led us to the brink of disaster. Patriotic legislators, do not slander suspicion. . . . Suspicion . . . is the guardian of the rights of the people; it is to a deep attachment to liberty what jealousy is to love.
   —*Robespierre, December 18, 1791*[1]

I went native from the first day, with an ease which revealed a profound affinity—not with French art, architecture, or literature—but with that most conservative and oppressive form of existence, the life of the French *petit bourgeois*. . . . My first impression of Paris was the sleep-swollen, unwashed faces of the crowd enveloped in the cosy stink of a second-class carriage of the Metro at eight thirty in the morning; the dreary *prix fixe* restaurants around the Bourse; the hopeless drudgery of the *nègres* in the basement. I saw their meanness towards each other and their unattractive mistresses; and, above all, I learnt the motto of the French little man: *il faut se défendre.* . . .

I soon began to suspect that this motto . . . was symbolic of the France of our day. The French, next to the Americans, are probably the most individualistic people in the world. But whereas American individualism is youthfully aggressive, aimed at outsmarting the other fellow, French individualism is resigned and defensive. French foreign policy between the wars was obsessed by the idea of *sécurité*, of hiding behind the Maginot Wall; the private life of the French little man was modelled on a similar pattern. He defended himself in his underpaid job; he defended himself against the State by cheating on income tax, against his fellow-men by an attitude of suspicion and defiance, a manner of sour surliness. He lived entrenched in his oppressive little flat, in his unaired clothes, like a cockroach in his carapace. And yet his manner of living attracted and fascinated me. Partly . . . because it was the opposite of mine: tenaciously rooted in his country, town, *quartier*, family and habits; and also because he never went abroad, had no curiosity about other countries and other lives; because he regarded any idea of change with contempt; because

[1] Robespierre, Jacobins; *Oeuvres*, vol. 8, pp. 58f. Robespierre never married.

he was smug and self-satisfied, and for all his narrow-mindedness and
meanness, lived in a profound harmony with himself, and enjoyed his
food, wine, fishing and sex in his grumbling, sour, deprecatory
manner more than people in any other human community that I had
seen.
    —*Arthur Koestler, 1952, on the basis of impressions from the 1930s*[2]

Treason comes naturally to a deputy, whatever his party.
    —*Alain, July 1931*[3]

When the Radical theoretician [Alain: Mounier is criticizing Alain and
"all the theologians of the Republic"] remarks that unchecked power
becomes crazy, and portrays his model citizen as a sort of chronic
victim of persecution, good sense . . . answers, "Yes, but any honest
Radical deputy will tell you that one year before the end of the
legislature, the checking functions of the committees turn him into an
idiot." And he will ask if the ideal official is M. Lebrun, foreign
minister of the Convention, who went to his office flanked by
policemen, and in the end was guillotined. Persecutor-persecuted: is
this the normal mode of relations between a nation and its
government and among citizens themselves?
    . . . There are times when individuals, like nations, exhaust their
substance in an effort to forge arms and defenses. There are times
when clubs and committees and grassroots organizations,
indispensable guardians of freedom, suffocate freedom by
surrounding it too closely. If one does not endow collective life with a
certain underlying consensus, limited of course to objective relations,
but uncontested and alive, if the individual never sees the collectivity
except through his peephole and then only as a dangerous universe
of potential thieves, then democracy should throw in the towel, for
feudalism has more to offer.
    —*Emmanuel Mounier, "Bilan sprituel: court traité de la mythique de
gauche," March 1938*[4]

    [2] Arthur Koestler, *Arrow in the Blue: An Autobiography* (New York: Macmillan, 1952),
pp. 208ff.
    [3] Alain, *Propos sur les pouvoirs: Eléments d'éthique politique*, ed. by Francis Kaplan (Paris:
Gallimard, 1932, 1938, 1985), p. 74. Like Robespierre, Alain believed that any power
corrupted absolutely, and that treason was by definition reactionary since it was always
motivated by self-interest: "[Interest] is not now here, now there; it always pulls toward
the right. And so he who betrays the people always appears dominated by luxury, by
the easy life, by praise, by the salary of the Statesman. The other party can offer nothing of the sort. Therefore there are not two forms of temptation, but only one. There
are not two kinds of treason, only one. All the weaknesses of any man pull him in the
same direction. The slope descends to the right" (March 12, 1914; in *Propos sur les
pouvoirs*, p. 62). Alain insists on these ideas, and they appear on nearly every page of
his writings.
    [4] Emmanuel Mounier, "Bilan spirituel: court traité de la mythique de gauche," orig-

"PATRIOTIC LEGISLATORS, never slander suspicion . . .": What Robespierre's compatriots made of the Incorruptible's views on love, we will never know; that many shared and passed on to their descendants his conception of liberty, however, there can be little doubt. From Robespierre to Alain and beyond, from the First Republic through at least the Fourth, not virtue, not property, but suspicion provided the cornerstone of the "conditional liberalism"[5] that became the political faith of Radical deputies and of the "little men" of Koestler's Paris.

Up to a certain point, suspicion and liberalism go hand in hand. What is problematic is the relationship between a political ideology and praxis defined in large part by its exclusionary elements on the one hand, and a political system based on representative institutions, individual rights, and limited government on the other. How then did Jacobinism contribute to and shape liberal outcomes in France?

In this book, we have compared revolutionary processes and outcomes in France, England, and America. The comparison seemed justified because in each case, political systems emerged that were based on liberal propositions regarding political authority, legitimacy, obligation, and action, and because (for presumably related reasons) all three countries became major industrial and international powers. In each country, governmental legitimacy came to rest on representative institutions, the limitation of state power, and the protection of individual rights. But comparability does not imply identity. In arriving at liberal solutions to the questions of political organization, political elites in the three countries built different ideological constructions around liberalism's basic philosophical positions. These different constructions in turn encouraged and legitimated different approaches to the key problem of political coalition building. We have called the particular combination of liberal ideology and praxis that emerged in England and America the politics of transaction. The politics of transaction added political stability to the liberal package because the structure of revolutionary opportunity allowed the revolutionary elites in England and America to establish the ideological hegemony of liberal positions in the postrevolutionary state. At this point in the argument, it should be clear why this first form of liberalism was unlikely to take hold in France. In its place, a second form appeared, in which political *instability* played an integral role. The politics of exclusion was both responsive to an initial situation that precluded the politics of transaction, and responsible for the long-term pattern that made political instability unavoidable. Liberalism in

inally published in *Esprit*, no. 66 (March 1938), pp. 873–90; reprinted in *Oeuvres de Mounier* (Paris: Le Seuil, 1961), vol. 4; cited passage is on pp. 60f.

[5] The expression is Stanley Hoffmann's; see *Le Mouvement poujade* (Paris: Armand Colin, 1956), pp. 381–87.

France leaned on an exclusionary model, and exclusionary politics depended on a constant current of suspicion.

Suspicion is a posture common to all liberals. Liberalism erects protective fences around the individual and his or her rights; the obvious assumption is that the safety of the individual depends on the careful maintenance of the fences. The Radical Whigs understood the positive political function of suspicion; John Adams's personality seconded his political convictions in supporting its practice; and even today the motto of the United States Navy reminds us that "eternal vigilance is the price of liberty." In England and America, however, the emphasis on the inviolability of property (and the sociopolitical structure that made that emphasis possible) permitted a concrete and therefore restricted specification of suspicious behavior and suspicious people. With its targets thus limited, suspicion did not hinder the development of that "underlying consensus" absent in France. In America, the Navy is vigilant, while civilians go about their business without concern; furthermore, the Navy's watchful eye is directed beyond our borders, trusting in the "underlying consensus" to guarantee domestic tranquillity.

The Terror of 1793–1794, like the Occupation and the final years of the Algerian War, was a time of exceptional external pressure on French politics, but the politics of exclusion that the Jacobins practiced and defended became in France a normal element of political life. Only its more lethal manifestations disappeared as the external pressure abated; the underlying political reflexes (and the compensatory measures that accompanied them) survived. The politics of exclusion, involving a particular ideological and institutional response to the problem of conflict and community, became the source of a persistent and regular pattern of political instability. The first episode in what became a recurrent story was the rise and fall of the Directory. The centrality of instability to this model raises a key problem, for it would appear that the model of liberal politics that we are now proposing includes both liberal positions and illiberal alternatives. This problem is aggravated by the interpretive difficulties associated with the Jacobin phenomenon.

It would be tendentious to present revolutionary Jacobinism—the Jacobinism of Robespierre and Saint-Just, of the revolutionary tribunals, and of the republican armies sent to "pacify" the Vendée[6]—

---

[6] General Westermann to the Convention, December 23, 1793: "The Vendée is no more. I have just buried it in the swamp of Savenay. I crushed children beneath the hooves of horses and massacred women. I have not a single prisoner on my conscience. I exterminated everything." Quoted in Jean Tulard et al., *Histoire et dictionnaire de la Révolution française* (Paris: Robert Laffont, 1987), p. 363.

itself as a form of liberalism, although after 1870, the jacobinism of large portions of the republican elites might accurately be so described. Rather, I will argue that the politics of exclusion, most easily analyzed during the period when the Jacobins put it on full display, mixed permanently with the more conventional liberal positions that moderate politics had been unable to establish but that continued to represent programmatically a revolutionary common denominator. The goals remained the same; the dynamic was distinctive. By shaping this dynamic, Jacobinism contributed decisively to the elaboration of an alternative model of liberal politics and set up a specific form of liberal political and social development.

In the first section of this chapter, I will argue that Jacobinism at last provided the revolutionaries with a psychologically and ideologically adequate means of responding to events. Here, I will speak interchangeably of Jacobinism and the politics of exclusion. The Jacobins' account of human nature and political causality, their dedication to the final eradication of the Old Regime, and their reading of current events credited exclusion as the only conceivable way of dealing with conflict. First directed against the defenders or the remnants of the Old Regime (the king, the Vendée rebels, the European powers), by the late spring of 1793 the politics of exclusion had also become the accepted way of "settling" conflicts *within* the revolutionary camp. The first victims were the Girondins; they were followed by the Hebertists, and finally by Danton and his friends. Relatively minor differences of political orientation, as well as conflicts of interest and ambition, were cast in ideological terms and resolved by the guillotine. Political resistance was impossible, in part because the victims shared the executioners' conception of politics and in part because there was no organizational base to sustain resistance.

Revolutionary Jacobinism was a complex phenomenon, and it is not the purpose of this chapter to provide a full analysis of its many facets. Such an analysis might build on distinctions between Jacobin policies and politics, between Jacobinism in power and Jacobinism in opposition, between routine and crisis Jacobinism, between grassroots and elite Jacobinism, between Parisian and provincial Jacobinism. To the extent that revolutionary Jacobinism in all its forms was primarily a punitive doctrine aimed at punishing the perceived abuse of power—to the extent, that is, that it was defined by its defensive and exclusionary functions—it had a relatively underdeveloped positive program. Jacobinism did nonetheless entail a positive set of common positions and postures. The combined positive and negative planks of the Jacobin program make *Jacobinism* a meaningful term despite the distinctions mentioned above, and despite the occasionally heavy dose of opportunism that sometimes seemed to drive Jacobin actions, sidelining the recommendations of conviction and ideological coherence.[7] In the second section of this chapter, I will insist on those elements of revolutionary Jacobinism that allowed it to mix with liberalism and underwrite a liberal route to modernity.[8] I will therefore argue against confusing Jacobinism, however virulent the policies of exclusion it justified, with protototalitarianism. Jacobin traditions remained, but France never veered toward totalitarianism, and she in fact showed little patience for authoritarian experiments, however often and under whatever guise they were tried. The Jacobins' views of political institutions, the kind of state they endeavored to build, their conception of virtue and of the limits and ends of political life, and the type of inclusionary rhetoric and policies that were the other side of their politics of exclusion profoundly affected what became the dominant view of the state, the public interest, and the national community in France. Combined with the politics of exclusion, that view constitutes an alternative understanding of liberalism.

Jacobinism did not, and could not, immediately produce stable liberal institutions. In that sense, the exclusionary violence of the French Revolution, unlike the violence of the English and American Revolutions, was uneconomical. The *pattern* of politics engendered by the politics of exclusion was functional in the sense that it interacted coherently with a broad range of French political and social expectations and thus explains the regularities of apparent French instability. But as we shall see in the final section of this chapter, from the perspective of the Directory, it appeared that the politics of exclusion had not "worked," for it had aggravated the problem of conflict without resolving the problem of community. It could not produce the kind of revolutionary settlement achieved in England and America.

The Politics of Exclusion: Negative Legitimacy

Although the Jacobins were in power during a time of constant unrest and foreign and civil war, their actions and reactions lacked the

[7] For an analysis that places greater emphasis on opportunistic motivations, see Lucien Jaume, *Le Discours jacobin et la démocratie* (Paris: Fayard, 1989).

[8] My thinking here has been stimulated, positively and negatively, by Michael Walzer's discussion of Jacobinism as an "ideology of transition" (comparable, in his view, to Puritanism and Bolshevism) in the Conclusion of *The Revolution of the Saints* (Cambridge, Mass.: Harvard University Press, 1965), as well as by Samuel Huntington's understanding of the relationship between institutions and the public interest, and his treatment of Leninism and revolutionary politics in *Political Order in Changing Societies* (New Haven: Yale University Press, 1968).

ad hoc character typical of the moderate response to events.[9] The Jacobins possessed what the moderates had so sorely lacked: an ideology constructed on the same scale as their political aspirations, and correspondingly powerful. Neither the Jacobins' institutional preferences nor their account of the ends of political life distinguished them fundamentally from other revolutionaries of more moderate reputation. What made the Jacobins different was their attitude toward politics as a human activity. Obsessed by the role played by individuals in history, professing a sure understanding of human motivation, always attentive to the "symbolic and projective side" of politics,[10] the Jacobins, like the American revolutionaries, proposed a convincing (if "objectively" erroneous) explanation of what had lately gone wrong in France and of what had to be done. Unlike the ideologies of the English and American revolutionaries, however, Jacobin ideology, through its account of human nature and its conception of politics, in effect denied the possibility of an uncorrupted revolutionary agent—whence the unceasing emphasis on suspicion and exclusion and the gloomy pessimism regarding both the present and the future fate of the Revolution. Moderates and Jacobins alike defended the sovereignty of the people as the foundation of political legitimacy; moderates and Jacobins alike argued the necessity of stable representative institutions. The moderates thought the system would work: The public interest would be hammered out through a process of debate and compromise, and then made effective by an impartial state. Everything in the Jacobin understanding of the human and political world told against such confidence.

There is no Jacobin version of the sociological analysis of events presented by Barnave in the first part of his *Introduction à la Révolution française*. The Jacobins' assessment of political causality was based instead on an account of individual psychology that minimized the historical importance of impersonal factors and forces. The Jacobins believed that men made history, that they knew the history they made, and that they made it in ways dictated either by human nature directly or by human nature as distorted by a given social and political environment.[11] Intellectually less sophisticated than Barnave's ac-

[9] My analysis of Jacobinism is based primarily on the speeches and writings of prominent members of the Paris Society, on the governmental record of the Committee of Public Safety during Robespierre's tenure in office, and on the secondary literature. For an account of Jacobin societies in the provinces, see Michael Kennedy, *The Jacobin Clubs in the French Revolution* (Princeton: Princeton University Press, 1982).

[10] The expression is Fritz Stern's in *The Failure of Illiberalism: Essays on the Political Culture of Modern Germany* (Chicago: University of Chicago Press, 1971), p. xxxiii.

[11] Cf. Lefebvre's description of "la mentalité révolutionnaire," cited above, pp. 120f.

count, the Jacobin account was by the same token more representative of and accessible to the intellectual capacities of the average member of the political class.

Human nature, the Jacobins argued, could lead in one of two directions. The results would depend on which path was chosen: on whether the individual, in seeking to promote his welfare, relied exclusively on his own productivity and resourcefulness, or instead invoked the devices of pride and power. Saint-Just, following Rousseau, attacked the Hobbesian contention that the state of nature resembled a state of war. That idea, Saint-Just argued, was but a self-serving invention of men intent on power: "Men were assumed to be savage and murderous in the state of nature, in order that rulers might have the right to enslave them."[12] "Natural man" was in fact inclined to be gentle, gullible, independent, a bit lazy, and easily satisfied. His safety, however, was always threatened by a minority eager to establish tyrannical rule. The reason was not the institution of property, but rather pride and politics, both inherent to the human condition. Government was necessary to ensure the external security of a people, but power awoke pride, and pride invited the abuse of power: "All the arts have produced their marvels; the art of governing has produced only monsters: the reason is that we have carefully searched for our pleasures in nature, and for our principles in our pride."[13]

Thus the Jacobin world divided neatly into two unequal and necessarily hostile parts: the powerless majority—"the people"—and the powerful minority. In each instance, action was informed by self-interest, but whereas the people relied on themselves, the powerful used the people. The Jacobins included prosperous merchants, rich bankers, large landholders, and affluent *rentiers* of various descriptions among the untrustworthy minority, but the most dangerous men by far were those vested with political authority:

> The ills of society never come from the people, but from government. How would it not be so? The interest of the people is the public good; the interest of the office-holder is a private interest. To be good, the people need only prefer itself to that which lies outside itself; to be good, the magistrate must immolate himself to the people.[14]

The conflict between the people and the powerful could never be definitively resolved, for no Jacobin leader ever predicted the with-

[12] Saint-Just, Convention, April 24, 1793; *Oeuvres complètes* (Paris: Gérard Lebovici, 1984), p. 417.
[13] Ibid., p. 416.
[14] Robespierre, Convention, May 10, 1793; *Oeuvres*, vol. 9, p. 496.

ering away of the state: The Jacobins were too preoccupied with the power-seeking character of individuals and the social need for discipline to imagine that structures of political dominance could ever be banished from human affairs. Political power could be limited; it could not be abolished. To limit power and so preserve freedom and security, institutional checks—and popular vigilance—would have to curb the inevitable illegitimate ambitions of those whose job it was to govern. The goal of the Revolution, for the Jacobins as for moderate revolutionaries to their "right," was therefore the establishment of appropriate institutions and the political education of a long-suffering and naive people. The difficulty, for the Jacobins, lay in their inability to identify a reliable revolutionary agent; this inability both reinforced their exclusionary politics and kept them within the liberal fold, since it was only with great difficulty that they could move beyond an essentially negative image of power.

A first reading of Jacobin politics would assign the role of revolutionary agent to the people. That reading, however, would be incorrect, for the defining characteristic of the people was precisely its distance from the daily exercise of political power. The people in power would no longer be the people, but rather a group of individuals, and as such, subject to the urgings of pride and the perverse forms of individual interest; the public interest could be constructed only by institutions and processes that could plausibly be represented as impersonal and egalitarian. By default, and because it was the only impersonal actor available, the state ended up with the responsibility of defending, representing, and occasionally defining the public interest that other, less impersonal political actors would necessarily subvert. The Jacobins, one might say, adopted the idea of the state as the artificer of the public interest, but rejected the notion of a universal class—not to mention a monarch. It is little wonder that they were more comfortable in opposition than in power, or that the oppositional aspects of their ideology shaped and constrained their use of power.

The Jacobins depended on the politics of exclusion to secure the Revolution against real and imagined enemies. There was nothing surprising about the Jacobins' distrust of the Court and of all those openly associated with it. To the Jacobins, however, the revolutionary elite itself—Assembly leaders, ministers, generals—seemed doubly suspect, and remained so after the fall of the monarchy and the execution of the king. The revolutionary leadership was suspect by virtue of the power it exercised, and because its members had grown to maturity under the Old Regime. The Old Regime, with its privatized politics, had made men wrongly self-interested even in their private

dealings: It had denigrated self-promotion achieved through indus-
try, thrift, and discipline, while encouraging manipulation and ex-
ploitation:

> As for us unhappy ones! We raise up the temple of liberty with hands still
> branded by the irons of servitude. What was our former education, if not
> an unending lesson in egoism and stupid vanity? What were our customs
> and our purported laws, if not a code of impertinence and baseness, where
> scorn for other men was subjected to a sort of tariff, and graduated ac-
> cording to rules as bizarre as they were numerous? Despise and be de-
> spised; grovel in order to dominate, slaves and tyrants by turn; now on
> one's knees before a master, now trampling the people beneath one's feet,
> such was our fate, such was our ambition, of all of us as we were, *well-born
> men or well-brought up men, honnêtes gens or respectable men, men of the law and
> financiers, nobles of the robe or of the sword.*[15]

Lafayette's background made him an obvious target of Jacobin suspicion:

> Connected to our former oppressors, related to a family famous in the
> glitter of the court for its hereditary command of intrigue and adulation,
> devoid of the masculine virtues that characterize free men, your soul could
> not be sensitive to the glory of reviving the human dignity and the power
> of the French people through the regenerative principles of justice and
> equality; you wanted only a revolution compatible with your aristocratic
> prejudices and your personal interest. Your means were worthy of your
> ends, of the upbringing you had received in the most corrupt of all courts,
> of the base passions and the innate dishonesty which you have already
> demonstrated.[16]

> You intrigue, you intrigue, you intrigue; you would be capable of a palace
> revolution, it is true; but stop a world revolution, that task is beyond your
> capacities![17]

Later, Camille Desmoulins' easy morals and rich marriage would
play a part in his downfall. The most common political insults in the
Jacobin vocabulary—"*intrigant,*" "*fripon,*" "*homme perfide*"—denounce
the alleged transfer of private vices rewarded by the Old Regime into

---

[15] Ibid., pp. 497f.
[16] Robespierre, *Le Défenseur de la Constitution*, no. 6 [June 22 or 23, 1792]; *Oeuvres*,
vol. 4, p. 170.
[17] Robespierre, *Le Défenseur de la Constitution*, no. 7 [end of June, 1792]; *Oeuvres*, vol.
4, p. 199.

the public life of the new republic.[18] They are political only if the revolutionaries' condemnation of the privatized political world of the Old Regime is understood, and their significance reflects the degree to which the Jacobins' political concepts were shaped by a culture they condemned. Free institutions, acting on the mores and morals of the people, would eventually create a virtuous circle, but the legacy of the Old Regime trapped the revolutionaries in a vicious one: "In order to create our political institutions, we would need to have the mores that those institutions will one day teach us."[19] Mirabeau too had indicted the moral heritage of the Old Regime, but had believed it could be overcome by compromise, leadership, and trust. The Jacobins disagreed. "Be the people!" Danton repeatedly admonished his colleagues of the Convention,[20] but ultimately that order represented both a necessary and an impossible demand.

By the end of 1792, the Revolution was clearly in trouble. As a first step toward remedying the situation, the Jacobins set out to identify the responsible elements. The first step rapidly became an all-consuming task. The Jacobins supposed the Revolution's enemies lacking in courage but not in intelligence, and assumed that they would operate by "intrigue and subtlety [*l'intrigue et la finesse*]." Like an (aristocratic) lover socializing in the company of his mistress's husband, the Revolution's enemies would opt for deceit over all other arms. It was a strategy Robespierre had denounced in detail as early as January 1792:

> The court and its servants will never betray you in a gross and vulgar manner, that is, in a manner that might arouse your suspicions. . . . But they will deceive you, they will lull you to sleep, they will exhaust you, they will lead you by degrees to the last moment of your political agony; they will betray you with art, with moderation, with patriotic gestures; they will betray you slowly, constitutionally, as they have done up to now; they will

[18] The preferred Girondin term seems to have been "*scélérat*," already more straightforwardly applicable to public life than the Jacobin epithets. Like the politics of exclusion, the Jacobin insults survived Thermidor.

[19] Robespierre, *Lettres à ses commettans*, no. 1 [around September 30, 1792]; *Oeuvres*, vol. 5, p. 20.

[20] For example, on March 27, 1793: "The Convention is a revolutionary body; this body must be '*peuple*' like the people itself." Later in the same speech: "Show yourselves terrible, show yourselves people, and you will save the people." And still later: ". . . I insist on what is more than a law: you must be the people [*il faut que vous soyez peuple*]. . . ." *Discours de Danton*, ed. André Fribourg (Paris: Société de l'histoire de la Révolution Française, 1910), pp. 300, 305, 310. Cf. Robespierre's remarks after Dumouriez went over to the enemy: "Let all Paris arm itself, let the sections and the people stand watch, let the Convention declare itself the people." Jacobins, April 3, 1793; *Oeuvres*, vol. 9, p. 359.

even beat [opposing foreign armies], if it is necessary, in order to betray you more successfully. How many kinds of treason the genius of tyranny has invented in a century of enlightenment![21]

Counterrevolutionaries and insincere revolutionaries would employ deceit to lull, seduce, corrupt, and abase the people. If they succeeded, the Revolution would be undone. In the Jacobin vision, politics appeared as a game played in the shadows for high stakes, where one side always said or did one thing but intended another. In such a setting, the primary activity of the patriot was to "unmask" (*démasquer, dévoiler*) and eventually eliminate the enemy. Isnard had reproached the moderates for failing to clothe revolutionary goals in compelling imagery. Jacobin discourse filled the breach: The Revolution would derive its legitimacy from the diligence with which it unmasked and punished the people's enemies.

At every stage of the Revolution, Jacobin accounts of its course provided lengthy portraits of the enemy, and of his misdeeds and motivation. The Jacobin explanation of events rested on three related theses about political opposition to the Revolution; these same theses informed the Jacobins' conduct of the Terror. Covert counterrevolutionary subversion, the Jacobins contended, had begun with the Revolution itself. All political critics ("conspirators") and all oppositional activities were bound together by an objective solidarity. Finally, the common purpose of the entire opposition was the reestablishment of the monarchy.

The Revolution's original constitutional arrangements had preserved the king and his court as a focal point of political life, and where there was temptation, the Jacobins believed, there would be sin. Palace intrigues and attractions had naturally rallied many would-be patriots whose sense of self-interest still conformed to Old Regime norms. Robespierre condemned Lafayette's "middling third party" (a pejorative description destined to a long future in French politics) as being composed of "all those who love liberty for themselves," and he traced its treasonous machinations back to the first days of the Revolution.[22] Similarly, he denounced the Girondins as men who had "embraced the Revolution like a profession and the Republic like a prize,"[23] while Saint-Just described Danton, Desmou-

---

[21] Robespierre refers to "*l'intrigue et la finesse*" in his denunciation of Lafayette, *Le Défenseur de la Constitution*, no. 6; *Oeuvres*, vol. 4, p. 170. The longer passage is from a speech to the Legislative Assembly on January 25, 1792; *Oeuvres*, vol. 8, p. 142.

[22] Robespierre, *Le Défenseur de la Constitution*, no. 6; *Oeuvres*, vol. 4, p. 178.

[23] Robespierre, Convention, February 5, 1794; *Oeuvres*, vol. 10, p. 356.

lins, Fabre d'Eglantine, Phillippeaux, and their co-accused as men who "had never known the fatherland":

> There is no crime that they have not hidden, no traitor whom they have not excused; avaricious, egotistical, apologists of vice, rhetoricians, and not friends of freedom, the Republic cannot coexist with them; they require pleasures that are acquired at the expense of equality; they have an insatiable thirst for influence.[24]

The emphasis on personal, rather than political, motivation allowed the Jacobins to argue (in this case through Saint-Just) that "all crimes are related."[25] Past plots and present, domestic troubles and foreign armies, *enragés* and *indulgents*, self-avowed counterrevolutionaries and dissident veterans of the revolutionary movement: All were the products of or participants in "a party composed of diverse but coinciding factions, . . . one sometimes unknown to the others."[26]

The emphasis on the self-interested character of "counterrevolutionary" action permitted the Jacobins to contend that all such action favored the restoration of the Old Regime, although not precisely the Old Regime as it had existed prior to 1789:

> Do they ["the enemies of our liberty"] wish to bathe France in blood in order to reestablish the Old Regime in all its deformity? No, they know very well that such an enterprise would be too difficult; and the heads of the dominant faction [in December 1791: Feuillants and Girondins] have no interest in reviving the Old Regime abuses that inconvenience them; they seek only, in the current situation, those changes demanded by their personal interest and their ambition.[27]

Since the material interests of those lumped together as counterrevolutionaries were known to differ, the social organization of a reestablished Old Regime could not be predicted with certainty. The political gains of the Revolution, however, would surely be erased: the sovereignty of the people denied, political equality and participation abolished, and the emerging autonomy of the political world destroyed.

Would the people not resist? "O people too good and too credulous," Robespierre exclaimed two weeks before the insurrection of August 10, 1792, "fear lest you be deceived again!"[28] The Jacobins never endorsed Marat's scornful and spiteful commentaries on the

---

[24] Saint-Just, Convention, March 31, 1794; *Oeuvres complètes*, p. 778.

[25] Saint-Just, Convention, March 13, 1794, *Oeuvres complètes*, p. 730.

[26] Saint-Just, Convention, March 31, 1794, *Oeuvres complètes*, p. 762.

[27] Robespierre, Jacobins, December 18, 1791; *Oeuvres*, vol. 8, p. 51.

[28] Robespierre, Jacobins, July 29, 1792; *Oeuvres*, vol. 8, p. 411.

people, not because they had more faith in popular judgment, but because they had no expectation that "the people" could or would regularly play an active political role. The normal role of those who governed was to deceive and betray, and the normal role of the governed was to be deceived and betrayed:

> France's misfortunes are extreme. Can their cause be identified? . . .
>
> Betrayed by the guardians of her authority, delivered by the government itself to the insults and the sword of foreign despots, abased, oppressed, stripped in the name of the laws, the French people is nervous, affected by a painful anxiety, without knowing either the source of its troubles, nor the means to end them. Eternal plaything of the intriguers who have governed it since the beginning of the Revolution, victim of its own ignorance or of its own prejudices, it has been now alarmed, now reassured by their vows; insignificant or perfidious acts of patriotism have made the people forget a thousand terrible attacks on its rights. Even today [July 29, 1792], in the final period of the crisis which torments it, it is ready to entrust its own salvation to partial and insufficient measures, to impotent or dangerous remedies. Amongst the multitude of public functionaries . . . , how many are there who show the people what course it must follow, and who are not ready to immolate the rights of the people to their own stupid pride? Those who call themselves its counselors are, for the most part, simply ignorant men who are deceived, or crafty men who strive to prolong its errors and its slumber. Its representatives themselves, in proclaiming the dangers to the fatherland [a reference to the decree of July 11, 1792], have dissimulated the cause [of those dangers]. . . . Since this time, what have these representatives done, except surround the fatherland with inescapable traps?[29]

If the world appears, in Emmanuel Mounier's words, as "a dangerous universe of potential thieves," the politics of transaction becomes inconceivable. The Jacobins could only believe that under such an arrangement, the people would always be had. To protect the people and at the same time to consolidate the (liberal) gains of the Revolution, the Jacobins resorted to what we have called the politics of exclusion. Since their understanding of political causality and the resulting interpretation of events left them unable to distinguish between different kinds of political opposition, they employed the politics of exclusion indiscriminately, against Danton as against the king. "I want to see in their past conduct," Robespierre wrote of Bris-

[29] Ibid., pp. 408f.

sot and his political allies in May 1792, "only a sovereign disregard of political reality."[30] That succinct and fitting description of the Girondins was not, however, allowed to stand, for events had now clarified the "mystery" of the Girondins' alleged earlier ties to Lafayette: The Girondins, Robespierre asserted, had been privy to "all the plots hatched over the last years by petty intriguers."[31] They were therefore traitors, not competitors, and to paint them as legitimate political rivals would itself be indicative of criminal intent. Thus Saint-Just charged Danton after the latter's indictment: "You accused Roland, but more as an acrimonious imbecile than as a traitor . . . ,"[32] Saint-Just cited this lapse as proof that Danton too was a traitor. The logic that prompted the transfer of the politics of exclusion from appropriate objects (the king) to inappropriate objects (the plausibly loyal opposition) discouraged the consolidation of liberal institutions, since the effect was perpetually to reopen revolutionary questions, forcing the opposition into ideological self-consciousness and intransigence, while fragmenting, isolating, and diminishing the supporters of the new regime. The effects cut all the more deeply because as a conception of political life, the politics of exclusion now permeated all sectors of French public opinion; as a model of political behavior, it affected the opposition(s) as much as it did the men and groups in power. To understand its short- and long-term impact on French political development, we must return to a selective examination of events: the trial and execution of the king in the winter of 1792–1793, the near-civil war between the Jacobins and the Girondins in April–May 1793, and finally the elimination of the "Dantonists" in the spring of 1794. Each episode marked a high point of political competition *within* the revolutionary camp, and each provoked a bitter debate regarding the immediate shape of politics. In each case, the Jacobin view of interest and conflict prevailed; the view was internally consistent, but unlikely by itself to lead anywhere except to a political system based on a continuing process of exclusion and an eternally "provisional" legality. The revolutionary opposition, motivated by ambition, fear, and fatigue (none necessarily incompatible with the public interest), was composed of Girondins and former Jacobins.[33] As early adepts of the politics of exclusion, the Girondins

---

[30] Robespierre, *Le Défenseur de la Constitution*, no. 1 [May 17 or 18, 1792]; *Oeuvres*, vol. 4, p. 13.

[31] Ibid.

[32] Saint-Just, Convention, March 31, 1794; *Oeuvres complètes*, p. 772.

[33] Until the departure of the Feuillants in July 1791, the Jacobin Club was the common property of the revolutionary elites. After that date, its ideology became more

were no more capable now than previously of formulating a viable alternative to Jacobin rule. Instead, as would Desmoulins and Danton after them, they covered their persecutors with ridicule and appealed to the compassionate instincts of those who shared their fatigue. Their impressive base of political support in the Convention, and in the country at large, was weakened by the familiar problems of ideology and organization, and, until the summer of 1794, effectively overawed by the pressure generated by Paris radicals.

In the first days of September 1792, rioting Parisians broke into the city's houses of detention. Before order was restored, the intruders put to death a large number of both common criminals and political prisoners. The event sent shock waves through the ranks of the revolutionary elites. At its opening session on September 21, 1792, the Convention abolished the monarchy; four days later, on Danton's motion, the Republic was declared "one and indivisible."[34] During the next month and a half, while Louis remained incarcerated in the Temple, the rivalry in the Convention between the Girondins and the Jacobins became increasingly intense. The former group, alarmed by the September Massacres and by the uncontrolled turn events seemed to be taking, hoped to avoid bringing the king to trial. Sensing the vulnerability of the Girondin position, the Jacobins pushed their advantage by accusing their opponents of repudiating a political program legitimated (according to the claims of Girondins and Jacobins alike) by the insurrection of August 10. As Georges Lefebvre has written:

> To save the King, it was necessary that the question be avoided: such was the desire of the Gironde. But striving to proscribe the Montagnards, the Gironde could not prevent the Montagnards from breaking the silence: the head of the King became the stake of party struggle.[35]

Formal debate on the various questions raised by Louis's status began on November 7, when Jean-Baptiste Mailhe reported out the recommendations of the Convention's Committee on Legislation.[36] Debate ended on January 20, 1793, when the Convention voted down a proposed stay of sentence. Louis was guillotined the next day.

Whatever their own position, the men of the Convention repeatedly denied the contention that their body's proceedings against the king were in any way comparable to the actions of Cromwell's High

sharply defined along the lines analyzed in this chapter. The Club remained the breeding ground of revolutionary leaders, all of whom now shared its exclusionary ideology.

[34] For these developments, see Le Moniteur, vol. 14, p. 8 and pp. 41–44.

[35] Lefebvre, La Révolution française, p. 290.

[36] For the text of Mailhe's report, see Le Moniteur, vol. 14, pp. 414–20.

Court. The court that had tried Charles I, the *conventionnels* argued, did not represent the English people; it was simply the instrument of Cromwell's ambition, and Cromwell was as much a tyrant as the king whose head he demanded.[37] By contrast, in France, the king had been overthrown by a popular insurrection and would be tried by an elected assembly; his punishment would contribute to the foundation of a republic based on the sovereignty of the people and the authority of representative institutions.

The Convention's understandable interest in self-justification blinded its members to more subtle, and relevant, points of comparison. In England as in France, the disintegration (temporary in the English case) of moderate unity and leadership made possible the trial of a king, but the domestic political ramifications of the two trials were different. In England, where the king had actually called troops into battle, the prudent reluctance of either party to alienate in definitive fashion moderate sympathies prevented the formulation of radical arguments. In France, the trial (like the war) was staged in part to clarify revolutionary divisions and to test revolutionary credentials; the trial's role as an indicator of revolutionary ardor encouraged the polarization of expressed opinions. In England, the interesting debate was, as one would expect, between the High Court and its royal prisoner. In France, that debate was all but absent. To charge after charge, Louis replied, "I do not recall . . . ," "I know nothing about it . . . ," "this fact is not my concern."[38] Desèze, one of the king's counsels, did, in addition to refuting the charges and questioning the validity of the evidence presented, insist on the absence of any applicable law, but the essence of his plea was that the king, even if guilty, should simply be returned to private life; he expressly denied any intention of contesting the right of the sovereign nation to determine its own political constitution.[39] Furthermore, neither Louis nor his lawyers were present during the truly crucial debates. The interesting exchanges in the French proceedings are those that opposed revolutionary and revolutionary, not revolutionary and king. Louis's guilt was from the beginning a foregone conclusion, and was eventually

---

[37] Two moments privileged negative commentary on Cromwell: Lafayette's effort to influence the Legislative Assembly in the late spring of 1792 (Robespierre: "Eh! What more did Cromwell, whose name is execrated by posterity, do?" *Le Défenseur de la Constitution*, no. 7; *Oeuvres*, vol. 4, p. 199) and the trial of the King (Barère: "It is convenient for English rulers to blame us for an act of national justice, when their history is covered with the blood of Charles I, spilled by a faction for the benefit of an infamous usurper." Convention, January 4, 1793; *Le Moniteur*, vol. 15, p. 61).

[38] Louis XVI, Convention, December 1, 1792; *Le Moniteur*, vol. 14, pp. 720–24.

[39] Desèze, Convention, December 26, 1792; *Le Moniteur*, vol. 14, pp. 841–44.

affirmed by a vote of 693 to 26.[40] Debate focused instead on the Girondin proposal to subject the Convention's sentence to a popular
referendum, and on the type and timing of punishment appropriate
in the event of a guilty verdict.

The Jacobin argument was forcefully articulated by Saint-Just and
Robespierre during the debates of November and December. Both
men contended that Louis must die, that popular ratification of the
sentence was theoretically unnecessary and politically inadvisable,
and that the sooner the execution took place, the better for the Republic. The Revolution's legitimacy, they believed, was under challenge from two quarters: the overt royalists and the Girondins. Since
the Jacobins wished to uphold revolutionary legitimacy as they understood it, they sought to answer both challenges. Their position
rested on two arguments. The first was directed against the Old Regime, as symbolized by its last king: Louis was an enemy, not a citizen,
and therefore not entitled to the protection positive laws accorded to
members of the political community. The second argument was directed against the Girondins: To debate the king's fate was in effect,
as Robespierre put it, to "put the Revolution itself on trial"[41]—that is,
was itself treasonous. Both arguments were exercises in the politics
of exclusion; the second foreshadows later Jacobin purges of the revolutionary movement.

Louis, the Jacobins argued, was guilty as specifically charged: The
record of his acts since May 1789 demonstrated that he had deliberately, deceitfully, and almost successfully endeavored to subvert liberty. The Romans, Saint-Just noted, had brought a comparable performance to a close "with no other formality but twenty-three dagger
blows, with no other law than the liberty of Rome":

> And today, we respectfully conduct a trial for a man who was the assassin
> of a people, [a man] taken *in flagrante*, his hand soaked with blood, his
> hand plunged in crime![42]

The past deviousness of the king and his partisans itself argued for
a sentence of death and a rapid execution. As Saint-Just admitted
before the Convention, conspiracies are inherently hard to prove:
"[Y]ou cannot call him to account for his hidden maliciousness; he
will lose you in the vicious circle you yourselves will draw in order to

---

[40] ". . . 693 votes declared *Louis guilty of treason against the nation, and of attacks against
the general security of the State*; 26 members did not cast votes, or qualified their vote."
Account of proceedings in the Convention, January 14, 1793; *Le Moniteur*, vol. 15, p.
144.

[41] Robespierre, Convention, December 3, 1792; *Oeuvres*, vol. 9, p. 122.

[42] Saint-Just, Convention, November 13, 1792; *Oeuvres complètes*, p. 377.

accuse him."[43] More importantly, there was the danger that if given time, Louis would find a way once again to trick the people into submission.

> Who does not see that the same spirit that presided formerly over this simple and sinuous tyranny, presides still over its defense? Then, no one provoked the people, and no one provokes you now: oppression was wrought with modesty; self-defense in the same way. . . .[44]

Robespierre, arguing against submitting the sentence to the consideration of the primary assemblies, reiterated his cautious appraisal of the people's political perspicacity:

> I do not doubt . . . that the people desire it [the death of Louis XVI], if by the people you mean the majority of the nation, without excluding the most numerous, most unfortunate, and purest portion of society, that portion on which all the crimes of egoism and tyranny weigh most heavily. That majority expressed its wishes at the moment when it threw off the yoke of your former king; it began and it upheld the revolution. That majority has character; it has courage; but it has neither subtlety nor eloquence; it strikes down tyrants, but it is often the dupe of rogues.[45]

The king's chances would be enhanced, Robespierre warned his colleagues, by the fact that the more reliable elements of the Revolution's natural constituency would never appear in full force in the primary assemblies: The best young men were bearing arms for the Republic, while the disinterested "little man" could ill afford to take time out from his daily labors. Sincere citizens who did attend the meetings would fall easy prey to the "intriguers":

> You [the Girondins] assure me that these discussions will be perfectly peaceful and exempt from any dangerous influences. But assure me then that bad citizens, that moderates, that *feuillants*, that aristocrats will find no access; that no wily and long-winded lawyer will take men of good faith by surprise and create pity for the tyrant in the hearts of simple men who cannot see the political consequences of so fateful an indulgence or so unconsidered a decision. What! Would not the weakness of the Assembly itself, not to use a stronger expression, be the surest means of rallying all royalists, all enemies of liberty, of whatever persuasion . . . ? Why would they not come to the defense of their leader, since the law itself calls upon all citizens to discuss this great question freely and fully? And who is more eloquent, more adroit, more rich in resources than the intriguers, the *hon-*

---

[43] Ibid., p. 378.
[44] Saint-Just, Convention, December 26, 1792; *Oeuvres complètes*, p. 393.
[45] Robespierre, Convention, December 28, 1792; *Oeuvres*, vol. 9, p. 193.

nêtes gens, . . . the scoundrels of the old and even the new regime? With what art they will declaim at first against the king, only to conclude finally in his favor! With what eloquence they will proclaim the sovereignty of the people, the rights of humanity, only to bring back monarchy and aristocracy![46]

Risking the people's virtue in such an unnecessary manner would surely be an inauspicious way to found a republic, and the Jacobins frequently reminded their listeners that the foundation of the Republic was indeed their primary task. The consolidation of a new regime, they realized, demanded something more than a conviction of the king based on the evidence and justified by standard legal procedure; it demanded more even than "protecting" the people from the danger of corruption. In his first words to the Convention, Saint-Just made his position on the king's trial clear:

> I shall undertake, citizens, to prove that the king can be judged, that the opinion of Morisson which would respect inviolability and that of the committee which would have him judged as a citizen are equally false, and that the king ought to be judged according to principles foreign to both propositions.
>
> . . . I say that the king should be judged as an enemy; that we must not so much judge him as combat him; that as he had no part in the contract that united the French people, the forms of judicial procedure here are not to be sought in positive law, but in the law of nations.[47]

Saint-Just and Robespierre did argue that Louis's actual conduct had been criminal, but at the heart of their argument lay a far more radical contention, one never articulated in the court that had tried Charles I. Between a king and a people, the Jacobins insisted, there could be no legitimate contract.

> A king should be held to account, not for the crimes of his administration, but for the crime of having been king, as that is a usurpation which nothing on earth can justify. With whatever illusions, whatever conventions, monarchy cloaks itself, it remains an eternal crime against which every man has the right to rise and to arm himself. Monarchy is an outrage which even the blindness of an entire people cannot justify. . . .
>
> No man can reign innocently. . . . Every king is a rebel and a usurper.[48]

Irrespective of his acts, Louis had been a tyrant simply through the pretensions of his office. On August 10, the people had responded to

[46] Ibid., p. 189.
[47] Saint-Just, Convention, November 13, 1792; *Oeuvres complètes,* p. 376.
[48] Ibid., p. 379.

tyranny with an "appeal to heaven," and force had decided the issue. As Robespierre put it:

> Louis was king, and the Republic is founded. The great question that concerns you is settled by this argument: Louis has been deposed by his crimes. Louis denounced the French people as rebels; to punish them he called upon the arms of his fellow tyrants. Victory and the people have decided that he alone was a rebel. Therefore, Louis cannot be judged; he has already been condemned. . . .
>
> When a nation has been forced to resort to its right of insurrection, it returns to the state of nature insofar as the tyrant is concerned. How could the tyrant invoke the social contract, when he abolished it? The nation, if it deems proper, may preserve the contract still, as it concerns the relations between citizens; but the effect of tyranny and of insurrection is to break completely all bonds with the tyrant and to reestablish the state of war between tyrant and people. Tribunals and legal procedures are meant only for the members of the polity. It is too great a contradiction to suppose that the Constitution might preside over this new order of things. That would be to suppose that it could outlive itself. What laws replace it? Those of nature, the one that is the basis of society itself: the salvation of the people. The right to punish the tyrant and the right to depose him are the same thing. Their forms are the same. For a tyrant, an insurrection is his trial; the end of his power is the verdict; his punishment is whatever the liberty of the people demands.[49]

Given Louis's political position, Saint-Just affirmed, the only appropriate way to treat him was "like a foreign enemy."[50] Both Robespierre and Saint-Just advocated the speedy execution of the king as a symbolic act of universal significance. It would teach the people to hold tyranny in contempt; it would set an example for other nations still ruled by kings; and it would serve as a gauge of the French people's determination to be free. Both men further maintained that Louis's death was necessary because the Revolution, a year and a half after Duport's speech, was still not finished. With Louis dead, Robespierre speculated, perhaps the Revolution could at last be brought to an end:

> It is time to leap over the fatal obstacle which has for so long barred our course. Then doubtless we will march together toward our common aim of public felicity; then the hateful passions which mutter too often in this

---

[49] Robespierre, Convention, December 3, 1792; *Oeuvres*, vol. 9, pp. 121f.
[50] Saint-Just, Convention, November 13, 1792; *Oeuvres complètes*, p. 381.

sanctuary of liberty will yield to love of the public good . . . ; and all the plots of enemies of public order will be confounded.[51]

Having (at least to their own satisfaction) cut the ground out from under any possible defense of the king, the Jacobins condemned all attempts to prolong the debates as counterrevolutionary in implication and effect, and probably in intention. "The constitution forbade all that you have done," Robespierre reminded his colleagues;[52] "[Louis] has already been condemned, otherwise the Republic is not cleared of guilt."[53] Either revolutionary government, and therefore the trial and punishment of the king, were legitimate, or else all that had transpired since August 10, including the convocation of the Convention, was illegitimate: "[T]he Constitution condemns you; go throw yourselves upon Louis' mercy."[54]

To its proponents, the Jacobin argument seemed watertight; since it was nonetheless contested, Robespierre concluded, as usual, that the opposition could be animated only by hidden and sinister motives:

> I saw all my fears and suspicions confirmed. At first we seemed troubled by the consequences that delays in the progress of this affair might bring. Now we risk rendering it interminable. We feared the unrest that each moment of delay might bring, and here we are guaranteed the overthrow of the Republic. Why, of what matter is it that a fatal plot be hidden beneath a veil of prudence or even beneath the pretext of respect for the sovereignty of the people? Such was the art of all tyrants who, from behind the mask of patriotism, have until now assassinated liberty and been the cause of all our ills.[55]

The Girondin reply made up in passion what it lacked in rigor. Forced to give battle on terrain they had wished to avoid, the Girondins temporized; threatened by the same politics of exclusion they had previously practiced, they could do little more than ridicule its present application. The Jacobins had sensed a political opportunity in the Girondins' efforts to circumvent the trial of an unpopular monarch; the Girondins detected a similar opportunity in the Jacobins' seeming distrust of the sovereign people. The Girondins could not, however, suddenly come up with the defense of a procedural conception of majority rule their situation now required. Their guarded

---

[51] Robespierre, Convention, December 28, 1792; *Oeuvres*, vol. 9, p. 187.
[52] Robespierre, Convention, December 3, 1792; *Oeuvres*, vol. 9, p. 126.
[53] Ibid., p. 121.
[54] Ibid., p. 126.
[55] Robespierre, Convention, December 28, 1792; *Oeuvres*, vol. 9, p. 188.

pleas for caution as concerned the king and the case they made for summoning the primary assemblies to deliberate on the death sentence were politically and theoretically weak, but the withering sarcasm to which they subjected the Jacobins, while in the end equally ineffective, at least makes for refreshing reading.

> But intrigue! Intrigue will save the king. You would be made to believe that the majority of the nation is composed of intriguers, aristocrats, *feuillants*, moderates, in short, of those counter-revolutionary *honnêtes gens* of whom Lafayette spoke at this bar. And to give credence to such a black slander against the majority of the people, who in other circumstances are so basely flattered, mankind has been impudently defamed. The cry goes up: "Virtue has always been in the minority on this earth [the reference is to a statement made by Robespierre in his speech of December 28[56]]." Citizens, Catiline was a minority in the Roman Senate, and if that conspiring minority had prevailed, it would have meant the end of Rome, of the Senate, of liberty. Citizens! In the Constituent Assembly, at least until the revision, Cazalès and Maury were also a minority, and if that minority, half from the nobility, half from the priesthood, had succeeded by its holy and noble insurrections in stifling the zeal of the majority, that would have been the end of the Revolution, and you would still today grovel at the feet of Louis, who retains of his former grandeur only the remorse of having abused it. Citizens! Kings are in the minority on earth, and to enslave nations, they too say that virtue is in the minority. They say as well that the majority of the people is composed of intriguers upon whom silence must be imposed by terror, if the empires of the world are to be preserved from a general upheaval.
>
> The majority of the nation, composed of intriguers, aristocrats, *feuillants*, and so forth! Thus, according to those who voice an opinion that reflects so honorably on their country, I see that there is no one in the entire land who is truly pure, truly virtuous, truly devoted to the people and to liberty, but themselves and perhaps a hundred of their friends whom they will have the generosity to associate with their glory. Thus, so that they might found a government worthy of the principles they profess, I think it will be quite fitting to banish from French soil all those families whose *feuillantisme* is so perfidious, whose corruption so deep; to change France into a vast desert and, for its more rapid regeneration and greater glory, to abandon it to their sublime conceptions.[57]

Rather late and still without proposing an alternative model of political interaction, the Girondins realized that the politics of exclusion

[56] See *Le Moniteur*, vol. 14, p. 880.
[57] Vergniaud, Convention, December 31, 1792; *Le Moniteur*, vol. 15, pp. 12f.

is attractive only if force and/or visible public opinion happen to coincide with one's own position. With their backs to the wall, the Girondins understood, as they had been unable to understand when
they themselves had attacked the Feuillants and the record of the
Constituent Assembly, the risks of indulging in Jacobin discourse
during dangerous times:

> Have you not heard, within these walls and elsewhere, men cry out furi-
> ously: "If bread is dear, the cause is to be found in the Temple; if coin is
> rare, if the army is ill-provisioned, the cause is in the Temple; if we have
> daily to suffer the spectacle of indigence, the cause is in the Temple?"
>   Those who speak this way are aware that the price of bread, the lack of
> money in circulation, the poor administration of the army, indigence . . . ,
> all have causes other than those of the Temple. What then are their plans?
> Who will guarantee that these same men, who continuously exert them-
> selves to vilify the Convention, . . . who proclaim everywhere that a new
> revolution is needed; . . . who say to the commune, that when the Conven-
> tion succeeded Louis, it was but an exchange of tyrants; . . . who declare in
> their sectional assemblies and in their writings that a *defender* of the Repub-
> lic must be named, that there is only one *leader* who can save it—who, I ask,
> will guarantee that these same men will not cry out with the greatest
> violence after the death of Louis . . . : "if bread is dear, the cause is
> to be found in the Convention; if coin is rare, if our armies are poorly
> supplied, the cause is in the Convention; if the wheels of government move
> hardly at all, the cause is in the Convention whose responsibility it is to
> lead . . . ?"[58]

For the Girondins, the king's trial and execution marked the beginning of the end. Since the Girondins, unlike the Feuillants, never appreciated the necessity, let alone the desirability, of political accommodation, their disappearance would not in itself appear causally
significant. The moderates of 1789–1791 had lost because Jacobin
ideology provided a more adequate account of the revolutionary situation, and the politics of exclusion it justified a more powerful political instrument, than did the ad hoc ideology and praxis the moderates offered. The Girondins lost because they played Jacobin
politics less effectively than did the Jacobins: They did not defend an
alternative form of politics. Their very inability to understand that
they were being hoisted on their own petard as they lost the desper-

---

[58] Ibid., pp. 14f. Cf. later Girondin efforts to distinguish between "good" insurrections and "bad" ones; e.g., Vergniaud, Convention, April 10, 1793, and Pétion, Convention, April 12, 1793; *Le Moniteur*, vol. 16, pp. 117, 126.

ate struggle for power during the spring of 1793[59] is important to our analysis, for it shows what the later trials of the Terror (seen here through the fate of the Dantonists) would repeatedly illustrate: the domestic dynamic set in place by the politics of exclusion. It was a dynamic that made coalition building virtually impossible; indeed, coalition building, which had been central to revolutionary politics in England and America, was not a major Jacobin concern.

Following their psychologically crucial victory at Valmy on September 20, 1792, republican armies had recovered the ground lost in the early days of the war. Taking the offensive, they had occupied Belgium. In Paris, no one dared make the case for peace, for to advocate accommodation with the European powers now would be to attract Jacobin suspicions. Instead, the Convention made the war a matter of revolutionary pride, wedding the ideological ambitions of the Revolution to the long-standing territorial and political aspirations of traditional French foreign policy.[60] On February 1, 1793 (a week and a half after the execution of the king), France declared war on England and Holland; on March 7, Spain was added to the list. Neither the government nor the economy was strong enough to sustain the military effort required, and the spring again saw the reversal of French fortunes in the field. On April 5, the republican general Dumouriez went over to the Austrians. The beginning of organized civil war in the Vendée (March 10) and rising prices in Paris amplified the political repercussions of military setbacks on the country's borders; all contributed to the continued political mobilization of Parisian radicals, to whom the Commune had imparted a taste for independent political authority. While Robespierre declaimed tirelessly against conspirators and conspiracies, substantive debate in the Convention crystallized around two issues. The first concerned the need to ensure governmental effectiveness; it led to the creation of the Committee of Public Safety on April 6, and is important for what it tells us about

[59] Like the Jacobins, the Girondins most often blamed counterrevolutionary conspirators for the bad turn the Revolution had taken. Very occasionally, they indicted fate: "I was hoping that Dumouriez' treason would provoke a fortunate crisis in that it would rally us all in the face of a common danger. I thought that instead of trying to condemn each other, we would apply ourselves to saving the country. By what fatality do petitions get written outside our walls which then come within to foment hate and division? By what fatality do the representatives of the people unceasingly turn this place into a forum for their calumnies and passions?" Vergniaud, Convention, April 10, 1793; *Le Moniteur*, vol. 16, p. 119.

[60] The classic work on this subject remains Albert Sorel's *L'Europe et la Révolution française* (Paris: Plon, 1885–1904, 8 vols.). See also Kyung-Won Kim, *Revolution and the International System: A Study in the Breakdown of International Stability* (New York: New York University Press, 1970).

dominant views of power and interest. The second focused attention on the relationship between representative politics and revolutionary legitimacy, for a militant extraparliamentary minority now forcefully laid claim to the latter. In part because of the prevailing view of power, this second issue could not be resolved by debate. It culminated in the insurrectionary *journées* of May 31–June 2 and the proscription of the Girondins, as the Jacobins lined up with the extraparliamentary radicals in an uneasy and unstable alliance motivated on both sides by a mix of conviction and perceived political necessity. The heightened sense of emergency helped tip the scales against the Girondins, who even in their last stand failed to maintain a united front.

Deepening divisions within the Convention precluded the election of an executive committee that would be both representative of parliamentary opinion and capable of action; governmental paralysis and the recriminations it engendered in turn aggravated parliamentary antagonisms. Thus, while the Convention dreaded the advent of a dictator, its fragmentation and polarization invited dictatorial intervention. The body that would become the Committee of Public Safety was proposed by Isnard, speaking for the Committee on General Defense, on April 3.[61] After a brief discussion, the proposal was sent back to committee, whence Isnard rescued it on April 5, asserting that the Committee was incapable of any action on any matter;[62] as Vergniaud would later explain, the Committee had been deliberately composed of representatives from opposing factions, on the incorrect hypothesis that the imperatives of republican defense would bring them together. Instead, the result had been boycotts (by Robespierre and his allies), leaks, and paralysis.[63] Barère came to the defense of the proposed Committee. The conventionnels could not, Barère argued, continue to conduct themselves as had the Athenians when threatened by Phillip's armies, unless they wished France to share Athens's fate:

> This committee, as it is presently composed, was the result of a sort of transaction between the most clearly delineated parties: you created a congress of passions, when we needed a congress of enlightenment [lumières].[64]

Governmental ineffectiveness had paved the way for the dictatorship Barère saw taking shape around him: that of slander and de-

[61] *Le Moniteur*, vol. 16, p. 57.
[62] Ibid., p. 70.
[63] Vergniaud, Convention, April 10, 1793; *Le Moniteur*, vol. 16, p. 116.
[64] Barère, Convention, April 5, 1793; *Le Moniteur*, vol. 16, p. 71.

nunciation, easily exploitable by specific individuals. Compared to the threat posed by potential dictators like Marat and Robespierre,[65] the proposed Committee would be innocuous. It would be, Barère said, a

> committee without authority over matters of civil liberty, deliberating behind closed doors, without the power of the purse, without any power independent of the national assembly, simply performing an oversight function, deliberating in emergencies on matters of public safety and reporting on them to the Convention, facilitating the work of the executive council, denouncing to the assembly suspected or unfaithful public agents, and provisionally suspending the orders of the executive council, when those orders seem contrary to the public good, with the obligation to report the reasons the same day to the Convention.[66]

In vain, Buzot (like Isnard, a "Girondin"), argued against the proposed measure. The Romans, he admitted, had resorted to dictatorship,

> but in Rome, a dictator was a virtuous man. Would you compare yourselves to a people who, in five hundred years of revolution [sic] never shed a drop of blood until Tiberius?[67]

When Marat lent his (probably unwelcome) support to the measure by arguing that "the time [had] come to organize the despotism of liberty to crush the despotism of kings," Birotteau (another Girondin) protested the notion "that it is by violence that liberty must be established" and added: "If, behind the curtain, there is an ambitious man, what will he not do once he has the revolutionary committee at his command . . . ?"[68]

The Convention could not square the circle: Since the politics of exclusion precluded bargaining and compromise as legitimate means of arriving at the common good, executive effectiveness presupposed either unanimity or the ability to govern without regard for opposing opinions. Despite the warnings of men like Buzot and Birotteau, Isnard's measure passed; its partisans had little difficulty persuading a majority that the country's survival was at risk and that an effective executive was indispensable to its salvation. The dangers of military defeat and domestic insurrection were real; dictatorship was still a hypothetical.

Almost immediately, the Convention turned to a question that

---

[65] During the debates of April–May 1793, both men were frequently accused, though not by Barère, of harboring such ambitions.

[66] Barère, Convention, April 5, 1793; *Le Moniteur*, vol. 16, p. 71.

[67] Ibid.

[68] Ibid., p. 76.

would help determine the shape of the dictatorship to come. On April 10, Pétion rose to read and denounce a lengthy petition written and circulated by the Halle-au-Blé section.[69] The petitioners announced that they spoke for the whole nation. This claim made, the petitioners held the Convention responsible for the dire straits into which the country had lately fallen, demanded the impeachment of Roland, and informed the Mountain that if it could not save the country, the petitioners would. Pétion denounced the manipulation and intimidation of the sections by a militant minority, and reacted with outrage to the applause with which some of his colleagues had greeted what he perceived as a treasonous petition. By what right could a handful of radicals claim to speak for the people? By what aberration, Pétion demanded, could the Convention congratulate those who sought its dissolution (a crime theoretically punishable by death)?

> I cannot understand how anyone can have the audacity to applaud his own dishonor. What will people say in the *départements*? What? the assembly did not rise up as one man when it was said that its majority was corrupt, when men pushed delirium and insolence to the point of telling you that they alone will save the country![70]

As the debate continued and became increasingly heated, Boyer-Fonfrède and Guadet both spoke in support of Pétion's position. Boyer-Fonfrède said he too would accuse the Convention's majority, "but of weakness" in the face of extraparliamentary subversion; he then accused the petitioners of lending objective support to Dumouriez, Orléans (still), foreign kings, and royalists of all descriptions.[71] Guadet argued against confusing public opinion with "the croaking of a few toads." Articulating a position that the Girondins would develop and to which they would cling desperately during the coming weeks, Guadet distinguished between the whole people, correctly revered as sovereign, and minorities, who could not legitimately claim to speak in the people's name.[72]

The Girondins now sought to elaborate, as they had not during the debates on the fate of the king, a theory of representation. They would argue that "the will of the people can only be expressed by the people's representatives [as a group] or by the whole people,"[73] and that once elected, a representative belonged to the republic one and

[69] Text of the petition in *Le Moniteur*, vol. 16, p. 100.
[70] Ibid., p. 102.
[71] Ibid., p. 103.
[72] Ibid., p. 104.
[73] Boyer-Fonfrède, Convention, April 15, 1793; *Le Moniteur*, vol. 16, p. 157.

indivisible and could not be recalled by his own district.[74] If irrecon-
cilable political differences arose within the Assembly, or if its effectiveness became irreparably compromised by repeated attacks on its
legitimacy, only what we would call a general election could provide
a legitimate solution. But in the combined context of the politics of
exclusion and a (causally connected) national emergency, a general
election meant civil war.

Guadet's speech of April 10 elicited a reply by Robespierre, in
which the latter, without going so far as to call part of the Convention
corrupt, predictably sought to explain events in terms of constant but
hidden motives.[75] Danton later got to the essence of Robespierre's
logic when he said, "I myself would not have made a denunciation
based only on political proofs."[76] In lengthy and impassioned
speeches, first Vergniaud and then Guadet attempted both to refute
Robespierre's "ridiculous accusations"[77] with a defense of the Girondin record and to condemn the Halle-au-Blé petition. When the
Jacobin Club in Paris circulated an address bearing Marat's signature
to its provincial affiliates, the Convention moved to impeach Marat,
for the views expressed in the Jacobin address were substantially similar to those of the Halle-au-Blé section.[78] By mid-April, all sides were
speaking explicitly in terms of civil war. It was in this context that the
Girondin theory of representation emerged. Thus the Girondin appeal to the provinces was not, even in the eyes of its advocates, a defense of political decentralization or routine representative politics. It
was a Lockeian appeal to heaven:

> In the state of division and hate into which we have been thrown, we can
> have no other judge than the people; it is the people's judgment I demand.
> . . . In the unfortunate circumstances in which we find ourselves, in keep-
> ing with the very principles of the Jacobin address, it is impossible to elude
> my proposal. The address contains a veritable appeal to the people against
> the people's representatives. It is signed by a part of the assembly, and
> therefore the dignity of the Convention, its respect for the sovereignty of
> the people, require that this appeal be made. . . . It is all too clear that the
> republic is divided. I do not know that it is possible to change this state of

[74] See Gensonné, Convention, April 20, 1793; *Le Moniteur*, vol. 16, pp. 190f.
[75] Robespierre, Convention, April 10, 1793; *Le Moniteur*, vol. 16, esp. pp. 105f.
[76] Danton, Convention, April 12, 1793; *Le Moniteur*, vol. 16, p. 136.
[77] Guadet, Convention, April 10, 1793; *Le Moniteur*, vol. 16, p. 113.
[78] The Jacobin letter called its readers to arms and asserted that "the counter-revolution is in the government, in the national Convention." See text (read aloud by
Guadet) in *Le Moniteur*, vol. 16, p. 136. For a summary of Marat's views, see text of
letter he addressed to the Convention while in hiding; in *Le Moniteur*, vol. 16, pp. 143f.

affairs except by the expression of the nation's wishes [*l'expression du voeu national*].[79]

The Girondins denounced the Jacobins' recourse to unsigned, unsubstantiated accusations and their constant readiness to assert guilt by association; they professed to see in the Convention "the center around which all citizens should rally."[80] Vergniaud's words offer a strange echo of Duport's earlier appeal, but Vergniaud fiercely denied the Jacobin charge that the Girondins were "moderates, Feuillants."[81] His argument did not persuade the Jacobins, but it does demonstrate the difficulties the Girondins experienced as they finally tried, for seemingly prudential reasons, to break out of the political framework imposed by the Jacobins. To the Jacobins who accused them of conspiring against the republic, the Girondins could do no better than to return the charge;[82] thus they claimed that the destabilizing tactics of the Jacobins and their extraparliamentary allies worked objectively in favor of the Duke d'Orléans's ambitions. The political menu the Girondins consulted featured only three entrées: The immediate choice lay between revolutionary unity (the proper response to the danger in which the Revolution found itself) and civil war (the only political answer the Girondins saw to the Jacobin challenge). And if unity were beyond reach? Faced with this possibility, Vergniaud came down *against* an appeal to the primary assemblies. Self-immolation—the third option—seemed to him preferable to an act that would demonstrate the final disintegration of revolutionary solidarity.

> Citizens, the convocation of the primary assemblies is a disastrous measure. It could ruin the Convention, the republic, and freedom. If we must either order this convocation or deliver ourselves up to the vengeance of our enemies—if you are reduced to this set of choices, citizens, do not hesitate between the lives of a few men and the public good. Throw us into the abyss, and save the fatherland! (Applause.)[83]

If the Revolution was going to find middle ground on which to stand, someone other than the Girondins would have to identify and

[79] Gensonné, Convention, April 13, 1793; *Le Moniteur*, vol. 16, p. 149.

[80] Vergniaud, Convention, April 10, 1793; *Le Moniteur*, vol. 16, p. 118.

[81] Ibid., p. 117.

[82] Pétion is a partial exception to this rule; see, for example, his speech of April 12, 1793; *Le Moniteur*, vol. 16, p. 126.

[83] Vergniaud, Convention, April 20, 1793; *Le Moniteur*, vol. 16, p. 198. It is hard to read this without being reminded of the identity problems Arthur Koestler assigns to Rubashov, the protagonist of his novel *Darkness at Noon*, trans. Daphne Hardy (New York: Macmillan, 1941).

propose a model of politics adequate to maintaining the Revolution on that ground. Neither the Jacobins—or the Montagnards, as their parliamentary partisans were called—nor the Girondins commanded a majority in the Convention. Barère, who would survive to write his memoirs, spoke for the ultimately pivotal "center" (known as the Plain, or, less generously, as the Swamp) in denouncing the divisions within the Convention and in reproaching the extremists for their intransigence:

> When all of you are attacked in the person of one of your colleagues [Lé-onard Bourdon had been attacked in Orléans on the previous day], I see passions, hideous passions, arising still in your midst; while you should be concerned with nothing except the means of avoiding the common danger. . . .
>   Part of the Assembly believes itself—with reason—to be in the midst of a revolution; the other part sees things differently. These two very disparate dispositions have produced internal divisions. . . . In a revolution, each has its place; the revolution cannot be the same for all. All minds are not the same, all souls do not act in the same way, all men do not envisage in identical manner the dangers which menace them. In light of these remarks, consider your present situation; the counter-revolution has begun, conspiracies are surfacing everywhere, troubles are spreading, and you deliberate only after events which it is your duty to foresee and prevent. Your situation is such that, if the Convention does not itself take hold of the revolutionary movement, liberty will regress; the Convention must no longer deliberate, it must act, it must fight. What would you think of an army, if you saw it quarrel in front of the enemy, if you heard some soldiers say to others: You are fanatical patriots, too prompt to fight; while the others reproached the lethargy of their comrades. Such an army would certainly be beaten by a more united foe. So! Let us go forward together, and things will not be so difficult.[84]

Barère was a political weathervane; Danton was a formidable leader. Like Barère, however, Danton believed, in the early spring of 1793, that the Revolution could already count enough enemies without needlessly creating more from within its own ranks. Like Barère, he condemned the "miserable passions"[85] that were paralyzing the Convention:

> Too long . . . a shared love of vengeance, inspired by distrust, has delayed the work of the Convention and, by the divisions it causes, diminished the Convention's energy. A strong argument is repulsed by one quarter or an-

[84] Barère, Convention, March 17, 1793; *Le Moniteur*, vol. 15, p. 739.
[85] Danton, Convention, March 27, 1793; *Discours*, p. 301.

other, simply because it was articulated by a rival. At long last then, may
danger unite you![86]

Danton did not yet seek to distance himself from the politics of
exclusion, any more than did Barère; he simply hoped that a sense
of shared danger might substitute for tolerance. Briefly, and before
the rivalry between the Jacobins and the Girondins reached its cli-
max, Danton's great political ambition was to rally the Convention's
two contending parties to a common position. The Jacobins, however,
had already classified the Girondins as enemies, and the sentiments
of the Parisian activists whose support the Jacobins had enlisted
would have made retreat difficult in the unlikely event that the Montagnard leaders should have deemed it advisable. In late March, the
Girondins aggravated their own isolation by imprudently accusing
Danton of improperly using public funds while on mission in Belgium and by questioning his relationship with Dumouriez. On April
1, Danton turned toward the Montagnard deputies and declared,
"you understood better than I."[87] In a speech punctuated by interruptions, he renounced his preferred role as revolutionary go-be-
tween. Abandoning those by whom he had been attacked, he fell back
on the politics of exclusion: "[T]here can no longer be a truce between the Mountain, between the patriots who demanded the death
of the tyrant and the cowards who, in trying to save him, slandered
us all across France."[88]

In England, Pride's Purge had entailed no loss of life, and middle
group strength in the provinces, instead of provoking civil war, had
served to moderate the moves of more radically inclined elements in
London. In the fall of 1791, when the moderate leadership was
eclipsed, political defeat did not yet carry with it the formal charge of
treason and a sentence of death. With the journées of May 31–June
2, 1793, the French Revolution began, in Vergniaud's words, to eat
its own children. The insurrection forced the expulsion and eventually the proscription of the Girondin deputies. Those who were
caught were executed in October 1793. The fierce partisanship of the
political players in the Convention, the increased influence of extra-

---

[86] Danton, Convention, March 30, 1793; *Discours*, p. 321. These sentiments would be
repeatedly echoed, after Danton had abandoned them, by less prominent members of
the Convention. Thus as Vergniaud sought to reply to the "perfidious fiction [*roman
perfide*]" (*Le Moniteur*, vol. 16, p. 113) woven by Robespierre, Joseph Lakanal exclaimed,
"[T]hese denunciations are killing the Republic," and Laurent Lecointre rejoined,
"The enemy takes our cities, and we denounce each other!" (*Le Moniteur*, vol. 16, p.
105).

[87] Danton, Convention; *Le Moniteur*, vol. 16, p. 25.

[88] Ibid., p. 27.

parliamentary activists, and the pressure of military and economic developments interacted and combined in the spring of 1793 to make the guillotine, rather than vehement speeches or parliamentary turnover, the accepted agent of political exclusion.

We have seen that as recriminations in the Convention grew more violent, the prospect of civil war became more real. On May 6, Vergniaud complained that "respect for the Convention [had] become a crime of *lèse-municipalité*,"[89] and on May 25, Isnard rashly rejoined by threatening the city with destruction:

> France made Paris the depository of the nation's representatives; Paris must respect them. . . . If ever the Convention were abased, if ever, through one of those insurrections which since March 10 have so frequently recurred, and of which the magistrates have never warned the Convention. . . . [Interruptions] I declare to you in the name of all of France . . . [Interruptions]: soon one would search on the banks of the Seine to see if Paris had ever existed.[90]

Both the Girondins and the Jacobins were now in a sense held hostage by the Parisian alliances they had been all but forced to contract. The strategy followed by the Girondins inadvertently strengthened the Jacobin case against them, and not just because it promoted civil war: Their rhetoric rallied the provincial and Parisian right, which previous revolutionary intransigence had rendered counterrevolutionary. And unlike the Jacobins, the Girondins had never developed the ability to break allies they could no longer use. The Jacobins, meanwhile, struggled both to eliminate the Girondins and to preserve for the Convention a semblance of institutional independence; in the process, they felt compelled to anticipate popular demands for repression: "Let us be terrible so that the people need not be so," declared Danton on March 10,[91] warning that only the creation of a special revolutionary tribunal could ensure against a repetition of the September Massacres; two weeks later, he advocated arming all citizens with a pike.[92] Beginning with the creation of the Revolutionary Tribunal on March 10, the Convention had, for reasons we have already examined, adopted measures that in effect institutionalized revolutionary government: On March 21, Surveillance Committees were set up; on April 6, the Committee of Public Safety was created. The Jacobins now stepped into the executive roles the Convention had set up.

---

89 Vergniaud, Convention; *Le Moniteur*, vol. 16, p. 322.
90 Isnard, Convention; *Le Moniteur*, vol. 16, pp. 479f.
91 Danton, Convention; *Discours*, p. 291.
92 See speech of March 27, 1793; *Discours*, p. 303.

Jacobin rule lasted for one year, from the summer of 1793 to the summer of 1794: Robespierre became a member of the Committee of Public Safety on July 27, 1793, and was overthrown on 9 Thermidor (also July 27) Year II. In the next section of this chapter, we will consider certain aspects of government under the Committee of Public Safety. For the moment, we must continue our analysis of domestic political competition as shaped by the politics of exclusion, and turn to the fate of Danton and his friends.

In September 1793, Danton had declined reelection to the Committee on Public Safety and had absented himself from Paris from mid-October until late November. Back in Paris during the winter of 1793–1794, Danton came in his turn to the conclusion that it was time to end the Revolution. Tired of Jacobin austerity and ill suited by temperament to an atmosphere of universal suspicion, Danton was ready, in R. R. Palmer's words, to accept a "relaxed and morally equivocal Republic."[93] To Danton, that early and vociferous advocate of the politics of exclusion, it now seemed that exclusion had fulfilled its proper function.

> Now that he had the Republic he wished to enjoy it. He saw no more need for wholesale guillotinings when Republican armies were victorious at home and on the frontiers. He considered that the war had come to a draw, and that peace might be made, especially if France took on a less fiercely revolutionary appearance. It is arguable that his judgment was correct: that the Terror was no longer needed for national defense, in the sense of protecting the country from the inroads of foreign powers. The great difficulty was the failure of the Mountaineers to agree. Danton would solve it by creating a vague and broad Republic, in which men of all kinds, good and bad, sound and tainted, might, after disposing of irreconcilable extremists, join together by not arguing over principles.[94]

The failure of Danton's project prefigures that of the Thermidorian Republic, and it should no longer seem surprising. From the opening moments of the Revolution, the structure of opportunity imposed by the Old Regime told against the emergence of a stable liberal polity based on the politics of transaction. The Old Regime had prevented the development of organized and independent groups within society, and the Revolution did not remedy that critical gap. The politics of exclusion, unchallenged from 1792 to 1794, promoted a tutelary view of the people, demeaned parliamentary institutions,

[93] R. R. Palmer, *Twelve Who Ruled* (1941; reprint, New York: Atheneum, 1965), p. 278.
[94] Ibid., p. 257.

pushed conservative opinion toward extremism, decimated the political elite, and constantly kept revolutionary dissenters off balance: On all counts, it favored ideological fragmentation and institutional fragility, when the politics of transaction would have required the opposite. Danton, whatever sympathies his protests against the continuation of the Terror may have aroused amongst the general population, never had a chance. His death, and the deaths of many others, were by-products of the complex political struggles of late 1793 and early 1794.

Unlike most of the other prominent figures of the revolutionary era, Danton tended to speak without a text and did not publish his speeches as pamphlets. The trial transcript tells us little of Danton's final positions, for the court all but gagged the defense. For a statement of the indulgents' case, we must therefore turn to Camille Desmoulins's journal *Le Vieux Cordelier*, which appeared regularly throughout December 1793 and into the first days of 1794. The case, it might be added, was not very complicated.

Condemning the left without condoning the right, Desmoulins argued against the more violent manifestations of revolutionary government; they were, he maintained, both morally offensive and politically counterproductive. The Revolution had not been undertaken, he reminded his readers, so that people might be guillotined with impunity, but rather so that all might enjoy liberty, equality, happiness, and peace. Cloaking his account of the current situation in citations from Tacitus and others, Desmoulins denounced a political world in which any action could be misconstrued and any individual treated as a suspect. Revolutionary justice had outlasted its utility; it had become a political liability as well as a moral disgrace:

> You want to exterminate all your enemies with the guillotine! But has there ever been a greater folly? Can you make a single one perish on the scaffold, without making ten enemies among his family or his friends? Do you think that it is these women, these old men, these sicklings, these egotists, these laggards of the revolution whom you are imprisoning, who are dangerous? Of your enemies, only the cowards and the sickly remain. The brave and the strong have emigrated. They have perished at Lyon or in the Vendée; as for all the others, they are unworthy of your anger.[95]

Desmoulins advocated the creation of a "clemency committee" to oversee the orderly release of the Revolution's political prisoners: "It

[95] Desmoulins, *Le Vieux Cordelier*, no. 4 [December 24, 1793]; Camille Desmoulins, *Le Vieux Cordelier*, ed. Albert Mathiez and Henri Calvet (Paris: Armand Colin, 1936), p. 116.

is this committee which will end the revolution; for clemency too is a revolutionary measure, and the most efficacious of all, when it is distributed with wisdom."[96]

The Dantonists were tried during the first week of April 1794, ten days after the trial and execution of the Hebertists. As if in direct response to Desmoulins, Saint-Just acknowledged that "courage is needed to speak to you [the Convention] once more of severity, after so much severity."[97] In such courage, however, Saint-Just seemed adequately endowed. For the purposes of condemnation and through what was by now a well-established form of argument, Hebertists and Dantonists were charged with conniving together to undo the Revolution:

> What was the first phase of this conspiracy? The very beginning of the Revolution. Who were its prime movers? All the royal courts leagued against us. The goal? The ruin of France. The victims? The people and you. The means? All manner of crimes.[98]

The arguments were, for the most part, the familiar ones Jacobins were by now accustomed to using against their opponents. Robespierre denounced the two groups, one (the Dantonists) guilty of "*modérantisme*," the other (the Hebertists) of "patriotically counter-revolutionary excesses,"[99] as

> factions opposed in appearance, but united . . . by a tacit pact . . . ; factions which, by their combined crimes, provided each other with excuses and support, and which, by opposite routes, tended toward the same goal: the destruction of the Republic and the ruin of liberty.[100]

Saint-Just in particular insisted on the self-interested motives of the accused: Danton, in addition to being a "run-of-the-mill conciliator,"[101] had sold himself to the likes of Mirabeau, Orléans, and Dumouriez, and had betrayed his true colors through his "cowardly and constant desertion of the public cause in the midst of crises."[102]

The Jacobin style of accusation had developed before the Jacobins gained power. The Jacobins, however, were no longer in opposition, and so to the old arguments, a new twist was now added. The politics

[96] Ibid., p. 119.
[97] Saint-Just, Convention, March 31, 1794; *Oeuvres complètes*, p. 761.
[98] Robespierre, undelivered speech, around March 20, 1794; *Oeuvres*, vol. 10, p. 398.
[99] Robespierre, undelivered speech, around January 15, 1794; *Oeuvres*, vol. 10, p. 326.
[100] Ibid., p. 334.
[101] Saint-Just, Convention, March 31, 1794; *Oeuvres complètes*, p. 770.
[102] Ibid., p. 768.

of exclusion had begun as a means of revolutionary self-definition and self-defense; it soon came to dominate intraparty relations; it now became an instrument of government.

> The triumph of one or the other party would be equally fatal to liberty *and to national authority*. If the first [the Hebertists] crushed the other, patriotism would be proscribed, the Convention would lose the energy which alone can save the Republic, and the common weal would fall again into the hands of intrigue, the aristocracy, and treason. If the second [the Dantonists] won out, confusion and anarchy, the debasement of the nation's representatives, the persecution of all courageous and wise patriots would be the fruits of its victory.
>
> To dissolve the Convention, to overthrow the republican regime, to proscribe energetic patriots and place both the command of the armed forces and the reins of revolutionary administration in the hands of rogues and traitors: such is, such will be the interest, the goal of all the tyrants in league against the Republic, until the last of them has expired under the blows of the French people. . . .
>
> A systematic attack was mounted against the Committee of Public Safety, from the moment it began to show characteristics truly troublesome to the enemies of the Republic.[103]

We would seem to be far removed from the days when Robespierre had warned that men in power are always the worst men around. So we may be, but we are also very close to the fall of Robespierre, though we are nowhere near the end of the politics of exclusion. As had the Girondins' dilemma a year earlier, Robespierre's words suggest some of the problems involved in formulating a positive political conception of the common good in a world defined simultaneously by the politics of exclusion and liberal aspirations.

The life of the Committee of Public Safety, which Robespierre wished for disinterested as well as interested reasons to prolong, depended on the Committee's ability to muster a parliamentary majority. The general impact of the politics of exclusion and the specific results of Jacobin policies combined to make a stable parliamentary majority unobtainable. Robespierre had profound programmatic differences with the Hebertist left: He condemned the left's campaign for dechristianization as needlessly provocative and subversive of public morals, he was uncomfortable with its social and economic positions, and he rejected its antiparliamentary tendencies and its excessive attachment to the punitive side of revolutionary government. For

---

[103] Robespierre, undelivered speech, around January 15, 1794; *Oeuvres*, vol. 10, p. 327.

his majority, Robespierre would have to look to the Plain, but the Plain, lacking organization, lacked fiber. In December, Robespierre seemed to be moving toward an alliance with Danton, but the consummation of such an alliance was prevented by blackmail from the pro-Terrorist left, represented on the Committee of Public Safety by Collot d'Herbois and Billaud-Varenne. The two great purge trials of Germinal were in fact episodes in what, given a different political framework, might have been a rather banal struggle for party and parliamentary power. Ultimately, the trials, which marked the beginning of the Great Terror (June 11–July 27, 1794), failed to give Robespierre the majority he needed. They also failed to contribute to the emergence of any other majority, except the Thermidorian one, based overwhelmingly on overwhelming fear, and correspondingly fragile. Its formation was made possible by the repression of the extraparliamentary left that had accompanied the execution of the Hebertists and by the favorable position of republican armies.

At the end of his speech against the Dantonists, Saint-Just presented his colleagues with a portrait of what life would be like after the Revolution:

> When the remains of the Orléans faction, today devoted to all the attacks against the fatherland, will have ceased to exist, you will no longer have to make examples; you will be peaceable; intrigue will no longer frequent your sacred surroundings; you will devote yourself to legislating and governing; . . . then, only patriots will remain; then, the illusion of intrigues that for five years assumed the mask of the Revolution and today would shift their opprobrium onto the Revolution by having it said that patriots will be dishonored one after the other, that illusion will be destroyed. . . .
>
> . . . Having abolished factions, give to this Republic gentle mores. Rekindle in civil society individual esteem and respect. Frenchmen, be happy and free, love each other. Hate all the enemies of the Republic, but be at peace with each other. Liberty calls you back to nature; and others would have you abandon it! Have you no wives to cherish, no children to raise? Respect each other. And you, representatives of the people, concern yourselves with government, and let everyone else enjoy freedom instead of governing.[104]

By the summer of 1794, it seemed to many that Jacobin politics were more likely to lead to the "vast desert" predicted by Vergniaud than to the peaceable Republic evoked by Saint-Just. The politics of exclusion remained the preferred way of limiting power. Trans-

[104] Saint-Just, Convention, March 31, 1794; *Oeuvres complètes*, p. 778.

formed into a tool of those in power, it was intolerable except under extreme circumstances. It would soon be undone by its own contradictions.

Jacobinism and Liberalism: Defining the Common Good

The Jacobins' propensity to recast domestic political conflict in the uncompromising language of war, their incorporation of a new democratic rhetoric into an equally new justification of revolutionary government, and their vision of a harmonious future political community in which unanimity would prevail because, as Saint-Just put it, only patriots would remain, have suggested to many students of European politics that Jacobinism, often viewed as a practical extension of Rousseau's theoretical formulations, should be seen not as providing the core of a second model of liberal politics, but rather as a precursor of modern totalitarianism.[105]

The argument linking revolutionary Jacobinism to totalitarianism is necessarily a retrospective one, for totalitarianism was not an eighteenth-century option. Postrevolutionary history tells against the argument, since the country that allegedly invented the totalitarian model would also seem to have acquired an immunity against it: The French right of the 1930s never made the leap from frantic conservatism to fascism, and the French Communist Party, Stalinist though it stubbornly remained, nonetheless consistently shied away from the possibility of seizing power.[106] Totalitarian regimes are not founded

[105] Even contemporary observers of the Revolution were left with an uncomfortable sense of disquieting political innovation: Thus Pitt, disturbed by the ideological overtones of revolutionary foreign policy, declaimed against "armed opinions." In the mid-nineteenth century, soon after publishing the finished parts of *L'Ancien régime et la Révolution*, Tocqueville confided to a friend: "There is . . . in this malady of the French Revolution something special which I sense without being able to describe it, or to analyze its causes. It is a *virus* of a new and unknown species. There have been violent revolutions in the world; but the immoderate, violent, radical, desperate, audacious, nearly demented yet powerful and efficacious character of these revolutionaries has no precedent, it seems to me, in the annals of the social disturbances of past centuries. From whence this new race? What produced it? What made it so effective? What perpetuates it? For the same men are still before us, although the circumstances are different; these men have sprung up throughout the civilized world" (cited by Furet, *Penser la Révolution française*, p. 222, n. 26). For contemporary statements of the argument linking Jacobinism to totalitarianism, see J. L. Talmon, *The Origins of Totalitarian Democracy* (New York: Praeger, 1960); Furet, *Penser la Révolution française*, and Fehér, *The Frozen Revolution*.

[106] See, for example, the conduct of the Party in 1944 and 1968.

simply on the power of ideological appeal and manipulation; they demand a certain type of society and require a specific form of political organization. While French liberalism's dependence on the politics of exclusion made the life of liberal institutions in postrevolutionary France a dangerous one, it also precluded the forms of social and political organization necessary not just to the development of totalitarianism, but even to stable authoritarian rule. In the preceding section, we looked at typically Jacobin forms of political competition. For a brief period, the use of terror as a means of everyday political control—perhaps the defining characteristic of modern totalitarian regimes[107]—did indeed seem the natural product of the Jacobin conception and practice of politics. But Jacobinism's Terrorist phase was remarkably short lived. The Bolsheviks relied on terror for decades, and Nazi terror ended only with Germany's defeat. Jacobin terror, on the other hand, undid itself—very quickly. It undid itself because its exclusionary politics remained tied to liberal goals. Jacobin politics were coherent, and extremely potent even if inherently destabilizing, when harnessed to the liberal goal of limiting power. In the setting in which they arose, they rapidly grew incoherent and intolerable when transmuted into a basis for power and policy.

Just as significantly for long-term French political development, Jacobinism limited the topics around which immediate statements of the public interest could be constructed, the terms in which those statements would be cast, and the actors who would be allowed to make them. To see French liberalism taking shape under the imprint of revolutionary Jacobinism, we must look at how the Jacobins thought about the ideal shape and proper functions of governmental institutions, the limits they drew around the place of politics in the daily existence of normal individuals, and the mix of conflict and community to which they aspired. The ultimate goals and fundamental assumptions of the Jacobins—including Robespierre and Saint-Just—will appear familiarly liberal. The more immediately operative political goals compatible with both liberalism and the politics of exclusion will be more distinctive: They will focus on foundational issues (defending the Republic against its ever-present internal enemies) and, derivatively, on France's international role (asserting a common French identity on an external stage). Whereas in England

[107] See in particular Hannah Arendt, *The Origins of Totalitarianism*, new ed. (New York: Harcourt Brace Jovanovich, 1973), esp. part III; Carl J. Friedrich, ed., *Totalitarianism* (Cambridge, Mass.: Harvard University Press, 1954); cf. Michael Walzer, "On Failed Totalitarianism," in Irving Howe, ed., *1984 Revisited: Totalitarianism in Our Century* (New York: Harper and Row, 1983), pp. 103–21.

and America, the public interest is understood to emerge from civil society, in France the state is the repository, the guardian, and (within the limits described above) the author of the public interest. It is the state that makes the community and articulates its collective will: Where there is no state, there is no nation and no general interest.[108] The privileged instruments of jacobinism as policy include public oratory, the bureaucracy (as the impersonal enforcer of common rules), the army (as an agent of civic education as well as external defense), and the school system—not, it must be repeated, a political movement of any sort. In this account, the politics of interest articulation divides; the state unites, and it is popular control through elected officials that keeps the state from being taken over by particular interests.

Revolutionary Jacobinism preached the virtues of representative institutions and practiced the rigors of revolutionary government. The irony of such a position was not lost on the actors. At the end of February 1794 (thus shortly before the trials of Germinal and the beginning of the bloodiest period of the Terror), Saint-Just came before the Convention to deliver a report on the Revolution's political prisoners. In a phrase that Albert Ollivier adopted for the title of his biography of Saint-Just,[109] Robespierre's young lieutenant acknowledged that "the logic of events [la force des choses] leads us perhaps towards results we never envisioned."[110] The central result toward which Jacobin thought spontaneously tended was the radical limitation of political power; the unapplied Constitution of 1793, with its lengthy enumeration of the rights of man and citizen, reflects the Jacobins' fundamental aspirations.[111] The result that the logic of events forced upon them—and to which certain characteristics of Jacobin ideology, as well as the prior structure of revolutionary opportunity,

---

[108] The contemporary French exponents of this view would be Charles de Gaulle and Michel Debré, but for a related academic view, cf. Samuel Huntington: "The legitimacy of governmental actions can be sought in the extent to which they reflect the interests of governmental institutions. In contrast to the theory of representative government, under this concept governmental institutions derive their legitimacy and authority not from the extent to which they represent the interests of the people or of any other group, but to the extent to which they have distinct interests of their own apart from all other groups" (*Political Order in Changing Societies*, p. 27); "Without strong political institutions, society [complex and conflictual] lacks the means to define and to realize its common interests. The capacity to create political institutions is the capacity to create public interests" (Ibid., p. 24).

[109] Albert Ollivier, *Saint-Just et la force des choses* (Paris: Gallimard, 1954).

[110] Saint-Just, Convention, February 26, 1794; *Oeuvres complètes*, p. 705.

[111] For text, see Godechot, *Les Constitutions*, pp. 79–92.

certainly contributed—was, in essence, dictatorial rule by a political minority; it was codified in the decree of 14 Frimaire Year II (December 4, 1793).[112] Ultimately, Jacobin arguments for the limitation of power subverted their defense of revolutionary dictatorship.

In the summer of 1793, on the eve of the formation of the "Great Committee," it seemed to the revolutionary leadership in Paris that the most pressing threat to the Revolution lay in spreading anarchy. Republican armies were ill equipped, and their command was poorly organized. For both the civilian population and military personnel, supplies of food and other necessities were at best unreliable. The political class, inside and outside the Convention, was as fragmented as ever, and its divisions were aggravated by the pressure of popular unrest. The events of the late spring and summer had disrupted the chain of command and communication between Paris and the provinces. The expulsion of the Girondin deputies, combined with the Jacobin alliance with the extraparliamentary radicals, had alienated local notables, who retained their power, their desire for autonomy, and their Girondin sympathies. The population as a whole adopted a hesitant attitude toward the latest revolutionary developments; as one contemporary report from the Tarentaise region put it, "public spirit remained as though in a deep freeze."[113] Meanwhile, of course, the war continued. On October 10, 1793, Saint-Just defined for the Convention the task facing the revolutionary leadership:

> Your Committee of Public Safety . . . has calculated the causes of our public misfortunes: it has found them in the weakness with which your decrees are executed, in the lack of economy in the administration, in the fickleness of the views of the State, in the vicissitudes of the passions which influence the government.
>
> The Committee has therefore resolved to describe to you the state of affairs, and to present to you the means which it believes appropriate to the goal of consolidating the Revolution, crushing federalism [that is, the Girondins], bringing relief to and procuring abundance for the people, strengthening the army, and cleansing the State of the conspiracies that infest it.[114]

Against a situation they perceived as desperate, the Jacobins advocated a four-pronged response, elaborated and implemented between March and December of 1793. Revolutionary government, as they called their plan, rested in the first instance on the reinforced

---

[112] For text, see *Le Moniteur*, vol. 18, pp. 610–13.

[113] Cited without attribution by Marc Bouloiseau, *La République jacobine* (Paris: Le Seuil, 1972), p. 83.

[114] Saint-Just; *Oeuvres complètes*, p. 520.

authority of the Committee of Public Safety; it also relied on the various committees, military units, and tribunals charged with meting out speedy and exemplary justice to those guilty of political or economic misdeeds, on the work of the *représentants en mission*,[115] and on the imposition of economic controls. Arguing in favor of the decree of 14 Frimaire, Billaud-Varenne affirmed that "any good government must have a single source of direction [*un centre de volonté*]":[116] In France, that source would be in Paris, and in Paris, it would be vested in the Committee of Public Safety. The decree stripped local communities of their autonomy, placing them instead under the authority of appointed officials responsible directly to the Committee in Paris, and through the Committee, to the Convention:

> Under an ordinary government, the people have the right to elect officials. Under an extraordinary government, it is from the central power that all impluses must emanate, it is from the Convention that elections must come. We live in extraordinary circumstances. Those who invoke the rights of the people would render false homage to popular sovereignty. As long as the revolutionary machine is still running, you would hurt the people by giving them the task of electing public functionaries, for the people might name men who would betray them.[117]

Revolutionary government was justified because France was still at war with herself: that was what Couthon's listeners were meant to understand when told that "the revolutionary machine is still running." The Republic did not yet exist; it was idle (to the Jacobins it seemed criminal) to clamor for legal formalities when the political community itself had yet to be founded and its republican identity established.

> The goal of constitutional government is to preserve the Republic; that of revolutionary government is to found the Republic. The Revolution is a war of liberty against its enemies: the Constitution is the regime of victorious and peaceful liberty. Revolutionary government requires an extraordinary level of activity, precisely because it is at war. It is subject to rules less uniform and less strict [than constitutional government], because the circumstances in which it finds itself are stormy and transient, and above

[115] Marc Bouloiseau reports that during the winter of 1793–1794, more than one-third of the members of the Convention were *en mission*; see *La République jacobine*, p. 101. The nineteenth-century editors of the reprinted edition of *Le Moniteur* estimated that about 300 deputies (under half of the total) were *en mission* in April 1793; see *Le Moniteur*, vol. 16, p. 151.

[116] Billaud-Varenne, Convention, November 18, 1793; *Le Moniteur*, vol. 18, p. 464.

[117] Couthon, Convention, December 4, 1793; *Le Moniteur*, vol. 18, p. 491.

all because it is constantly forced rapidly to deploy new resources against new and pressing dangers.

Constitutional government is concerned chiefly with civil liberty: and revolutionary government, with public liberty. Under a constitutional regime, it is enough to protect individuals against the abuse of public power: under a revolutionary regime, public power itself is obliged to defend itself against all the factions that assail it.[118]

Robespierre defined the goal of the Revolution negatively as the moral and political obverse of the Old Regime, and positively as "the peaceful enjoyment of liberty and equality."[119] These goals could only be achieved within the framework of a democracy:

a state where the sovereign people, guided by laws of their own making, do themselves everything which they can do well, and leave to their delegates what they cannot do themselves.[120]

The means to this end were both less familiar and less attractive than the end itself. Robespierre defended terror—"prompt, severe, inflexible justice"[121]—as necessary, given the strength and strategy of the adversary:

People want to regulate revolutions with the subtleties characteristic of the Court; people view plots against the Republic as if they were comparable to litigation between individuals. Tyranny kills, and liberty pleads; and the code written by the conspirators themselves is the law by which they are judged.[122]

Nor did Robespierre feel the need to apologize at any length for tactics deemed temporarily necessary. Instead, he reaffirmed the exclusionary nature of revolutionary politics:

Social protection is due only to peaceful citizens: the only citizens of a Republic are the republicans. Royalists and conspirators are but foreigners, or rather they are enemies, in the eyes of the Republic. This terrible war which liberty has engaged against tyranny, is it not indivisible? Are not domestic enemies the allies of our external enemies?[123]

Yet despite the perceived need for a strong central authority and despite their willingness to resort to radical means, the advocates of

---

[118] Robespierre, Convention, December 25, 1793; *Oeuvres*, vol. 10, p. 274.
[119] Robespierre, Convention, February 5, 1794; *Oeuvres*, vol. 10, p. 352.
[120] Ibid., p. 353.
[121] Ibid., p. 357.
[122] Ibid., p. 358.
[123] Ibid., p. 357.

the decree of 14 Frimaire declined to rename the Committee of Public Safety the "committee of government":

> The Convention governs alone and alone must govern; the Committee of Public Safety is not the only instrument in its hands. . . . We are the outpost of the Convention; we are the arms which allow it to act, but we are not the government. To call us the committee of government would therefore be to give us a name which is not ours; it would give the committee a negative coloration which might damage the confidence invested in it, and which it needs; finally, it would change its elements and place us, we the individuals who compose it, outside the Convention, putting us instead among the class of executive agents.[124]

In their reports to the Convention, Committee members invariably used the expression "your Committee," reversing the reference of divine right kings to "their" parliaments.

To the Jacobins, the ultimate, unconquerable enemy remained men in power: "the class of executive agents," with whom Barère and his colleagues did not wish to be confused. It was precisely because "all the enemies of the Republic are in its government"[125] that Saint-Just urged the Convention to "tighten all the knots of responsibility, to direct the use of power."[126] Even during the grimmest days of the spring of 1794, the Jacobins never forgot their consuming fear of the corrupting influence of power, and five tumultuous years of revolutionary experience amply suggested that a strong state apparatus set up to further the aims of a group in power might still be there to serve the hostile purposes of the rival group that followed. The Jacobins had not, in fact, rushed to embrace revolutionary government when it first became an option, just as they had not rushed to lead the popular insurrections from which they sometimes benefited. In May 1792, Robespierre had deliberately entitled his journal *Le Défenseur de la Constitution,* and had informed his readers that he intended to defend the Constitution "as it is."[127] Robespierre's argument was reminiscent of Duport's: "[G]ood citizens need a point of reference and a mark of unity; I see no other but the Constitution."[128] Less than a month before the insurrection of August 10, 1792, Robespierre urged caution on the *fédérés:*

[124] Barère, Convention, November 29, 1793; *Le Moniteur,* vol. 18, p. 559.

[125] Saint-Just, October 10, 1793; *Oeuvres complètes,* p. 522.

[126] Ibid., p. 525.

[127] Robespierre, *Le Défenseur de la Constitution,* no. 1 [July 25, 1792]; *Oeuvres,* vol. 4, p. 5.

[128] Ibid., p. 7.

It would be an absurdity to believe that the constitution does not give the national assembly [the Legislative Assembly] the means of defending it [the constitution], when it is obvious that the national assembly still has far to go in employing all the resources that the constitution gives it; it would be sovereignly impolitic to begin by demanding more than the constitution, when one cannot secure the constitution itself; it would be even more impolitic to try to demand, by apparently unconstitutional means, that to which one has a right by virtue of a formal text within the constitution. . . .

Citizens-*fédérés*, combat your common enemies only with the sword of the law. Present legally before the Legislative Assembly the wish of the people of your *départements* and the alarm of the country in peril. . . .

It is only through this wise and firm process that you can save your country. Impatience and indignation might counsel measures in appearance more prompt and vigorous; the public safety and the rights of the people might justify such measures; but only the others are recommended by a healthy sense of the politic, and adapted to the circumstances in which we find ourselves. One must not always do everything that is legitimate.[129]

"The logic of events"—including, finally, their own desperate efforts to remain in power—later led Robespierre and the Jacobins of the Committee of Public Safety to change their tune. Robespierre's early reluctance to step outside the legally sanctioned channels of political action, frequently demonstrated before and during the summer of 1792, seems hard to reconcile with the law of 22 Prairial Year II (June 10, 1794).[130] It is, however, no accident that only six weeks separate the Convention's reluctant acceptance of the Terror's most threatening *loi des suspects* from Thermidor. The Thermidorians— conventionnels who had voted every month for a year to confirm the personnel and powers of the Committee of Public Safety—could (and did) condemn Robespierre without repudiating the Jacobin model of politics. The imperatives of that model were summarized by Robespierre as late as two months prior to his election to the Committee, during the debate over the new constitution. "Flee the ancient mania of governments that always want to govern too much," Robespierre admonished his colleagues;

leave to individuals, leave to families the right to do whatever does not harm others; leave to towns the power to regulate their own affairs in any matter that does not directly concern the general administration of the Republic. In a word, give to individual liberty whatever does not belong nat-

[129] Robespierre, *Le Défenseur de la Constitution*, no. 10 [July 25, 1792]; *Oeuvres*, vol. 4, pp. 296ff.

[130] For text, see *Le Moniteur*, vol. 20, pp. 696f.

urally to public authority, and you will have deprived ambition and arbitrariness of a foothold.[131]

The Jacobins' enduring preference for limited government and representative institutions was reflected in and reinforced both by the limited personal returns they expected to draw from politics as an inherently fulfilling human activity and by their vision of postrevolutionary society. Totalitarianism holds society in a constant frenzy of political activity and defines virtue so as to require the annihilation of the private individual, with his or her particular constellation of interests and pleasures and his or her autonomous will. Closer in time and culture to the revolutionary Jacobins, Rousseau's republic would have devalued the individual and permanently elevated politics to the status of a full-time occupation. Casting Rousseau as an intellectual forerunner of totalitarian thinking poses the same problems of retrospective argument as does placing the Jacobins in that role. Whatever one's assessment of Rousseau's twentieth-century legacy, however, it is important to note that the Jacobins, indebted to Rousseau in other areas, parted company with him on the crucial issue of the place of politics in the general economy of an individual's life.

Rousseau rejected the notion of natural rights, repudiated representative government, and doubted that any individual could reconcile the conflicting vocations of man and citizen. The foundation of the Republic would therefore require the "mutilation"[132] of the individual, and the Republic's prosperity would depend on its ability to maintain the individual in that mutilated condition:

> Good social institutions are those that best know how to denature man, to take his absolute existence from him in order to give him a relative one and transport the *I* into the common unity, with the result that each individual believes himself no longer one but a part of the unity and no longer

[131] Robespierre, Convention, May 10, 1793; *Oeuvres*, vol. 9, pp. 501f.

[132] In a draft of the *Contrat social* (the so-called "Manuscrit de Genève"), Rousseau defined the Legislator's task: "He who would found a people must feel himself capable . . . of changing human nature. He must transform each individual, who by himself constitutes a perfect and solitary whole, into a part of a greater whole from which the individual receives, so to speak, his life and his being; he must *mutilate*, as it were, the constitution of man so as to reinforce it; he must substitute a partial and moral existence for the physical and independent existence that we all receive from nature." "Manuscrit de Genève," II, 2, in Rousseau, *Oeuvres complètes*, vol. 2, p. 407; emphasis added.

feels except within the whole. A citizen of Rome was neither Caius nor Lucius; he was a Roman. He even loved the country exclusive of himself.[133]

Rousseau would not have abolished private life, but he idealized Sparta and dreamed of a republic in which private life and its satisfactions would disappear of themselves:

> The better constituted the State, the more public affairs dominate private ones in the minds of the citizens. There is even less private business, be- cause since the sum of common happiness furnishes a larger portion of each individual's happiness, the individual has less to seek through private efforts. In a well-run polity, everyone flies to assemblies. . . .[134]

As public life became more genuine, it would also become more absorbing; private life, on the other hand, would seem less and less attractive.

The Jacobin formula is the exact inverse of Rousseau's. Only during the Revolution—which sooner or later somebody would succeed in bringing to completion—would it be necessary for anyone to fly to the assemblies. Explicitly rejecting Rousseau's vision of the republic while at the same time denouncing the extraparliamentary radicals' antiparliamentary abuse of political activism, Robespierre argued:

> Democracy is not a condition in which the people, continuously assembled, decide themselves every public question; still less is it that condition in which a hundred thousand fractions of the people, by isolated, precipitous, and contradictory measures, decide the fate of the entire society: such a government has never existed, and it could exist only as a step on the road back to despotism.[135]

Saint-Just, whom we have already heard suggesting that people had better and more pleasant things to do than govern, defended what was, in an as yet overwhelmingly agricultural society, a view of happiness that we would today express in different terms and identify as solidly middle class: "a plow, a field, a cottage safe from the tax-collector, a family safe from the rapacity of a bandit, now *there* is happiness."[136]

The Jacobin Republic, founded through terror, would depend after its foundation on the virtue of its citizens. The virtue demanded, however, was entirely consonant with Saint-Just's portrait of happiness. "We have no wish to cast the French Republic in the Spartan

---

[133] Rousseau, *Emile*, in *Oeuvres complètes*, vol. 3, p. 21.

[134] Rousseau, *Contrat social*, III, 15; *Oeuvres complètes*, vol. 2, p. 558.

[135] Robespierre, Convention, February 5, 1794; *Oeuvres*, vol. 10, pp. 352f.

[136] Saint-Just, Convention, March 13, 1794; *Oeuvres complètes*, p. 730.

mold," Robespierre affirmed; "we do not want to give it either the austerity or the corruption of the cloisters."[137] Instead of the self-denying, martial virtues stressed by classical republican theory, Jacobin discourse emphasized "modesty"—a codeword signifying the opposite of Old Regime manners[138]—and independence.

Rousseau would have banned political parties from his republic, and the Jacobins shared his distrust of organized political opinion (their own sometimes, but not always, excepted). The Jacobins, however, were not purchasing an end to political conflict at the price of minimizing the articulation of private interests throughout society as a whole; rather, they were separating politics from society, seeking to ensure that conflicting private interests would not use the power of the state to settle their disputes. Their assumption was that if everyone minded their own business, political assemblies would have little to do, and since they did not think that under normal circumstances—when political loyalty and the security of republican institutions could be taken for granted—political assemblies should have much to do, that was all to the better. If the state limited itself to the task of preserving formal equality, it would not excite controversy; if it did not so limit itself, it was probably on the way to subverting liberty. Thus the Constitution of 1793 stipulated that "each deputy belongs to the entire nation."[139] Particular interests would differ from one constituency to the next, but keeping a vigilant eye on those in power was indeed in the interest of the entire nation. Far from being on the road to an unknown totalitarian destination, we are in a world in which only one type of authoritarianism would be tried, and then only briefly.

The Jacobins were too preoccupied by the realities of conflict and exclusion to devote extensive consideration to the problem of how

[137] Robespierre, Convention, February 5, 1794; *Oeuvres*, vol. 10, pp. 354f.

[138] The reference to modesty survived Thermidor. Thus, on July 29, 1794, Barère asked the Convention to name "faithful team players [*des coopérateurs fidèles*] and modest republicans" to replace the three executed members of the Committee of Public Safety. He added: "They should not hold national office, those who think more of their personal glory than of the welfare of their country, who occupy prominent places as one walks out upon a brilliant stage, and who look to patriotism only for ostentation, and to the republic only for power. Revolutionary government does not need egotists or indifferent men, it does not need frigid souls for whom authority is nothing but an amusement, for whom great interests are without interest, and who, more concerned with staying in power than with serving the country, are neither zealous republicans nor public administrators. We are no longer in an age when one would sacrifice a nation to a man and the happiness of future generations to the pleasures of a power-seeker [*un ambitieux*]." *Le Moniteur*, vol. 21, p. 361.

[139] Constitution of 1793, Article 29; Godechot, *Les Constitutions*, p. 85.

community would be maintained in the liberal society of the postrevolutionary era. Emmanuel Mounier suggests, and not in jest, that on the issue of solidarity, feudalism's record compares favorably to that of French republicanism. The Jacobins did not find a promising situation when they arrived in power, and the situation they handed down to their successors was scarcely improved. Insofar as they did address the problem of community, however, the means they thought to employ were also those used in England and America. The effect was different because revolutionary processes made community more problematic. The Jacobins intended to institute compulsory public schooling for all children: In school, children of all social classes would learn mutual respect and acquire the necessary habits of discipline, thrift, hard work, and respect for those in authority.[140] The Third Republic would finally establish such a school system; Catholic and conservative resistance would make its teachers feel like soldiers of the Republic. Anglo-American liberalism relied perhaps even more heavily on the Protestant churches than on public schools to act as agents of social discipline and solidarity; obviously unable to call upon the Catholic Church for aid, Robespierre tried to invent a civil religion that would inspire "in man that religious respect for his fellow man, and that deep sentiment of duty, which alone can guarantee public felicity."[141] Far more easily adopted, although of ambiguous efficacy in resolving the problem of community, was Jacobin nationalism, symbolized by the praise lavished upon the "volunteers of the Year II." From its birth, however, French nationalism implied an appeal away from the existing state of domestic political affairs. The volunteers of the Year II were fighting for freedom; yet factions continued to battle one another in Paris: The politicians, critics claimed, were a dishonor to the sovereign people for whom the volunteers were valiantly fighting and dying. More often than not in the years since the Revolution, nationalism has been a weapon used by the opposition of the day to discredit the regime in power.

To the many men and women who perished needlessly during the Terror, the knowledge that neither Jacobin ideology nor the basic structure of French society would long sustain the dictatorship of a revolutionary minority might not have provided much consolation.

[140] On the educational policies proposed during the revolutionary period, see Bronislaw Baczko, comp., *Une éducation pour la démocratie: Textes et projets de l'époque révolutionnaire* (Paris: Garnier Frères, 1982).

[141] Robespierre, Convention, May 7, 1794; *Oeuvres*, vol. 10, p. 458.

From our vantage point, however, Jacobinism would seem to constitute the defining strand of a second model of liberal politics, even
more wary of political power than its Anglo-American counterpart,
and, because of its own tendency to generate fragmentation and polarization, rather less able to compensate for liberalism's disintegrat-
ing effects. Jacobinism established the primacy of the liberal agenda
in France; as the experience of the Directory promptly and amply
demonstrated, it did not sponsor stable liberal institutions. Alternative arrangements could not escape the standard and now fatal liberal
critique: All would be attacked as arbitrary and authoritarian. And all
French regimes—liberal and illiberal—would be attacked as somehow
unworthy of the nation: constitutional regimes (or would-be constitutional regimes) as squabbling cartels of particular interests offering
but a petty version of the national identity,[142] and Bonapartist regimes as ultimately unable to sustain the populistic, militaristic nationalism on which they based their legitimacy.

Conflict and Community? A Preliminary Verdict

In the two centuries that have elapsed since the Thermidorian coup,
the term *Jacobin* has proved remarkably elastic. It has been casually
applied to or invoked by leaders as different as Napoleon and de
Gaulle and groups as distinct in time and character as the Sociétés
des Jacobins, which subsisted after the overthrow of Robespierre, and
the Club des Jacobins of the 1950s.[143] For some, the term evokes a
certain conception of the state; for others, a form of political action;
for yet others, a political program. It is above all the assimilation of
Jacobinism with a conception of the state in large part inherited from
the Old Regime that accounts for the casual extension of the term to
men and groups in postrevolutionary France. Yet for all the obvious
continuities, the revolutionary Jacobins profoundly altered the Old
Regime notions of sovereignty, unity, and the general interest to
which they were indebted. The Jacobins were liberals; Louis XIV was

[142] Lest this judgment appear the exclusive property of political extremists, cf. Alfred Cobban's assessment of the July Monarchy: "On the afternoon of 24 February
[1848], collapsing in senile despair, Louis-Philippe abdicated in favour of his grandson,
the little comte de Paris. It was the end of a régime that had been so lacking in principle that it could only be known by the name of the month of its founding, as the July
Monarchy." Cobban, *A History of Modern France*, vol. 2, 1799–1871 (Harmondsworth,
Middlesex: Penguin, 1961, 1965), p. 131.

[143] Founded in 1951, the Club des Jacobins supported Pierre Mendès France and
eventually joined the Convention des institutions républicaines. See Janine Mossuz, *Les
Clubs politiques en France* (Paris: Armand Colin, 1970), esp. pp. 31–34.

not. The Jacobins' conception of the state was, as we have seen, intimately tied to a form of political action and a political program, which together formed a coherent package quite distinct from its Old Regime antecedents or its Bonapartist counterpoint. The Jacobins, like liberals in England and America, were determined to limit state power and to create a public world to which all individuals would (theoretically) have equal access. Unlike liberals in England and America, the Jacobins combined their understanding of the state and their political program with a permanent reliance on the politics of exclusion.

In the postrevolutionary period, Jacobin liberalism was by no means the only liberal tradition present in France, and liberal positions themselves remained under sustained challenge throughout the nineteenth century and on into the twentieth century. This instability, I have argued, was a necessary element of the exclusionary model of liberal politics. Jacobinism was most compelling as an opposition ideology; it could not serve as the basis of an expanding coalition around which the new liberal order could be institutionally consolidated. At the same time, its influence on other groups and its impact on political competition were too strong to be circumvented. The Jacobins were relentlessly but ineffectively exclusionary; their inability to delimit and then definitively destroy political options incompatible with their own aspirations had a splintering effect on political opinion both within and outside the revolutionary camp. Their view of the state—shared, as we have noted, by men and groups hostile or indifferent to liberal values—made the institutional management of political fragmentation particularly difficult. Finally, with the Anglo-American appeals to property and a shared religious culture unavailable, Jacobinism could not propose a comparably positive and powerful account of the moral foundations of liberalism in general and of ethical and political individualism in particular. The sociological leanings of nineteenth-century French liberals were directly proportional to their inability to prevail on the basis of normative arguments, but their sociological insights could easily be confiscated by men who did not share their normative positions.[144]

Thus the Revolution left French liberalism strong enough to call the shots in politics, but not strong enough to hit its target on every try. More formally, we could say that the liberal agenda prevailed (placing France in the same political category as England and Amer-

[144] This happened most obviously with the socialist adoption of class analysis; see Larry Siedentop, "Two Liberal Traditions," in Alan Ryan, ed., *The Idea of Freedom: Essays in Honor of Isaiah Berlin* (Oxford: Oxford University Press, 1979).

ica) but that its demands were only partially met—even when the Third Republic finally achieved the measure of stability that had eluded the constitutional monarchies of the nineteenth century. The structural factors that had led to liberal revolution in the first place precluded the emergence of any form of political regime immune to liberal demands—in other words, any form of totalitarianism. But there is plenty of political space between liberal stability and totalitarian unfreedom. Revolutionary outcomes precluded a return to the Old Regime, but they both encouraged and abbreviated the Bonapartist interludes that punctuate nineteenth-century French history and cast their shadow over much of twentieth-century French history.

The political constraints the Jacobin experience would impose on subsequent political actors became apparent even as Jacobin heads rolled. The announced purpose of the Terror had been to secure the Republic once and for all against its many internal and external adversaries. Its immediate effect was instead to compromise the reputation of the entire revolutionary enterprise and to extend the range of political dissent on both ends of the ideological spectrum. Jacobin apologists during and after the revolutionary period pointed to the victories of republican armies to vindicate the repression employed by the Committee of Public Safety, but that argument is only slightly less spurious than a more recent one crediting the purge trials of 1938 for the successful defense of Stalingrad four years later: In the French case, nothing proves that the Terror was a necessary condition of more effective government.

In the months following Robespierre's downfall, the Convention attempted to bury its bitter memories of the Terror. It sought to strike a constitutional arrangement that would guarantee limited government and representative institutions and exclude both a royalist restoration and a return of the Jacobins. The sorry political record of the Thermidorian Republic provides a preliminary balance sheet on revolutionary Jacobinism, for the Thermidorians could escape neither the mentality nor the practical consequences of the political model the Jacobins had developed.

The coup which led to the execution of Robespierre, Saint-Just, Couthon, and nineteen of their partisans was defended before the Convention in terms and through arguments worthy of any account the executed men might themselves have delivered to justify the liquidation of a rival group. This is perhaps not surprising, since the report was Barère's work. "Citizens," he began, "the representatives of the nation have saved themselves in one day from conspiracies incubated for over a year. . . ." He denounced "this atrocious plot," concocted by men whom two days earlier he had still recognized as colleagues, and set himself to unmasking and decoding the hidden maneuvers of "their abominable counter-revolution." His conclusion was familiar: "Thus everything was to contribute to re-establishing tyranny on a bloody throne."[145] After summarizing the initial measures the Committee of Public Safety had taken in the hours following the coup, Barère reaffirmed the parliamentary supremacy he knew it had been the purpose of Thermidor to reassert:

> The Committee . . . will soon issue a report to make known in definite terms the state of the Republic and of the government, in order to put the Convention in a position to take all the great measures rendered necessary by the current situation, past commotion, and the dangers which the aristocracy and foreigners will not hesitate to create, if we are not vigilant and of one mind. For great measures must and can come only from you. The Convention is the depository of the authority that the people have created. The committees are but secondary organs, auxiliary arms, and supplementary means at the disposal of national authority and the Convention, which alone exercises authority and alone has the right to do so.[146]

Having paid his respects to the authority of the Convention, Barère added some emphatic advice. The demise of Robespierre should not, Barère argued, discredit the politics of exclusion.

> Beware above all of that fatal modérantisme which knows how, when speaking of peace and clemency, to take advantage of all circumstances, even of the most rigorous developments. . . . May the revolutionary movement not cease in its cleansing course, and may the Convention continue to cause traitors and kings, domestic conspirators and foreign despotisms, to tremble.[147]

For several weeks, the Convention tried simply to dismantle the machinery of the Terror, without inquiring too far into the personal responsibilities of men still alive. The law of 22 Prairial Year II was quickly repealed (Barère himself condemning "senseless terror"[148]) and the committee system reorganized. On August 29, however, Lecointre demanded the indictment of men who had figured prominently in the Committees of Public Safety and General Security: Billaud-Varenne, Collot d'Herbois, Barère, Vadier, Amar, Voulland, and David. His terse speech included the enumeration of twenty-six counts against one or more of the accused men. Goujon's immediate

---

[145] Barère, July 29, 1794; *Le Moniteur*, vol. 21, p. 358.
[146] Ibid., p. 359.
[147] Ibid.
[148] Barère, Convention, August 1, 1794; *Le Moniteur*, vol. 21, p. 369.

reaction translated the unpleasant position in which the convention-nels found themselves:

> My heart stops when I see with what calm tranquillity people sow within
> our midst the seeds of division. . . . Note well, fellow citizens, that most of
> the reproaches levelled against them [against the men Lecointre would
> have indicted] are equally valid against the Convention itself. Yes, it is the
> Convention that is being indicted, it is the French people who are being
> put on trial, since they tolerated the tyranny of the infamous Robes-
> pierre.[149]

Amidst interruptions and growing agitation, Cambon repeated Goujon's warning:

> This accusation is truly a child's game. The extension of Committee powers
> serves as grounds for accusation, yet each month you unanimously ex-
> tended those powers: you are therefore all guilty.[150]

While the Convention wrestled inconclusively with its conscience, society, in Georges Lefebvre's felicitous expression, ceded to its desire to "se décarêmer."[151] With the release came the drive for revenge, and the desire for revenge rapidly precluded the pursuit of any coherent political strategy aimed at stabilizing the political situation.[152] The various components of the extraparliamentary right resurfaced, reorganized, and effectively brought their pressure to bear on an assembly whose fears were for the moment focused exclusively on the possibility of a new threat from the left. In November 1794, the Jacobin Club in Paris was ordered closed. A month later, the seventy-three deputies who had been excluded from the Legislative Assembly because they had formally protested against the expulsion of their Girondin colleagues were readmitted to their seats. In late December,

---

[149] Goujon, Convention; Le Moniteur, vol. 21, p. 622.

[150] Cambon; Le Moniteur, vol. 21, p. 623.

[151] Lefebvre, La Révolution française, p. 435. The word comes from "la Carême," Lent.

[152] For a stimulating discussion of the political debates and developments of the immediate post-Thermidor period, see Bronislaw Baczko, Comment sortir de la Terreur: Thermidor et la Révolution (Paris: Gallimard, 1989), summarized in Baczko, "Thermidoriens," in François Furet and Mona Ozouf, eds., Dictionnaire critique de la Révolution française (Paris: Flammarion, 1988), pp. 425–39. On 3 Sans-culottide Year II (September 19, 1794), Robert Lindet pleaded eloquently for a strategy that would have lowered the stakes of politics, widened the circles of political tolerance, and permitted the consolidation of constitutional government; his strategy was quickly abandoned. For text of speech, see Le Moniteur, vol. 22, pp. 18–26; for analysis, see Anne Sa'adah, "After the Terror: The French Revolution and Political Development" (Paper delivered at 1989 APSA Annual Meeting, Atlanta, Georgia, August 31, 1989); and Baczko, Comment sortir de la Terreur, pp. 164–79.

price controls were lifted. In February 1795, Marat's remains were removed from the Pantheon, as the revolutionaries revised their list of "*grands hommes*."[153] In early March, Billaud-Varenne, Collot, and Barère were finally arrested for their conduct during the Terror. Alarm generated by popular unrest allowed the Convention to deport the three ex-members of Robespierre's Committee of Public Safety before the conclusion of their trial (Barère escaped before the convoy reached the boat) and provided an excuse for further repressive measures against the left. In the provinces, Jacobins were assassinated, as those who had suffered at their hands settled their accounts. As for the leaderless Parisian demonstrators, they were subdued in both April and May by troops and took their leave of the revolutionary stage.

Soon after the Paris journées, other events intervened to remind the conventionnels that they still had enemies on their right. On June 8, the young Louis XVII died in his Paris prison. His death left constitutional monarchists without a candidate for the throne. Two weeks later, the new pretender made public his political positions in a manifesto issued from Verona. Jacques Godechot summarizes this document as follows:

> Louis XVIII declared that he extended his pardon to the errors of the people, but that the regicides would be excepted. As a consequence, he threatened with death half the members of the Convention. He then affirmed that France would purely and simply return to its former constitution, that is to the Old Regime, though abuses would be corrected. The Catholic faith would be reestablished as the state religion, with other religions merely tolerated. Royal power would once again be hereditary, the three orders would be reconstituted; the Estates-General would be called, but only to vote new taxes or to increase old ones. The Estates-General would be allowed to articulate their wishes, but their meetings could always be dissolved by the King. The parlements would be restored and would become the guardians of the law. Since there was no mention of *biens nationaux*, one could assume that they would be returned to their former owners.[154]

The contrast with Charles II's conciliatory Declaration of Breda could not be more complete.[155] In France, if not in the cities of the emigration, constitutional monarchists vastly outnumbered the "ul-

[153] The inscription on the Pantheon reads: "*Aux grands hommes la patrie reconnaissante.*"

[154] Jacques Godechot, *La Contre-Révolution* (Paris: Presses universitaires de France, 1961), p. 183.

[155] For text of the Declaration of Breda, see Kenyon, *Stuart Constitution*, pp. 357f.

tras" to their right. They participated openly in public life and were not opposed on principle to the liberal aspirations that formed the basis of the revolutionary platform; eighty years and several regimes later, they would reach an accommodation of convenience with the republicans. To the ultras of the 1790s, however, the constitutionalists were just one more revolutionary faction, and it was the ultras, not the constitutionalists, who were in a position to create events. The political repercussions of the Verona Manifesto were soon compounded by an attempted invasion at Quiberon, led by émigrés wearing English uniforms and intended to rekindle the war in the Vendée, and by a royalist insurrection in Paris at the beginning of October 1795. The Convention responded by relaxing earlier measures against the left, but it could draw scant comfort from the provisional aid proffered by men it had recently treated as enemies. Once again—and for a century and a half to come—the Republic was beseiged from both left and right.

Such were the inauspicious beginnings of the Directory. The Directory's problems, like those of the Fourth Republic, are frequently attributed to the shortcomings of its constitution. Again like the Fourth Republic, however, the Directory's real problems were political, not constitutional: The Constitution of 1795 did not create the fragmentation and polarization that were its undoing.[156] Drafted and ratified in 1795,[157] the text sought to parry dictatorial impulses from all quarters: It would have guarded equally against an overweening executive, an ambitious assembly, and a militant extraparliamentary minority. It provided for a rigorous separation and limitation of governmental powers. The legislature was divided into two chambers, with one-third of each house up for election each year and no member eligible to stand for reelection immediately after serving two consecutive three-year terms. Executive powers were vested in a council of five members, individually elected to five-year terms by the upper house from nominees proposed by the lower house. The Directors could neither dissolve the legislature nor initiate legislation. The ministers were responsible to the Directors, not to the assemblies, and were not to act as a cabinet (Article 151). The procedure for amending the Constitution, set forth under Title 13, was de-

---

[156] Philip Williams develops a similar argument about the Fourth Republic throughout *Crisis and Compromise: Politics in the Fourth Republic* (New York: Doubleday, 1966).

[157] For text of the Constitution, see Godechot, *Les Constitutions*, pp. 101–41. Boissy d'Anglas opened debate with a report delivered on 5 Messidor Year III (June 23, 1795) and reproduced in *Le Moniteur*, vol. 25, pp. 81–84, 90–95, 98–101, 106–10, and 113–15; discussion extended through the summer, until the adoption of the final text on 5 Fructidor Year III (August 22, 1795).

signed to serve as a deterrent to ill-considered changes: The process required at least nine years.

The Constitution did not lend either legitimacy or stability to the Republic because its procedural provisions alone could not cope with either the quantity or the quality of the conflicts first aggravated by the Terror and then released by its end. The government would therefore be forced to defend itself through extraconstitutional measures. The right acquiesced to the Constitution only because it calculated on riding public opinion back to power and a restoration. Fearing precisely this possibility, the Convention stipulated in a decree of late August 1795 that two-thirds of the new deputies would have to be chosen from among the members of the old. Nor did the Convention stop there. Elections were invalidated in September 1797 (at the expense of the right) and again in May of 1798 (at the expense of the left). As Georges Lefebvre put it:

> The Thermidorians wanted the Republic to live, but they shunned those who had founded it; they wanted it to be bourgeois, but they deprived part of the bourgeoisie of power; they wanted it to be authoritarian, but to appear liberal.[158]

The Terror set up a situation in which the Thermidorians could not escape the foundational tasks that comforted Jacobinism in its fundamental assumptions and reflexes; the context created by the Terror encouraged the continuation of revolutionary legality and thus postponed the institutional and ideological consolidation the Thermidorians sought. Beset by apparently irreducible opposition on its right, weakened by the hostility of the left, perpetuating both, and burdened by a war its own contradictions prevented it from concluding, the Directory in the end fell victim to the careful constitutional clauses devised to preclude a repetition of 1793.

Thus ideological rifts and the war continued under this supposedly centrist regime. So, too, did the politics of exclusion, unabated if less bloody (and less boastful) than in the days of the Committee of Public Safety. Previously, representative politics had not worked or had not been allowed to work. Now, its inadequacies gave rise within the political class to a widespread and articulate wave of antiparliamentarism—the beginning of a long French political tradition. François Furet and Denis Richet analyze its origins:

> An abyss lay between the Convention and public opinion. . . . Bourgeois opinion was itself divided, segmented, truncated; it no longer recognized itself in the Assembly, and yet the Assembly was a faithful reflection of the

[158] Lefebvre, *La Révolution française*, p. 458.

bourgeoisie's own divisions. Between the legal country and its delegates there was a divorce, not on the grounds of incompatibility, but because of an excessive resemblance. Public opinion wanted to be led by its representatives; it did not want to see them adopt its own weaknesses.[159]

For the first but not the last time, Frenchmen discovered that the present determination of political allegiance, national solidarity, and even immediate policy was in part a function of the way a burdensome and ambiguous past could be remembered, analyzed, and accepted—or forgotten.[160] Mona Ozouf has described the difficulties the Thermidorians encountered during their brief tenure as they selected and reselected the public holidays destined to commemorate the great moments of the recent revolution. Their purpose was clear: "Public holidays would be based . . . only on what could strengthen the bonds of national reconciliation by emphasizing the idea of a completed revolution."[161] Because the Revolution was still not "finished," however, the goal was inevitably elusive:

> The triumphs celebrated . . . by revolutionary memory presuppose a defeated party. The seeds of division are therefore present in the celebrations: they confirm an exclusion and sometimes tend even to perpetuate it, by exasperating those whom they banish.[162]

The Revolution's formal conclusion was shaped by the course it had taken, and that course was itself the product, as we have seen, of the interaction between liberal aspirations and the sociopolitical structure of the Old Regime. Sieyès, whose signal achievement it had been first to open the Revolution with *What Is the Third Estate?* and then to survive the next ten years, engineered on his own behalf the coup that inadvertently brought Napoleon to power. With the 18th Brumaire, we may declare the Revolution interrupted, although still not "finished." Napoleon had no use for either individual rights or genuine representative institutions; if the French Revolution was indeed a liberal revolution, Bonaparte's retention of civil equality hardly suffices to classify him on the side of the Revolution. Napoleon proposed a new model of authority, neither liberal nor imitative of the Old Re-

[159] François Furet and Denis Richet, *La Révolution française* (Paris: Fayard, 1973), pp. 268f.
[160] See Sa'adah, "After the Terror."
[161] Mona Ozouf, "De Thermidor à brumaire: Le Discours de la Révolution sur elle-même," *Revue historique*, no. 493 (Janvier–Mars 1970), p. 38.
[162] Ibid., p. 35.

gime, and he has no opposite number in England because the model of authority he incarnated was the privileged counterpoint to the French model of liberal politics, which England, like America, had sidestepped. Bonapartism can be seen as representing the favorite fallback position of men and women detached (ideologically and materially) from the Old Regime but disappointed with the French version of liberalism. In power and out, its rhetoric was populist, unkind to elites, scornful of "petty" politics and "divisive" parties, and nationalistic.[163]

The difficulties of finding English equivalents to either Thermidor or Brumaire should now be clear. The New Model Army had no counterpart in France, a point reinforced by the differences of purpose and outlook between Bonaparte and Cromwell. Equally unable to dispense with parliaments entirely or to control the ones it called, the New Model of the 1650s was not as powerful as it sometimes appeared. It was constrained in part by the persistence of other centers of power in society, in part by its own political past. That past distinguished the New Model not only from Bonaparte's army, but from the sans-culottes of the earlier 1790s. The sans-culottes favored direct democracy based on mutual surveillance, while their social ideas were nostalgically precapitalist. In contrast, the mobilizing planks of the old New Model platform—legal reform, religious toleration, the abolition of tithes, a broader franchise and a more equitable distribution of parliamentary seats, like the Leveller program they resembled, tended to anticipate the liberal reforms of the nineteenth century. The policies of political and moral repression and heavy taxation imposed by the Major-Generals hardly exercised the same appeal. Meanwhile, the middle group remained: present in London and powerful in the provinces. The French political class of the post-Thermidor period had to come to terms with its Terrorist past; it had long since fissured ideologically; and during the Directory it concentrated its disillusion not just on a supposedly parliamentary regime, but on parliamentary politics in general. What Napoleon then "saved" were not constitutional clauses on which no one could agree, but the authority of the state, civil equality, and national pride.

In France, the politics of exclusion aggravated and perpetuated the disagreements of the revolutionary era, making conflict all the more

---

[163] The two Empires, and the Bonapartist tradition in general, remain relatively understudied. See Louis Bergeron, *L'Episode napoléonien, 1799–1815*, 2 vols. (Paris: Le Seuil, 1972); Alain Plessis, *De la fête impériale au mur des fédérés, 1852–1871* (Paris: Le Seuil, 1973); René Rémond, *Les Droites en France*, 4th ed. (Paris: Aubier Montaigne, 1987); Theodore Zeldin, *France 1848–1945*, vol. 1 (Oxford: Oxford University Press, 1973), ch. 18.

difficult to tame and rendering far more compelling than in England or America both the continued recourse to exclusion and the need for an alternate political model that would stress a unity purportedly blind to class differences and above politics—that would, in other words, periodically adjourn, or at least mute, both the political aspirations and the political conflicts that had become the fixtures of national political life.

England in 1660 and France in 1799 were both politically exhausted countries, but the different nature of their exhaustion elicited different remedies. Napoleon tapped his compatriots' readiness to set aside conflicts that seemingly could not be resolved. Inside the logic of Jacobin liberalism, the conflicts in fact could not be resolved. Napoleon's account is self-serving, but not inaccurate:

> When a deplorable weakness and an interminable versatility display themselves in the circles of power; when, yielding alternately to the counsels of contradictory parties, and living from day to day, without a predetermined plan, without a firm step, power demonstrates its inadequacies and citizens are forced to see that the State is not governed; when, to its domestic impotence the administration adds the most serious wrong it can acquire in the eyes of a proud people—I mean foreign abasement—then a vague anxiousness spreads through society: the need to preserve society agitates its members, and looking around within itself, society seems to seek a man who could save it.[164]

Napoleon abolished freedom of expression and even-handedly repressed opposition wherever he found it. He did not, however, engage in the politics of exclusion as had the revolutionary governments of the previous decade. Uninterested in ideology, unimpressed by the dangers of power, Napoleon applied exclusion to individuals only in the last resort: he considered cooptation a far more desirable route, and he found many potential opponents among the elites more than willing to serve his regime. Many became officials in the reinforced bureaucracy through which Napoleon ensured that the country was "governed."

Behind Napoleon's refusal to accept the ideological choices the Revolution had generated as exhaustive and exclusive, there was clearly an element of opportunism: "To rule by way of a party leads eventually to dependence on that party. I won't be caught in the trap. I belong to the nation."[165] As the last sentence indicates, however, Napoleon also proposed a distinctive way of understanding the na-

---

[164] Napoleon, *Vues politiques*, pp. 53f.
[165] Ibid., p. 69.

tional community. Robespierre would have found it incomprehensible, even though Jacobin nationalism invited it and even though it built on the Jacobin allergy to institutionalized conflict. In 1809, Napoleon wrote:

> I do not separate myself from my predecessors and . . . from Clovis through the Committee of Public Safety, I identify with all, and . . . the ill that is gaily spoken of governments which came before my own, I take as uttered with the intention of offending me.[166]

Some 140 years later, Charles de Gaulle, who did not abandon liberal freedoms or destroy representative institutions, marched down the Champs-Elysées of liberated Paris and left us this account:

> With each step that I take on the most illustrious artery in the world, it seems to me that past glories combine with the glory of today. Under the Arc, in our honor, the flame leaps joyfully. This avenue, down which the triumphant army paraded twenty-five years ago, seems radiant before us. On his pedestal, Clemenceau, whom I salute as I pass, seems ready to bound to our side. The chestnut trees of the Champs-Elysées, of which the imprisoned Aiglon dreamed and which witnessed, through so many ages, the display of French grace and prestige, offer viewing-posts to thousands of spectators. The Tuileries, which provided the setting for the majesty of the State under two Emperors and two monarchies, the Concorde and the Carrousel which watched the wild expressions of revolutionary enthusiasm and the reviews of victorious regiments; the streets and bridges named for battles won; on the other bank of the Seine, the Invalides, its dome sparkling still with the splendor of the Sun-King, the tomb of Turenne, of Napoleon, of Foch. . . . And there, in their turn: the Louvre, where the succession of kings succeeded in constructing France; in their place the statues of Joan of Arc and Henry IV; the palace of Saint Louis, whose feast-day happened to be yesterday; Notre-Dame, the prayer of Paris, and the Cité, its cradle. . . .[167]

The farther away the world of the Revolution seemed politically and socially, the easier it became in France to complete the Jacobin model of politics with elements stolen from its Bonapartist *frère ennemi*, and to have both limited conflict and limited community. For a long time, however, important aspects of the revolutionary world lingered, sustained in large part by the patterns of politics that had crystallized during the Revolution. From Tocqueville to Mounier, liberal

---

[166] Ibid., p. 70.
[167] Charles de Gaulle, *Mémoires de guerre*, vol. 2: *L'Unité, 1942–1944* (Paris: Plon, 1956), p. 313.

critics dissatisfied with both Jacobin liberalism and its Bonapartist counterpoint would warn of the effects the politics of exclusion would have on the country's human resources. When Mounier wrote of the Radical Republic that "feudalism has more to offer," he was advocating a different sort of Republic, not the return to feudalism that Vichy would soon attempt, ridiculously and tragically.

As we turn in the Conclusion to a brief consideration of why the patterns Mounier deplored persisted, it is perhaps well to bear in mind Koestler's final verdict on a style of life he too found oppressive: the suspicious, defensive "little man," Koestler reminds us, "lived in a profound harmony with himself, and enjoyed his food, wine, fishing, and sex . . . more than people in any other human community that I had seen."

IV

Conclusion: Liberal Politics over Time

IN SEVENTEENTH-CENTURY ENGLAND and in eighteenth-century America and France, demands for liberal political institutions and practices—limited government, the protection of individual rights, representative politics—pressed in on political systems that had been fashioned by different sets of expectations. In each case, the confrontation between the new demands and existing political arrangements led to revolution. The revolutions produced a new distribution of power. The new distribution was expressed in new institutional arrangements, new patterns of behavior and expectation, and new ways of justifying authority and obligation. In England and America, revolutionary settlements both consecrated the victory of liberal politics and led to political stability. In France, the revolutionary process privileged a form of liberal politics that precluded a similarly definitive revolutionary settlement and instead set up a pattern of political instability. In the analysis of each case presented in the preceding chapters, we focused on the different patterns of revolutionary competition that prevailed and on the nature and logic of the two different types of liberal politics that developed. What, if anything, can the arguments developed tell us about political development beyond the revolutionary period or outside our small set of countries?

The origins of liberal politics are usually discussed in terms of the triumph of either a social class or a set of ideas. The stability or instability of the resulting regime is then attributed to the balance of power among social groups or to the character of the dominant political culture. Until recently, the categories and assumptions of Marxist analysis dominated twentieth-century French scholarship on the Revolution. For many years, in France and beyond her borders, they also shaped the terms in which the debate over the origins and nature of liberal institutions was cast.[1] In analyzing the causes, course, and outcomes of revolution in England, America, and France, I have adopted a different approach. I hope that this ap-

---

[1] By way of example, see C. B. Macpherson, *The Political Theory of Possessive Individualism* (Oxford: Oxford University Press, 1962), around which a long and lively debate arose.

proach, by borrowing from both strategies evoked above, has produced a convincing argument about the revolutionary periods. I also hope it provides a useful window on developments that occurred later or elsewhere. Within the limits explained in the Introduction, I have emphasized the causal importance of ideology. While it is often hard to explain persuasively how ideas are transmuted into a political culture and thus become politically operative, an ideology is espoused by identifiable groups and is by definition tied to political action. Initially formulated around political ideals and patterns of political understanding, under a favorable distribution of power it becomes embedded in patterns of political interaction and institutional development. In using ideology to get at the logic of revolutionary events and outcomes, I have tried to offer an account that shows where the political cultures associated with each country—and too often invoked as though they were the result of some eternal "national character"—came from and why they "worked" for the actors.

In an earlier chapter, I suggested that historically, liberal revolutions have occurred when a broadly based group in civil society attained independent moral and material power and then employed that power to limit permanently the power of the state. Non-Marxist as well as Marxist scholars usually identify the "broadly based group" as the bourgeoisie, or the middle class. Marxists and non-Marxists alike tend to assume that the bourgeoisie is a product of economic development and is defined by its economic role. Gordon Craig cites the demographic and political impact of the Thirty Years War and the Treaty of Westphalia in his effort to account for the failure of liberalism in Germany two and three centuries later,[2] but Ralf Dahrendorf is more typical when he argues for a different chronology:

> The crossroads of decision for the development of liberalism may . . . be found in the age of industrialization. It is only at this point that a society decides which political path it is going to take; a nation, which social path it will follow.[3]

Dahrendorf accepts the categories of Marxist interpretation while rejecting Marxist determinism; he argues that Germany "developed into an industrial, but not into a capitalist society,"[4] and that "there emerged a bourgeoisie that was not really a bourgeoisie."[5]

[2] See Gordon Craig, *The Germans* (New York: G. P. Putnam's Sons, 1982), chap. 1.
[3] Ralf Dahrendorf, *Society and Democracy in Germany* (Garden City, N. J.: Doubleday, 1967), p. 32.
[4] Ibid., p. 41.
[5] Ibid., p. 49.

Just as the economy of Imperial Germany became industrial but not capitalist, the German society of the time remained quasi-feudal. Industrialization in Germany failed to produce a self-confident bourgeoisie with its own political aspirations. In so far as a bourgeoisie emerged at all, it remained relatively small and, what is more, unsure of itself and dependent in its social and political standards. As a result, German society lacked the stratum that in England and America, and to a lesser extent even in France, had been the moving force of a development in the direction of greater modernity and liberalism.[6]

Dahrendorf states what the historical record confirms in Marx's despite: that only in England and America, and "to a lesser extent even in France," was industrialization accompanied by the development of a "real" bourgeoisie. That observation, combined with the developmental experience of communist countries, would seem to suggest that the group whose self-assertion was so crucial to liberalism's success was *not* a product of economic development, nor should it be seen as defined primarily by its economic role; it would also seem to suggest that the "crossroads of decision for the development of liberalism" may not lie in the "age of industrialization."[7] In the first two chapters of this book, I argued that the prerevolutionary state played a crucial role in determining the structure of revolutionary opportunity, and was thus instrumental in shaping, well before capitalism reached adolescence (let alone maturity), the character of the "middle class." The group elaborating and sustaining liberal demands turned out in each country to be socially heterogeneous and most relevantly defined by its relationship to the state, not to the means of production. In prerevolutionary England and America, political authority was both decentralized and divorced from the major tasks of social regulation. In each country, the revolution consolidated but did not have to create the autonomous political world essential to liberalism. The revolutionaries were already possessed of an institutional power base, and with the exercise of power had come a coherent and widely disseminated set of expectations concerning its use. The men who challenged the legitimacy of the prerevolutionary state could therefore gamble for power and win without ever creating a power vacuum. Both the type of revolutionary competition and the nature of the revolutionary settlement pointed toward the politics of transac-

[6] Ibid., appears above previous quote.

[7] The most persuasive argument linking later political outcomes to patterns of social interaction during the early phases of industrialization remains Barrington Moore's *Social Origins of Dictatorship and Democracy: Lord and Peasant in the Making of the Modern World* (Boston: Beacon Press, 1966).

tion. In France, the policies of the Old Regime generated a different structure of revolutionary opportunity and a correspondingly different bourgeoisie, denigrated by its contemporaries for its dependent qualities, less "real" than its English or American counterparts, but more "real" than the class produced by the fragmented political world of the German states.

If the structure of revolutionary opportunity was determined by the sociopolitical character of the old regime, the structure of post-revolutionary political opportunity was shaped by the ideas and attitudes with which liberalism's advocates were stamped during the revolutionary years, and by a distribution of power that made those ideas and attitudes count. In the initial stages of modern political development, state and society—material conditions as Montesquieu or Tocqueville, rather than Marx, might have understood them—played the major causal role; after the revolution broadened the scope of participation, the fears, aspirations, and expectations of an increasingly wide segment of the population shaped the contours of both politics and society.

Parliamentary democracy, Bagehot once wrote, requires nerve.[8] He might more accurately have asserted that it requires trust. Where trust—either in the self-restraint of rule-obeying and/or duty-conscious individuals and groups, or in the automatic restraining power of institutional mechanisms and competitive interactions—exists, conflict can take place within the context of community. Men and women can pursue and use power without being constantly suspected of abusing it. Liberalism can then team up with political stability. Where trust seems a bad bet, the liberal preoccupation with limiting power will lead instead to political instability. Englishmen and Americans were not inherently more inclined to take risks or to trust one another than were the French; rather, the process by which they arrived at liberalism, and the kind of liberalism that ensued, made a certain kind of nerve seem less risky in England and America than it did in France.

In England, the "century of revolution" left a narrow segment of society in a highly advantageous political and economic position. The eighteenth century is not a particularly edifying period in English his-

[8] "Parliamentary Government is not a thing which always succeeds in the world; on the contrary, the lesson of experience is that it often fails, and seldom answers, and this is because the necessary combination of elements is rare and complex. First, Parliamentary Government requires that a nation should have the nerve to endure incessant discussion and frequent change of rulers." Cited by Fritz Stern in *The Failure of Illiberalism: Essays on the Political Culture of Modern Germany* (Chicago: University of Chicago Press, 1971), p. xv.

tory. It was a century of oligarchic rule and rampant political corruption, and it tolerated a still impressive amount of legal, illegal, and extralegal violence. Yet however unappealing, the eighteenth century contributed crucially to the consolidation of the politics of transaction, and it did so in ways that reveal the long-term importance of the particular ideology that allowed revolutionary groups to impose their claims in the seventeenth century. The eighteenth century reassured the ruling elites of their hold on power, while at the same time reinforcing their attachment to and dependence upon an ideology that celebrated not power, with its lonely, tragic heroes and its harsh necessities, but liberty: the restraint of power, the inviolability of the individual, and the rule of law. British elites had inherited both the power and the ideology from the prior century of revolution, and by the nineteenth century, the interdependence of the two was widely recognized within the political class.[9] The Reform Bill of 1831 did not pass because of the eloquence of Lord Macaulay's addresses; it passed because (as Macaulay understood) the power of the elites both allowed and depended on it and (as Earl Grey repeatedly reminded his king) their ideology left them little choice.[10] Macaulay and Grey were

[9] This point is persuasively argued by E. P. Thompson in *Whigs and Hunters: The Origins of the Black Act* (New York: Pantheon Books, 1975): "Turn where you will, the rhetoric of eighteenth-century England is saturated with the notion of law. Royal absolutism was placed behind a high hedge of law; landed estates were tied together with entails and marriage settlements made up of elaborate tissues of law; authority and property punctuated their power by regular 'examples' made upon the public gallows. More than this, immense efforts were made . . . to project the image of a ruling class which was itself subject to the rule of law, and whose legitimacy rested upon the equity and universality of those legal forms. And the rulers were, in serious senses, whether willingly or unwillingly, the prisoners of their own rhetoric; they played the games of power according to rules which suited them, but they could not break those rules or the whole game would be thrown away. And, finally, so far from the ruled shrugging off this rhetoric as a hypocrisy, some part of it at least was taken over as part of the rhetoric of the plebeian crowd, of the 'free-born Englishman' with his inviolable privacy, his *habeas corpus*, his equality before the law. If this rhetoric was a mask, it was a mask which John Wilkes was to borrow, at the head of ten thousand masked supporters.

". . . In the sixteenth and seventeenth centuries the law had been less an instrument of class power than a central arena of conflict. In the course of conflict the law itself had been changed; inherited by the eighteenth-century gentry, this changed law was, literally, central to their whole purchase upon power and upon the means of life. . . . But it was inherent in the very nature of the medium which they had selected for their own self-defence that it could not be reserved for the exclusive use only of their own class. The law, in its forms and traditions, entailed principles of equity and universality which, perforce, had to be extended to all sorts and degrees of men" (pp. 263f.).

[10] See Charles, [2nd] Earl Grey, *The Reform Act, 1832: The Correspondence of the late Earl Grey with H.M. King William IV and with Sir Herbert Taylor, from Nov. 1830 to June 1832*, 2 vols., ed. Henry, Earl Grey (London: J. Murray, 1867).

as confident that the demands of the middle classes enfranchised by the Reform Bill could be accommodated within the system as they were certain that the continued exclusion of those classes would simply breed a far more dangerous form of political competition. Locked out of legitimate politics, the new groups would inevitably seek allies among their social inferiors, who would then be politicized on terms hostile to the institutions and classes Macaulay and Grey sought to defend. The two men could successfully appeal to their colleagues to open up the political system because, as Macaulay put it, the "heart of England" was still "sound"; the "old feelings and old associations"[11] cherished by those already within the system (whatever disagreements might otherwise divide them) were also shared by those seeking entrance. The newcomers entered the system as reinforcements rather than as rebels. England ended up a country of political subcultures, but not a country divided amongst political countercultures.

Thus the power of the English ruling classes, combined with and guided by the ideology that those classes had used to conquer power, created a virtuous circle as egalitarian demands bore down on the political system. Potential participants framed their claims in the universal terms that liberalism provided. Those standing guard at the doors of the political class stood back, obviating the need for a new and hostile ideology. The new participants added new items to the political agenda and built institutions suited to the new tasks. Thus strengthened, the system could accommodate still more former outsiders, who in turn contributed to the system's continued resilience. It was inevitable that this method of defending power would ultimately transform the way it was employed, and then the manner in which it would be defended, but as England journeyed from the night-watchman state to the welfare state, the politics of transaction was never seriously jeopardized.

In the United States, the impact of the liberal victory was modified by circumstances unique to America: the decentralized character of power in a still-expanding state, the relative equality of condition and opportunity enjoyed by white Americans, and the existence of slavery. The triumph of revolutionary principles made slavery an increasingly untenable anomaly; slavery, in turn, provides the most flagrant example of an issue that the politics of transaction was incompetent to solve—as not only the Civil War, but the failure of Reconstruction demonstrated. Yet liberalism survived the prolonged and bitter debate over slavery, the bloodletting of 1861–1865, and

[11] Thomas Babington Macaulay, *Selected Writings*, ed. John Clive and Thomas Pinney (Chicago: University of Chicago Press, 1972), p. 180.

the rampant racial oppression that the postbellum South eventually wrote into its laws.[12] Even more threatening to liberal politics than the secession of the Confederate states would have been the formation of an authoritarian coalition uniting southern planters and northern industrialists; the established habits (and benefits) of liberal politics, however, made the northerners unwilling partners. With the war over and slavery officially abolished, the politics of transaction returned—and alongside it, the violence of which we spoke in the Introduction continued, decentralized, unavowed, and generally unhindered.

In France, the Revolution did not lead to the politics of transaction because the Old Regime had not permitted the development of a "real" middle class; after the Revolution, a "real" middle class was a long time in developing because its substitute had armed itself with a coherent set of rival values, now transmitted through established behavioral and institutional patterns and powerful enough to deflect whatever domestic influences might have moved it in the direction of the Anglo-American model. The same "nerve" that was lacking in the political world was also lacking in the economic realm; the risk-averse, slightly paranoid Radical denounced by Mounier also preferred security to profit in the economic side of life—a trait which prompted further criticism from other quarters:

> The concept of free enterprise as developed in the England of the nineteenth century and transplanted to the United States, with its postulate of a competitive struggle for markets and drastic penalties for failure, and with its emphasis on earning more and more through producing more and more for less and less, has never really been accepted in France. Instead France . . . has continued to cherish the precapitalist ideology that underlay the guild organization of the pre-Revolutionary period. . . .
>
> The result . . . has been to create an environment hostile to the development of a capitalistic business structure. But more important for our present purpose, it has formed to a significant degree the mind of the businessman himself, who has never fully accepted the principles of risk and competition that are at the root of a free-enterprise system as we understand it.[13]

[12] On the gradual imposition of legal segregation, see C. Vann Woodward, *The Strange Career of Jim Crow*, 2d rev. ed. (Oxford: Oxford University Press, 1955, 1966).

[13] David Landes, "French Business and the Businessman: A Social and Cultural Analysis," in Edward Mead Earle, ed., *Modern France: Problems of the Third and Fourth Republics* (Princeton: Princeton University Press, 1951), p. 348. For futher discussion of prevalent values, see Zeldin, *France, 1848–1945*, vol. I, part I, particularly chap. 7; Jesse Pitts, "Continuity and Change in Bourgeois France," in Stanley Hoffmann et al., *In Search of France* (Cambridge, Mass.: Harvard University Press, 1963), particularly

In France, there were no commonly recognized "old feelings and old associations" to provide a secure base from which reformers could safely venture. By 1799, the Revolution had distributed bitter memories all around, but just as no faction had clearly won, no faction had clearly and completely lost. The elites emerged profoundly fragmented from the years of revolutionary strife and Napoleonic muzzling to renew their frustrating search for a formula that would guarantee constitutional government and representative institutions. Their fragmentation perpetuated the politics of exclusion through its impact on the relationship between power and law and on the way political participation was opened up. The instrumental understanding of constitutional legality inherited from the "unfinished" Revolution, compounded by each group's realistic appraisal of its own weakness in a situation of potentially unlimited competition, left the elites less constrained than their English or American counterparts in their use of political power and made political solutions based on fair play and open compromise a very poor bet. The Church complicated matters by reaffirming at regular intervals throughout most of the nineteenth century its unmitigated hostility to both liberal political principles and the new society slowly taking shape in Europe. The political class looked outside its own ranks for support, but its fragmentation meant that new political participants would be socialized as new combatants in the country's political wars. Thus used, the working class was never an equal beneficiary of the coalitions it joined, and it eventually sought satisfaction in its own ideology and organizations.

Commenting on pervasive patterns of French collective behavior, Michel Crozier has written:

> The development of cooperative forms of social action depends in large part on the attitude individuals adopt with regard to participation. . . .
> . . . A bureaucratic system of organization . . . offers individuals a felicitous mixture of independence and security. The modern observer tends to see only the dysfunctional aspect of a bureaucratic system. He is struck by the high price exacted both from those within the organization and from those who rely on it. But if one takes into account a realistic assessment both of the values and demands of the members of the organization and

pp. 235–62; Edmond Goblot, *La Barrière et le niveau* (1925; reprint, Paris: Presses universitaires de France, 1967); and, of course, Crozier, *Le Phénomène bureaucratique* (Paris: Le Seuil, 1963), chap. 7 to the end of the book.

of the necessary limits of social action, the arrangement is not so bad for the participants.[14]

Political regimes, especially those based on consent, tend to reflect the values of their citizens. Tocqueville, who often emphasized the causal importance of what he called mores, examined French political development before the quarrel between Marxists and non-Marxixts relegated the role of the state to the background and transformed the attribution of causal primacy to either ideas or economic structures from an empirical judgment into an exclusive and philosophical decision. He also wrote before academic specialization made it possible for arguments about the past to disregard relevant evidence from the present. Observing his country as both citizen and scholar, Tocqueville summarized the circular causal chain that in his opinion had all but killed freedom's chances in France:

> The division of classes was the crime of the late monarchy, before becoming its excuse; for when all those who compose the rich and enlightened part of the nation can no longer act in concert or help each other in public life, self-government is impossible, and a master must take charge.[15]

Tocqueville's assessment of the Revolution's impact is substantively different and rather more pessimistic than the one presented in this book. Tocqueville argued that the Revolution had only accelerated the egalitarian and centralizing trends that the Old Regime had initiated. Growing equality destroyed the solidarities inherent to aristocratic society, while centralization eliminated intermediary bodies by depriving them of their powers and functions. Tocqueville foresaw a society progressively more atomized and consequently increasingly prone to bureaucratic and autocratic rule.

Such a society would have been ripe for fascism in the 1930s; yet France avoided that disaster. Tocqueville's conception of freedom was based on positive moral aspiration; he underestimated the strength of a conception of freedom based on fear. In extending his model of French organizational behavior to other areas of French collective life, Michel Crozier identified the functional and therefore stabilizing aspects of a form of social organization and interaction that Tocqueville could only deplore.[16] In politics as in other spheres, Crozier argues, the prevalent organizational pattern grants the

[14] Michel Crozier, *Le Phénomène bureaucratique*, pp. 251, 253, my translation. Cf. author's translation, *The Bureaucratic Phenomenon* (Chicago: Chicago University Press, 1964), pp. 204, 206.

[15] Alexis de Tocqueville, *L'Ancien régime et la Révolution* (1856; reprint, Paris: Gallimard, 1967), Book I, chap. 10, p. 189.

[16] For Crozier's model, see in particular *Le Phénomène bureaucratique*, chap. 7–end.

French what they want most: independence, security, and a certain form of equality—the primary benefits of liberalism, but without the dynamism and insecurity that liberalism usually implies. Stanley Hoffmann describes the fit between values and institutions, and notes the limited loyalty political institutions commanded:

Routine authority, despite its tendency toward paralysis, nevertheless functioned, and the two parliamentary Republics [the Third and the Fourth] showed a remarkable aptitude for self-preservation. The colorful deadlock of parliaments and cabinets should make us forget neither the bureaucracy, grinding out impersonal rules at a distance from the public and also taking part in the game of parallel relations, nor the consensus on which the Republics rested. Among social groups and political forces, beneath all the ideological differences about the ideal society and the best regime, there was a broad consensus favoring a limited state, congruent with the prevailing style of authority; *in most circumstances*, a career bureaucracy together with a parliamentary system more adept at checking than at moving that bureaucracy corresponded exactly to what was desired. Legitimacy was conditional; to most social or political groups and forces the regime was acceptable as long as its activities left intact their sphere of independence while settling conflicts to their satisfaction.[17]

In another context, a less detached Hoffmann described the result of France's conditional liberalism as "catastrophic" in every way, regardless of how well it accommodated—and indeed in part because it perpetuated—the conservative values of those for whom it had been nothing but "a means of protecting their status and their advantages"[18]:

The result was catastrophic. Catastrophic for the republican state: being in no way reformist, it was condemned on the one hand to passivity where positive action in the social and economic spheres would have been desirable, and, on the other hand, to ideological excesses. All this only confirmed social divisions. . . .

Catastrophic too for the citizens: they were encouraged to abdicate and to despise elected officials who, far from representing the "rational and moral will" of the people, represent the appetites of the voters. . . .

Finally, the result was catastrophic for the liberal philosophy of power itself: the social conservatism of the regime also conserved the enemies of liberal philosophy, those on the left and those on the right. Liberalism's partisans could only rally their troops around negative slogans of "repub-

[17] Stanley Hoffmann, *Decline or Renewal? France since the 1930's* (New York: Viking Press, 1974), p. 75.

[18] Stanley Hoffmann, *Le Mouvement Poujade* (Paris: Armand Colin, 1956), p. 382.

lican defense." They did not perceive in the representative system a means of reconciling opposing interests or a method of peaceful social integration.[19]

The patterns set up by the politics of exclusion and analyzed in their more contemporary manifestations by Crozier and Hoffmann seem decreasingly descriptive of France in the late twentieth century.[20] The models of liberal politics suggested here still stand as models, but the cases that fit the models have changed or may change. To understand why, we would have to consider for the current period the mix of variables we examined when we sought to recover the structure of revolutionary opportunity and the differential impact of transnational trends and ideas. If the Fifth Republic, whose founder was not especially fond of either parliaments or parties (at least not outside of their English setting), proves more skilled than its predecessors at organizing conflict without compromising community, it will be primarily because of both the postwar social transformation that has changed the face of Europe, and the behavioral incentives created—in the midst of crisis—by the new institutions de Gaulle imposed on the French in 1958. But it will also be because de Gaulle incessantly lectured his compatriots about what they had in common and what they might accomplish together. In 1940, Marc Bloch wrote:

> There are two kinds of Frenchmen who will never understand French history: those who feel no thrill at the memory of the *sacre* of Reims and those who can read without emotion the description of the *fête de la Fédération*.[21]

History is not so insistently taught as it once was. But insofar as the French are still learning their own history, the reading of French history that Bloch desired seems infinitely more plausible toward the end of the twentieth century than at any time since the first Fédérés gathered in Paris in the summer of 1790. De Gaulle's unprecedented attempt to reunite Frenchmen without silencing them may eventually stand out as the first politically visible phase of a transition from the politics of exclusion to the politics of transaction. That was never de Gaulle's primary goal; but then it was not the primary goal of English and American revolutionaries, either.

[19] Ibid., p. 386.
[20] Similarly, it is hard to describe Mrs. Thatcher's England as a country characterized by the politics of transaction.
[21] Marc Bloch, *L'Etrange défaite* (Paris: Armand Colin, 1957), p. 210.

Bibliography

THE THREE REVOLUTIONS analyzed in the preceding pages have inspired a massive literature, as have many of the theoretical topics considered. The bibliography provided here includes all works cited in the text. Otherwise, it is intended to be useful rather than exhaustive.

Research Aids (France)

Caron, Pierre. *Manuel pratique pour l'étude de la Révolution française*. Paris: A. and J. Picard, 1947.
Godechot, Jacques. *Les Révolutions (1770–1799)*. 3d ed. Paris: Presses universitaires de France, 1970.
Mandrou, Robert. *La France aux XVIIe et XVIIIe siècles*. Paris: Presses universitaires de France, 1974.
Martin, André, and Gérard Walter. *Catalogue de l'histoire de la Révolution française*. 5 vols. Paris: Bibliothèque nationale, 1936–1955.
Tourneux, Maurice. *Bibliographie de l'histoire de Paris pendant la Révolution française*. 5 vols. Paris: Imprimerie nationale, 1890–1913.
Tuetey, Alexandre. *Répertoire général des sources manuscrites de l'histoire de Paris pendant la Révolution française*. 11 vols. Paris: Imprimerie nationale, 1890–1914.

Primary Sources

Periodicals from the French Revolution

L'ami du peuple.
La Chronique de Paris.
La Gazette nationale ou le Moniteur universel, and reprinted edition: *Réimpression de l'Ancien Moniteur, seule histoire authentique et inaltérée de la Révolution française depuis la réunion des Etats généraux jusqu'au Consulat, mai 1789–novembre 1799*. 30 vols. Paris: Au Bureau Central, 1863–1870.
Journal du Club des Cordeliers.
Journal des débats et des décrets.
Journal des débats de la société des amis de la Constitution.
Journal de la Société de 1789.
Le Patriote français.
Le Père Duchesne.
Les Révolutions de Paris et de Brabant.
Le Vieux Cordelier. Ed. Albert Mathiez and Henri Calvet. Paris: Armand Colin, 1936.

Other Primary Sources

Alain [Emile Chartier]. *Propos sur les pouvoirs: Eléments d'éthique politique.* Paris: Gallimard, 1985.

Archives parlementaires de 1787 à 1860. 1st Series (1787–1799), vols. I–XCIII. Paris: Dupont, CNRS, 1867–1982.

Aulard, Francois, comp. *Paris pendant le Réaction thermidorienne et sous le Directoire. Recueil de documents pour l'histoire de l'esprit public à Paris.* 5 vols. Paris: L. Cerf, 1898–1902.

————, comp. *La Société des Jacobins. Recueil de documents pour l'histoire du Club des Jacobins de Paris.* 6 vols. Paris: Librairie Jouaust, Librairie Noblet, Maison Quantin, 1889–1897.

————, comp. *Recueil des Actes du comité de salut public, avec la correspondance officielle des représentants en mission et le registre du Conseil exécutif provisoire.* 27 vols. Paris: Imprimerie nationale, 1889–1933.

Baczko, Bronislaw, comp. *Une éducation pour la démocratie: Textes et projets de l'époque révolutionnaire.* Paris: Garnier Frères, 1982.

Bailyn, Bernard, ed. *Pamphlets of the American Revolution.* Cambridge, Mass.: Harvard University Press, 1965.

Barnave, Antoine. *Oeuvres de Barnave.* 4 vols. Ed. H. Bérenger de la Drome. Paris: Jules Chapelle et Builler, 1843.

Beecher, Lyman. *A Plea for the West.* 2d ed. Cincinnati: Truman and Smith, 1835.

Bertaud, Jean-Paul, comp. *Valmy: La Démocratie en armes.* Paris: Julliard, 1970.

Brasillach, Robert. *Notre avant-guerre.* Paris, 1942.

Buchez, P.-J.-B., and P.-C. Roux, comp. *Histoire parlementaire de la Révolution française.* 40 vols. Paris: Paulin, 1834–1838.

Burke, Edmund. *Reflections on the Revolution in France.* 1790; reprint, Harmondsworth, Middlesex: Penguin Books, 1969.

Clarendon, Edward Hyde, Earl of. *Selections from "The History of the Rebellion" and "The Life by Himself."* Ed. Gertrude Huehns. Oxford: Oxford University Press, 1978.

Cobbett, W., and T. B. Howell, eds. *A Complete Collection of State Trials,* vols. III, IV. London, 1809–1826.

Cromwell, Oliver. *The Writings and Speeches of Oliver Cromwell.* Ed. Wilbur C. Abbott. 4 vols. Cambridge, Mass.: Harvard University Press, 1937–1947.

Dahl, Robert. *Polyarchy: Participation and Opposition.* New Haven: Yale University Press, 1971.

Danton, Georges-Jacques. *Discours de Danton.* Ed. André Fribourg. Paris: Société de l'histoire de la Révolution française, 1910.

Durkheim, Emile. *L'Education morale.* Paris: Presses universitaires de France, 1974.

Filmer, Robert. *Patriarcha and Other Political Works of Sir Robert Filmer.* Ed. Peter Laslett. Oxford: Basil Blackwell, 1949.

Flammermont, Jules, ed. *Remontrances du Parlement de Paris au XVIIe siècle,* vol. 2 (1755–1768). Paris: Imprimerie Nationale, 1895.

Godechot, Jacques, comp. *Les Constitutions de la France depuis 1789*. Paris: Garnier-Flammarion, 1970.

Goubert, Pierre, and Michel Denis, comp. *1789: Les Français ont la parole: Cahiers de doléances des Etats généraux*. Paris: Julliard, 1964.

Grey [Charles Grey], 2d Earl. *The Reform Act, 1832: The Correspondence of the late Earl Grey with His Majesty William IV and with Sir Herbert Taylor, from Nov. 1830 to June 1832*. Ed. Henry, Earl Grey. 2 vols. London: J. Murray, 1867.

Guyot, Pierre. *Répertoire universel et raisonné de jurisprudence civile, criminelle, canonique et bénéficiale*, vol. 36. Paris: J. D. Dorez, 1775.

Hamilton, Alexander, et al. *The Federalist*. New York: Random House, n.d.

Handlin, Oscar and Mary, eds. *The Popular Sources of Political Authority: Documents on the Massachusetts Constitution of 1780*. Cambridge, Mass.: Harvard University Press, 1966.

Harrington, James. *The Political Writings of James Harrington*. Ed. Charles Blitzer. New York: The Liberal Arts Press, 1955.

Hobbes, Thomas. *Leviathan*. Ed. C. B. Macpherson. 1651; reprint, Harmondsworth, Middlesex, England: Penguin Books, 1968.

Jacobson, David L., ed. *The English Libertarian Heritage: From the Writings of John Trenchard and Thomas Gordon in "The Independent Whig" and "Cato's Letters."* New York: Bobbs-Merrill, 1965.

Jensen, Merrill, ed. *Tracts of the American Revolution, 1763–1776*. New York: Bobbs-Merrill, 1967.

Keayne, Robert. *The Apologia of Robert Keayne: The Self-Portrait of a Puritan Merchant*. Ed. Bernard Bailyn. New York: Harper and Row, 1965.

Kenyon, J. P., ed. *The Stuart Constitution, 1603–1688: Documents and Commentary*. Cambridge: Cambridge University Press, 1966.

Lepaige, Louis-Adrien. *Lettres historiques, sur le Parlement, sur le droit des pairs, et sur les loix fondamentales du Royaume*. 2 parts. Amsterdam: n.p., 1753–54.

Locke, John. *A Letter Concerning Toleration*. 1689; reprint, Indianapolis: Bobbs-Merrill, 1955, 1950.

―――. *An Essay Concerning Human Understanding*. 2 vols. 1690; reprint, New York: Dover Publications, 1959.

―――. *Two Treatises of Government*. Introd. Peter Laslett. Revised ed. Cambridge: Cambridge University Press, 1960.

Macaulay, Thomas Babington. *Selected Writings*. Ed. John Clive and Thomas Pinney. Chicago: University of Chicago Press, 1972.

Mavidal, M. J., and M. E. Laurent, comps. *Archives parlementaires de 1787 à 1860. Recueil complet des débats législatifs et politiques des chambres françaises, Première série (1787 à 1799)*, vol. I. 2d ed. Paris: Paul Dupont, 1879.

Merleau-Ponty, Maurice. *Humanisme et Terreur: Essai sur le problème communiste*. 1947; reprint, Paris: Gallimard, 1980.

Mill, John Stuart. *Considerations on Representative Government*. 1861; reprint, New York: Bobbs-Merrill, 1958.

―――. *The Philosophy of John Stuart Mill*. Ed. Marshall Cohen. New York: Modern Library, 1961.

Mirabeau, Honoré-Gabriel de. *Discours*. Introd. and ed. François Furet. Paris: Gallimard, 1973.

———. *Mirabeau entre le roi et la Révolution: Notes à la cour suivies de Discours*. Ed. Guy Chaussinand-Nogaret. Paris: Hachette, 1986.

Montesquieu, Charles Secondat de. *Oeuvres complètes*. Paris: Le Seuil, 1964.

Mounier, Emmanuel. *Oeuvres de Mounier*, vol. 4. Paris: Le Seuil, 1961.

Napoleon. *Vues politiques*. Americ = Edit., 1939.

Quatre Procès de trahison. Paris: Les Editions de Paris, 1947.

Rawls, John. *A Theory of Justice*. Cambridge, Mass.: Harvard University Press, 1971.

Robespierre, Maximilien. *Oeuvres de Maximilien Robespierre*. 10 vols. Paris: Presses universitaires de France, and other publishers, 1912–1967.

Rousseau, Jean-Jacques. *Oeuvres complètes*. 3 vols. Paris: Le Seuil, 1967–1971.

Saint-Just, Louis Antoine de. *Oeuvres choisies, discours, rapports, institutions républicaines, proclamations, lettres*. Ed. Jean Gratien. Paris: Gallimard, 1968.

———. *Oeuvres complètes*. Paris: Ed. Gérard Lebovici, 1984.

Sandel, Michael. *Liberalism and the Limits of Justice*. Cambridge: Cambridge University Press, 1982.

Sieyès, Emmanuel. *Qu'est-ce que le Tiers etat?* Introd. and ed. Roberto Zapperi. 1789; reprint, Geneva: Librairie Droz, 1970.

———. *Ecrits politiques*. Ed. Roberto Zapperi. Paris: Editions des Archives contemporaines, 1985.

Tanner, J. R., ed. *Constitutional Documents of the Reign of James I*. Cambridge: Cambridge University Press, 1931.

Tocqueville, Alexis de. *Oeuvres complètes*. Ed. J. P. Mayer. 12 vols. Paris: Gallimard, 1961–1964.

Verucci, Guido, comp. *L'Avenir, 1830–1831*. Rome: Edizioni di Storia e Letteratura, 1967.

Walzer, Michael L., introd. *Regicide and Revolution: Speeches at the Trial of Louis XVI*. Cambridge: Cambridge University Press, 1974.

Woodhouse, A. S. P., comp. *Puritanism and Liberty*. Chicago: University of Chicago Press, 1951.

Secondary Sources

Adam, Antoine. *Du Mysticisme à la révolte: Les jansénistes du XVIIe siècle*. Paris: Fayard, 1968.

Althusser, Louis. *Montesquieu: La politique et l'histoire*. Paris: Presses universitaires de France, 1974.

Appleby, Joyce. *Economic Thought and Ideology in Seventeenth Century England*. Princeton: Princeton University Press, 1978.

———. "The Social Origins of American Revolutionary Ideology." *Journal of American History* 64 (1978): 935–58.

———. *Capitalism and a New Social Order: The Republican Vision of the 1790's*. New York: New York University Press, 1984.

Arendt, Hannah. *On Revolution*. New York: Viking, 1963, 1965.

————. *Crises of the Republic*. New York: Harcourt Brace Jovanovich, 1969, 1970, 1971, 1972.

————. *The Origins of Totalitarianism*. New ed. New York: Harcourt Brace Jovanovich, 1973.

Ashcraft, Richard. *Revolutionary Politics and Locke's "Two Treatises of Government."* Princeton: Princeton University Press, 1986.

Aulard, François. *L'Eloquence parlementaire pendant la Révolution française: Les Orateurs de la Législative et de la Convention*. 2 vols. Paris: Hachette, 1885–1886.

Baczko, Bronislaw. *Comment sortir de la Terreur: Thermidor et la Révolution*. Paris: Gallimard, 1989.

Bailyn, Bernard. *The Ideological Origins of the American Revolution*. Cambridge, Mass.: Harvard University Press, 1967.

————. *The Origins of American Politics*. New York: Random House, 1968.

————. *Religion and Revolution: Three Biographical Studies*. Perspectives in American History, vol. IV, 1970, pp. 85–169.

————. *The Ordeal of Thomas Hutchinson*. Cambridge, Mass.: Harvard University Press, 1974.

Bailyn, Bernard, et al. *The Great Republic*. Lexington, Mass.: D. C. Heath, 1977.

Baker, Keith Michael. *Condorcet: From Natural Philosophy to Social Mathematics*. Chicago: University of Chicago Press, 1975.

————, ed. *The French Revolution and the Creation of Modern Political Culture*. Vol. 1, *The Political Culture of the Old Regime*. Oxford: Pergamon Press, 1987.

Barnes, Thomas G. *Somerset 1625–1640*. Cambridge, Mass.: Harvard University Press, 1961.

Beeman, Richard, Stephen Botein, and Edward C. Carter II, eds. *Beyond Confederation: Origins of the Constitution and American National Identity*. Chapel Hill: University of North Carolina Press, 1987.

Beer, Samuel. *Modern British Politics*. (Reprint of *British Politics in the Collectivist Age*) New York: Norton, 1965, 1969, 1982.

Beer, Samuel, et al. *Patterns of Government: The Major Political Systems of Europe*. 3d ed. New York: Random House, 1973.

Bergeron, Louis. *L'Episode napoléonien: Aspects intérieurs, 1799–1815*. Paris: Le Seuil, 1972.

Berlin, Isaiah. *The Hedgehog and the Fox: An Essay on Tolstoy's View of History*. New York: Simon and Schuster, 1953.

————. *Four Essays on Liberty*. Oxford: Oxford University Press, 1969.

Birnbaum, Pierre, and Jean Leca, eds. *Sur l'individualisme*. Paris: Presses de la Fondation nationale des sciences politiques, 1986.

Bloch, Marc. *Les Rois thaumaturges*. Strasbourg, 1924.

————. *L'Etrange défaite*. Paris: Armand Colin, 1957.

Bluche, François. *Louis XIV*. Paris: Fayard, 1986.

Bois, Paul. *Paysans de l'Ouest: Des structures économiques et sociales aux options politiques depuis l'époque révolutionnaire dans la Sarthe.* Paris: Flammarion, 1971.

Bouloiseau, Marc. *La République jacobine, 10 août 1792–9 thermidor an II.* Paris: Le Seuil, 1972.

Braesch, F. *La Commune du Dix Août 1792: Etude sur l'histoire de Paris du 20 juin au 2 décembre 1792.* Paris: Hachette, 1911.

Brailsford, H. N. *The Levellers and the English Revolution.* London: The Cresset Press, 1961.

Braudel, Fernand, Ernest Labrousse et al. *Histoire économique et sociale de la France,* vols. II, III. Paris: Presses universitaires de France, 1970–1976.

Breen, T. H. *Puritans and Adventurers: Change and Persistence in Early America.* Oxford: Oxford University Press, 1980.

———. *Tobacco Culture: The Mentality of the Great Tidewater Planters on the Eve of the Revolution.* Princeton: Princeton University Press, 1985.

Brinton, Crane. *The Jacobins: An Essay in the New History.* New York: Russell & Russell, 1961.

———. *The Anatomy of Revolution.* New York: Knopf, 1938, 1952, 1965.

Brown, Richard D. *Revolutionary Politics in Massachusetts: The Boston Committee of Correspondence and the Towns, 1772–1774.* New York: Norton, 1970, 1976.

Bushman, Richard L. *King and People in Provincial Massachusetts.* Chapel Hill: University of North Carolina Press, 1985.

Challamel, Augustin. *Le Clubs contre-révolutionnaires: Cercles, comités, sociétés, salons, réunions, cafés, restaurants et librairies.* Paris: L. Cerf, Charles Noblet, Maison Quantin, 1895.

Chevallier, Jean-Jacques. *Barnave ou les deux faces de la Révolution.* Paris: Payot, 1936.

———. *Histoire des institutions et des régimes politiques de la France moderne (1789–1958).* 3d ed. Paris: Dalloz, 1967.

Church, William F. *Richelieu and Reason of State.* Princeton: Princeton University Press, 1972.

Clark, G. Kitson. *The Making of Victorian England.* New York: Atheneum, 1979.

Cobb, Richard. *Les Armées révolutionnaires: Instrument de la Terreur dans les départements. Avril 1793–Floréal An II.* 2 vols. Paris: Mouton, 1961–1963.

Cobban, Alfred. *A History of Modern France.* 3 vols. Harmondsworth, Middlesex: Penguin Books, 1963.

———. *The Social Interpretation of the French Revolution.* Cambridge: Cambridge University Press, 1964.

Colman, John. *John Locke's Moral Philosophy.* Edinburgh: Edinburgh University Press, 1983.

Condon, Ann Gorman. *The Envy of the American States: The Loyalist Dream for New Brunswick.* Frederickton, N.B.: New Ireland Press, 1984.

Countryman, Edward. "A Review Article: The Problem of the Early American Crowd." *Journal of American Studies* 7 (1973): 77–90.

———. "Consolidating Power in Revolutionary America: The Case of New

York, 1775–1783." *Journal of Interdisciplinary History* 6 (Spring 1976): 645–77.

——. *A People in Revolution: The American Revolution and Political Society in New York, 1760–1790.* Baltimore: Johns Hopkins University Press, 1981.

——. *The American Revolution.* New York: Hill and Wang, 1985.

Craig, Gordon A. *The Germans.* New York: G. P. Putnam's Sons, 1982.

Crozier, Michel. *Le Phénomène bureaucratique.* Paris: Le Seuil, 1963.

Dahrendorf, Ralf. *Society and Democracy in Germany. (Gesellschaft und Demokratie in Deutschland,* Munich, 1965). Garden City, N. Y.: Doubleday and Co., 1967.

Darnton, Robert. *Mesmerism and the End of the Enlightenment in France.* Cambridge, Mass.: Harvard University Press, 1968.

——. *The Business of the Enlightenment: A Publishing History of the Encyclopédie 1775–1800.* Cambridge, Mass.: Harvard University Press, 1979.

de Gaulle, Charles. *Mémoires de guerre.* 3 vols. Paris: Plon, 1954–1959.

de Jouvenel, Robert. *La République des camarades.* Paris: Bernard Grasset, 1914.

Delumeau, Jean. *Le Catholicisme entre Luther et Voltaire.* Paris: Presses universitaires de France, 1971.

Demos, John. *A Little Commonwealth: Family Life in Plymouth Colony.* Oxford: Oxford University Press, 1970.

Doyle, William. *Origins of the French Revolution.* Oxford: Oxford University Press, 1980.

Dunn, John. *The Political Thought of John Locke: An Historical Account of the Argument of the "Two Treatises of Government."* Cambridge: Cambridge University Press, 1969.

——. *Western Political Theory in the Face of the Future.* Cambridge: Cambridge University Press, 1979.

——. *Rethinking Modern Political Theory.* Cambridge: Cambridge University Press, 1985.

Earle, Edward Mead, ed. *Modern France: Problems of the Third and Fourth Republics.* Princeton: Princeton University Press, 1951.

Echevarria, Durand. *Mirage in the West: A History of the French Image of American Society to 1815.* Princeton: Princeton University Press, 1957.

Egret, Jean. *La Révolution des Notables: Mounier et les Monarchiens, 1789.* Paris: Armand Colin, 1950.

——. *La Pré-Révolution française (1787–1788).* Paris: Presses universitaires de France, 1962.

——. *Louis XV et l'opposition parlementaire, 1715–1774.* Paris: Armand Colin, 1970.

Elton, G. R. *Policy and Police: The Enforcement of the Reformation in the Age of Thomas Cromwell.* Cambridge: Cambridge University Press, 1972.

Everitt, Alan. *The Community of Kent and the Great Rebellion, 1640–60.* N.p.: Leicester University Press, 1966.

Farrand, Max. *The Framing of the Constitution of the United States.* New Haven: Yale University Press, 1913.

Fehér, Ferenc. *The Frozen Revolution: An Essay on Jacobinism.* Cambridge: Cambridge University Press, 1987.

————, ed. *The French Revolution and the Birth of Modernity.* Special issue of *Social Research* 56 (Spring 1989).

Fischer, David Hackett. *The Revolution of American Conservatism.* New York: Harper and Row, 1965.

Foner, Eric. *Free Soil, Free Labor, Free Men: The Ideology of the Republican Party before the Civil War.* Oxford: Oxford University Press, 1970.

————. *Politics and Ideology in the Age of the Civil War.* Oxford: Oxford University Press, 1980.

Friedrich, Carl J., ed. *Totalitarianism.* Cambridge, Mass.: Harvard University Press, 1953.

Fugier, André. *La Révolution française et l'Empire napoléonien.* Paris: Hachette, 1954.

Furet, François. *Penser la Révolution française.* Paris: Gallimard, 1978.

————. "La Révolution sans la Terreur? Le débat des historiens du XIXe siècle," in "L'Héritage jacobin," in *Le Débat*, no. 13, June 1981, pp. 40–54.

————. *La gauche et la révolution au milieu du XIXᵉ siècle: Edgar Quinet et la question du Jacobinisme, 1865–1870.* Paris: Hachette, 1986.

————. *Marx et la Révolution française.* Paris: Flammarion, 1986.

Furet, François, Jacques Julliard, and Pierre Rosanvallon. *La République du centre: La fin de l'exception française.* Paris: Calmann-Lévy, 1988.

Furet, François, and Mona Ozouf, eds. *Dictionnaire critique de la Révolution française.* Paris: Flammarion, 1988.

Furet, François, and Denis Richet. *La Révolution française.* Paris: Fayard, 1973.

Gardiner, Samuel Rawson. *The First Two Stuarts and the Puritan Revolution, 1603–1660.* 1876; reprint, New York: Thomas Y. Crowell, 1970.

Garrisson, Janine. *L'Edit de Nantes et sa révocation.* Paris: Le Seuil, 1985.

Geertz, Clifford. *The Interpretation of Cultures.* New York: Basic Books, 1973.

Goblot, Edmond. *La Barrière et le niveau: Etude sociologique sur la bourgeoisie française moderne.* 1925; reprint, Paris: Presses universitaires de France, 1967.

Godechot, Jacques. *La Grande Révolution: l'expansion révolutionnaire de la France dans le monde.* Paris: Aubier, 1956.

————. *La Contre-Révolution: Doctrine et Action, 1789–1804.* Paris: Presses universitaires de France, 1961.

Goldmann, Lucien. *Le Dieu caché; étude sur la vision tragique dans les Pensées de Pascal et dans le théâtre de Racine.* Paris: Gallimard, 1955.

Goubert, Pierre. *Louis XIV et vingt millions de Français.* Paris: Fayard, 1966.

————. *Cent mille provinciaux au XVIIᵉ siècle: Beauvais et le Beauvaisis de 1600 à 1730.* Paris: Flammarion, 1968.

————. *L'Ancien Régime.* 2 vols. Paris: Armand Colin, 1969–1973.

Green, Jack P., and J. R. Pole, eds. *Colonial British America: Essays in the New History of the Modern Era.* Baltimore: Johns Hopkins University Press, 1984.

Greer, Donald. *The Incidence of the Terror during the French Revolution: A Statistical Interpretation*. 1935; reprint, Gloucester, Mass.: Peter Smith, 1966.

Greven, Philip J., Jr. *Four Generations: Population, Land, and Family in Colonial Andover, Massachusetts*. Ithaca: Cornell University Press, 1970.

———. *The Protestant Temperament: Patterns of Child-Rearing, Religious Experience, and the Self in Early America*. New York: Knopf, 1977.

Gross, Robert A. *The Minutemen and Their World*. New York: Hill and Wang, 1976.

Halévy, Daniel. *The Birth of Methodism in England*. (1906) Trans. by Bernard Semmel. Chicago: University of Chicago Press, 1971.

Haller, William. *The Rise of Puritanism*. Philadelphia: University of Philadelphia Press, 1938.

———. *Liberty and Reformation in the Puritan Revolution*. New York: Columbia University Press, 1955.

Hartz, Louis. *The Liberal Tradition in America: An Interpretation of American Political Thought since the Revolution*. New York: Harcourt Brace Jovanovich, 1955.

Hazard, Paul. *La Crise de la conscience européenne, 1680–1715*. Paris: Fayard, 1961.

Hexter, J. H. *The Reign of King Pym*. Cambridge, Mass.: Harvard University Press, 1941.

———. *Reappraisals in History*. 2d ed. Chicago: University of Chicago Press, 1979.

Higham, John. "Hanging Together: Divergent Unities in American History." *Journal of American History* 61 (1974): 5–28.

Higonnet, Patrice. *Class, Ideology, and the Rights of Nobles during the French Revolution*. Oxford: Oxford University Press, 1981.

———. *Sister Republics: The Origins of French and American Republicanism*. Cambridge, Mass.: Harvard University Press, 1988.

Hill, Christopher. *The Century of Revolution, 1603–1714*. New York: W. W. Norton, 1961.

———. *God's Englishman: Oliver Cromwell and the English Revolution*. New York: Harper and Row, 1970.

Hirschman, Albert O. *The Passions and the Interests: Arguments for Capitalism before its Triumph*. Princeton: Princeton University Press, 1977.

Hirst, Derek. *Authority and Conflict: England, 1603–1658*. Cambridge, Mass.: Harvard University Press, 1986.

Hoerder, Dirk. *Crowd Action in Revolutionary Massachusetts*. New York: Academic Press, 1977.

Hoffmann, Stanley. *Le Mouvement poujade*. Paris: Armand Colin, 1956.

———. *Gulliver's Troubles or the Setting of American Foreign Policy*. New York: Council on Foreign Relations/McGraw-Hill, 1968.

———. *Decline or Renewal? France since the 1930's*. New York: Viking Press, 1974.

Hoffmann, Stanley, et al. *In Search of France*. Cambridge, Mass.: Harvard University Press, 1963.

Hofstadter, Richard. *The American Political Tradition and the Men Who Made It.* New York: Knopf, 1948, 1973.

————. *The Progressive Historians: Turner, Beard, Parrington.* New York: Vintage Books, 1968.

Holmes, Stephen. *Benjamin Constant and the Making of Modern Liberalism.* New Haven: Yale University Press, 1984.

Howe, Irving, ed. *1984 Revisited: Totalitarianism in Our Century.* New York: Harper and Row, 1983.

Howe, John R., Jr. *The Changing Political Thought of John Adams.* Princeton: Princeton University Press, 1966.

Hunt, Lynn Avery. *Revolution and Urban Politics in Provincial France: Troyes and Reims, 1786–1790.* Stanford: Stanford University Press, 1978.

————. *Politics, Culture, and Class in the French Revolution.* Berkeley: University of California Press, 1984.

Hunt, William. *The Puritan Moment: The Coming of Revolution in an English County.* Cambridge, Mass.: Harvard University Press, 1983.

Huntington, Samuel P. *Political Order in Changing Societies.* New Haven: Yale University Press, 1968.

————. *American Politics: The Promise of Disharmony.* Cambridge, Mass.: Harvard University Press, 1981.

Isaac, Rhys. "Dramatizing the Ideology of Revolution: Popular Mobilization in Virginia, 1774 to 1776." *William and Mary Quarterly,* Third Series 33 (July 1976): 357–85.

————. *The Transformation of Virginia, 1740–1790.* Chapel Hill: University of North Carolina Press, 1982.

Jaume, Lucien. *Le discours jacobin et la démocratie.* Paris: Fayard, 1989.

Jaurès, Jean. *Histoire socialiste de la Révolution française.* 7 vols. Ed. Albert Soboul. Paris: Editions sociales, 1968–1973.

Jellison, Richard M., ed. *Society, Freedom, and Conscience: The American Revolution in Virginia, Massachusetts, and New York.* New York: Norton, 1976.

Jensen, Merrill. *The New Nation: A History of the United States During the Confederation, 1781–1789.* New York: Vintage Books, 1950.

Jones, J. R. *The First Whigs: The Politics of the Exclusion Crisis (1678–1683).* London: Oxford University Press, 1961.

————. *The Revolution of 1688 in England.* New York: W. W. Norton, 1972.

————, ed. *The Restored Monarchy, 1660–1688.* Totowa, N. J.: Rowman and Littlefield, 1979.

Judson, Margaret Atwood. *The Crisis of the Constitution: An Essay in Constitutional and Political Thought in England, 1603–1645.* New Brunswick, N. J.: Rutgers University Press, 1949.

Julliard, Jacques. *La Faute à Rousseau: Essai sur les conséquences historiques de l'idée de souveraineté populaire.* Paris: Le Seuil, 1985.

Kantorowicz, Ernst H. *The King's Two Bodies: A Study in Medieval Political Theology.* Princeton: Princeton University Press, 1957.

Kates, Gary. *The Cercle Social, the Girondins, and the French Revolution.* Princeton: Princeton University Press, 1985.

Katz, Stanley, ed. *Colonial America: Essays in Politics and Social Development*. 2d ed. Boston: Little, Brown, and Co., 1971, 1976.

Kelley, Robert. *The Cultural Pattern in American Politics: The First Century*. New York: Knopf, 1979.

Kelly, George Armstrong. *Victims, Authority, and Terror: The Parallel Deaths of d'Orleans, Custine, Bailly, and Malesherbes*. Chapel Hill: University of North Carolina Press, 1982.

Kennan, George F. *American Diplomacy 1900–1950*. Chicago: University of Chicago Press, 1951.

Kennedy, Michael L. *The Jacobin Clubs in the French Revolution: The First Years*. Princeton: Princeton University Press, 1982.

Kenyon, Cecilia. "Men of Little Faith: The Anti-Federalists on the Nature of Representative Government." *William and Mary Quarterly*, Third Series 12 (January 1955): 3–43.

Keohane, Nannerl O. *Philosophy and the State in France: The Renaissance to the Enlightenment*. Princeton: Princeton University Press, 1980.

Kim, Kyung-Won. *Revolution and International System: A Study in the Breakdown of International Stability*. New York: New York University Press, 1970.

Kintzler, Catherine. *Condorcet: l'instruction publique et la naissance du citoyen*. Paris: Le Sycomore, SFIED, 1984.

Kirchheimer, Otto. *Political Justice: The Use of Legal Procedure for Political Ends*. Princeton: Princeton University Press, 1961.

Kishlansky, Mark. *The Rise of the New Model Army*. Cambridge: Cambridge University Press, 1979.

―――. "Community and Continuity: A Review of Selected Work on English Social History." *William and Mary Quarterly*, Third Series 37 (1980): 139–46.

Koestler, Arthur. *Darkness at Noon*. Trans. by Daphne Hardy. New York: Macmillan, 1941.

―――. *Arrow in the Blue: An Autobiography*. New York: Macmillan, 1952.

Kurtz, Stephen G., and James H. Hutson, eds. *Essays on the American Revolution*. Chapel Hill: University of North Carolina Press, 1973.

Labrousse, Ernest. *La Crise de l'économie française à la fin de l'Ancien régime et au début de la Révolution*. Paris: Presses universitaires de France, 1944.

―――, ed. *Ordres et Classes*. Paris: Ecole pratique des hautes études et Mouton, 1973.

Laslett, Peter. *The World We Have Lost: England before the Industrial Age*. 2d ed. New York: Charles Scribner's Sons, 1965, 1971.

Lefebvre, Georges. *Etudes sur la Révolution française*. 2d ed. Paris: Presses universitaires de France, 1963.

―――. *La Révolution française*. 3d ed. Paris: Presses universitaires de France, 1963.

―――. *La Grande Peur de 1789*. New ed. Paris: Armand Colin, 1970.

Lefort, Claude. *L'Invention démocratique*. Paris: Fayard, 1981.

―――. *Essais sur le politique (XIXe–XXe siècles)*. Paris: Le Seuil, 1986.

Le Goff, Jacques, and Pierre Nora, eds. *Faire l'histoire*. Vol. 1, *Nouveaux pro-blèmes*. Paris: Gallimard, 1974.

Lewis, Gwynne, and Colin Lucas, eds. *Beyond the Terror: Essays in French Regional and Social History, 1794–1815*. Cambridge: Cambridge University Press, 1983.

Lockridge, Kenneth. *A New England Town, the First Hundred Years: Dedham, Massachusetts, 1636–1736*. Expanded ed. New York: Norton, 1970, 1985.

———. *Settlement and Unsettlement in Early America: The Crisis of Political Legitimacy and the Revolution*. Cambridge: Cambridge University Press, 1981.

Lucas, Colin, ed. *The French Revolution and the Creation of Modern Political Culture*. Vol. 2, *The Political Culture of the French Revolution*. Oxford: Pergamon Press, 1988.

Macpherson, C. B. *The Political Theory of Possessive Individualism*. Oxford: Oxford University Press, 1962.

Maier, Pauline. *From Resistance to Revolution: Colonial Radicals and the Development of American Opposition to Britain, 1765–1776*. New York: Random House, 1972.

———. *The Old Revolutionaries: Political Lives in the Age of Samuel Adams*. New York: Knopf, 1980.

Mandrou, Robert. *Louis XIV en son temps, 1661–1715*. Paris: Presses universitaires de France, 1973.

———. *L'Europe "absolutiste": Raison et raison d'Etat, 1649–1775*. Paris: Fayard, 1977.

Manent, Pierre. *Histoire intellectuelle du libéralisme: Dix leçons*. Paris: Calmann-Lévy, 1987.

Marrus, Michael R., and Robert O. Paxton. *Vichy France and the Jews*. New York: Basic Books, 1981.

Mathiez, Albert. *Etudes sur Robespierre (1758–1794)*. Paris: Editions sociales, 1973.

Mautouchet, Paul. *Le Gouvernement Révolutionnaire (10 août 1792–4 brumaire an IV)*. Paris: Edouard Cornely, 1912.

McCoy, Drew R. *The Elusive Republic: Political Economy in Jeffersonian America*. New York: Norton, 1980, 1982.

McCusker, John J., and Russell R. Menard. *The Economy of British America, 1607–1789*. Chapel Hill: University of North Carolina Press, 1985.

McDonald, Forrest. *Novus Ordo Seclorum: The Intellectual Origins of the Constitution*. Lawrence: University Press of Kansas, 1985.

Michon, Georges. *Robespierre et la guerre révolutionnaire, 1791–1792*. Paris: Marcel Rivière, 1937.

Milgate, Murray, and Cheryl B. Welch, eds. *Critical Issues in Social Thought*. London: Academic Press/Harcourt Brace Jovanovich, 1989.

Miller, Perry. *The New England Mind*. 2 vols. 1939; reprint, Cambridge, Mass.: Harvard University Press, 1954.

Moore, Barrington, Jr. *Social Origins of Dictatorship and Democracy: Lord and Peasant in the Making of the Modern World*. Boston: Beacon Press, 1966.

Moote, A. Lloyd. *The Revolt of the Judges: The Parlement of Paris and the Fronde, 1643–1652*. Princeton: Princeton University Press, 1971.

Mornet, Daniel. *Les Origines intellectuelles de la Révolution française (1715–1787)*. Paris: Armand Colin, 1933.

Mossuz, Janine. *Les Clubs et la politique en France*. Paris: Armand Colin, 1970.

Mounier, Emmanuel. *Oeuvres de Mounier*. 4 vols. Paris: Le Seuil, 1961.

Mousnier, Roland, and Ernest Labrousse. *Le XVIIIᵉ siècle: Révolution intellectuelle, technique et politique (1715–1815)*. Paris: Presses universitaires de France, 1953.

Nash, Gary. *The Urban Crucible: Social Change, Political Consciousness, and the Origins of the American Revolution*. Cambridge, Mass.: Harvard University Press, 1979.

———. *Race, Class, and Politics: Essays on American Colonial and Revolutionary Society*. Urbana: University of Illinois Press, 1986.

Nicolet, Claude. *L'idée républicaine en France (1789–1924): Essai d'histoire critique*. Paris: Gallimard, 1982.

Nora, Pierre, ed. *Les Lieux de mémoire*. 4 vols. Paris: Gallimard, 1984–1986.

Norton, Mary Beth. *The British-Americans: The Loyalist Exiles in England*. Boston: Little Brown, 1972.

———. "The Loyalist Critique of the Revolution." In *The Development of a Revolutionary Mentality*. Washington, D. C.: Library of Congress Symposia on the American Revolution, 1972.

Notestein, Wallace. *The Winning of the Initiative by the House of Commons*. N.p., 1924.

Ollivier, Albert. *Saint-Just et la force des choses*. Paris: Gallimard, 1954.

Ozouf, Mona. "De Thermidor à brumaire: Le discours de la Révolution sur elle-même." *Revue historique*, no. 493 (Janvier–Mars 1970), pp. 31–66.

———. "L'Héritage jacobin: Fortune et infortunes d'un mot." In "L'Héritage jacobin," in *Le Débat*, no. 13, June 1981, pp. 28–39.

———. *L'école de la France: Essais sur la Révolution, l'utopie et l'enseignement*. Paris: Gallimard, 1984.

Palmer, R. R. *The Age of the Democratic Revolution*. 2 vols. Princeton: Princeton University Press, 1959, 1964.

———. *Twelve Who Ruled: The Year of the Terror in the French Révolution*. 1941; reprint, New York: Atheneum, 1965.

Paxton, Robert O. *Vichy France: Old Guard and New Order, 1940–1944*. New York: Knopf, 1972.

Pearl, Valerie. *London and the Outbreak of the Puritan Revolution: City Government and National Politics, 1625–43*. London: Oxford University Press, 1961.

———. "The 'Royal Independents' in the English Civil War." *Transactions of the Royal Historical Society*, Fifth Series 18 (1968): 69–96.

Pennington, Donald, and Keith Thomas, eds. *Puritans and Revolutionaries: Essays in Seventeenth-Century History Presented to Christopher Hill*. Oxford: Oxford University Press, 1978.

Pitkin, Hanna Fenichel. *The Concept of Representation*. Berkeley: University of California Press, 1967.

Plessis, Alain. *De la fête impériale au mur des fédérés, 1852–1871*. Paris: Le Seuil, 1973.

Plumb, J. H. *The Growth of Political Stability in England, 1675–1725*. London: Penguin Books, 1967.

Pocock, J.G.A. *The Ancient Constitution and the Feudal Law*. Cambridge: Cambridge University Press, 1957.

————. "Virtue and Commerce in the Eighteenth Century." *Journal of Interdisciplinary History* 3 (Summer 1972): 119–34.

————. *Politics, Language and Time*. New York: Atheneum, 1973.

————. *The Machiavellian Moment: Florentine Political Thought and the Atlantic Republican Tradition*. Princeton: Princeton University Press, 1975.

————. *Virtue, Commerce, and History*. Cambridge: Cambridge University Press, 1985.

Polanyi, Karl. *The Great Transformation: The Political and Economic Origins of Our Time*. Boston: Beacon Press, 1944.

Porter, Roy. *English Society in the Eighteenth Century*. Harmondsworth, Middlesex: Penguin, 1982.

Potter, Janice. *The Liberty We Seek: Loyalist Ideology in Colonial New York and Massachusetts*. Cambridge, Mass.: Harvard University Press, 1983.

Prélot, Marcel, and F. Gallouedec Genuys, comps. *Le Libéralisme catholique*. Paris: Armand Colin, 1969.

Projet (coll.). "L'Héritage de la Révolution française aujourd'hui." *Projet* 213, September–October 1988.

Rémond, René. *Les Droites en France*. 4th ed. Paris: Aubier Montaigne, 1987.

Revault d'Allonnes, Myriam. "Le Jacobinisme ou les apories du politique." *Revue française de science politique* 36 (August 1986): 519–26.

Richet, Denis. *La France moderne: L'Esprit des institutions*. Paris: Flammarion, 1973.

Robbins, Caroline. " 'Discordant Parties:' A Study of the Acceptance of Party by Englishmen." *Political Science Quarterly* 73 (December 1958): 505–29.

Roots, Ivan. *Commonwealth and Protectorate*. New York: Schocken Books, 1966.

Rosenblum, Nancy. *Bentham's Theory of the Modern State*. Cambridge, Mass.: Harvard University Press, 1978.

————. *Another Liberalism: Romanticism and the Reconstruction of Liberal Thought*. Cambridge, Mass.: Harvard University Press, 1987.

Rothkrug, Lionel. *Opposition to Louis XIV: The Political and Social Origins of the French Enlightenment*. Princeton: Princeton University Press, 1965.

Rousso, Henry. *Le Syndrôme de Vichy, 1944–198. . . .* Paris: Le Seuil, 1987.

Rudelle, Odile. *La République absolue: Aux origines de l'instabilité constitutionnelle de la France républicaine, 1870–1889*. Paris: Publications de la Sorbonne, 1982.

Russell, Conrad. *Parliaments and English Politics, 1621–1629*. Oxford: Oxford University Press, 1979.

Rutman, Darrett B. "Assessing the Little Communities of Early America." *William and Mary Quarterly*, Third Series 43 (April 1986): 163–78.

Ryan, Alan, ed. *The Idea of Freedom: Essays in Honor of Isaiah Berlin*. Oxford: Oxford University Press, 1979.

———. *Property and Political Theory*. London: Basil Blackwell, 1984.

Sa'adah, Anne. "After the Terror: The French Revolution and Political Development." Paper delivered at the 1989 Annual Meeting of the APSA, Atlanta, Georgia, August 31, 1989.

Schama, Simon. *Citizens: A Chronicle of the French Revolution*. New York: Knopf, 1989.

Schmitt, Carl. *The Concept of the Political (Der Begriff des Politischen)*. Trans. by George Schwab. Hamburg, 1932; reprint, New Brunswick, N. J.: 1976.

Schochet, Gordon J. *Patriarchalism in Political Thought: The Authoritarian Family and Political Speculation and Attitudes Especially in Seventeenth-Century England*. New York: Basic Books, 1975.

Shalhope, Robert E. "Republicanism and Early American Historiography." *William and Mary Quarterly*, Third Series 39 (April 1982): 334–56.

Shklar, Judith N. *Legalism: Law, Morals, and Political Trials*. Cambridge, Mass.: Harvard University Press, 1964, 1986.

———. *Men and Citizens: A Study of Rousseau's Social Theory*. Cambridge: Cambridge University Press, 1969.

Shy, John. *A People Numerous and Armed: Reflections on the Military Struggle for American Independence*. New York: Oxford University Press, 1976.

Skinner, Quentin. *The Foundations of Modern Political Thought*. 2 vols. Cambridge: Cambridge University Press, 1978.

Skocpol, Theda. *States and Social Revolutions: A Comparative Analysis of France, Russia, and China*. Cambridge: Cambridge University Press, 1979.

Smith, Paul H. "The American Loyalists: Notes on their Organization and Numerical Strength." *William and Mary Quarterly*, Third Series 25 (April 1968): 259–77.

Soboul Albert. *L'Europe et la Révolution française*. 8 vols. Paris: Plon, 1885–1904.

———. *Les Sans-culottes*. Paris: Le Seuil, 1968.

———. *Mouvement populaire et Gouvernement révolutionnaire en l'An II (1793–1794)*. Paris: Flammarion, 1973.

Starzinger, Vincent E. *Middlingness: "Juste Milieu" Political Theory in France and England, 1815–1848*. Charlottesville: University Press of Virginia, 1965.

Stern, Fritz. *The Failure of Illiberalism: Essays on the Political Culture of Modern Germany*. Chicago: University of Chicago Press, 1971.

Stone, Lawrence. *The Crisis of the Aristocracy, 1558–1641*. Oxford: Oxford University Press, 1965.

———. "The English Revolution." In *Preconditions of Revolution in Early Modern Europe*. Ed. Robert Forster and Jack Greene. Baltimore: Johns Hopkins Press, 1970, pp. 55–108.

Stourzh, Gerald. *Alexander Hamilton and the Idea of Republican Government*. Stanford: Stanford University Press, 1970.

Strout, Cushing. *The New Heavens and New Earth: Political Religion in America.* New York: Harper and Row, 1974.

Sydenham, M. J. *The Girondins.* London: The Athlone Press (University of London), 1961.

Tackett, Timothy. *Religion, Revolution, and Regional Culture in Eighteenth Century France: The Ecclesiastical Oath of 1791.* Princeton: Princeton University Press, 1985.

Taft, Barbara, ed. *Absolute Liberty: A Selection from the Articles and Papers of Caroline Robbins.* Hamden, Conn.: Archon Books, 1982.

Talmon, J. L. *The Origins of Totalitarian Democracy.* New York: Praeger, 1960.

Tapie, Victor L. *La France de Louis XIII et de Richelieu.* Paris: Flammarion, 1967.

Thompson, E. P. *The Making of the English Working Class.* New York: Knopf, 1963.

―――. *Whigs and Hunters: The Origins of the Black Act.* New York: Pantheon Books, 1975.

Thuau, Etienne. *Raison d'état et pensée politique à l'époque de Richelieu.* Paris: Athenes, 1966.

Tiedemann, Joseph S. "Patriots by Default: Queens County, New York, and the British Army, 1776–1783." *William and Mary Quarterly,* Third Series 43 (January 1986): 35–63.

Tilly, Charles, ed. *The Formation of National States in Western Europe.* Princeton: Princeton University Press, 1975.

―――. *The Vendée.* Cambridge, Mass.: Harvard University Press, 1976.

Tocqueville, Alexis de. *Souvenirs.* Vol. 12, *Oeuvres complètes.* Paris: Gallimard, 1964.

―――. *L'ancien régime et la Révolution.* vol. 2, *Oeuvres complètes.* 1856; reprint, Paris: Gallimard, 1967.

Underdown, David. "The Independents Reconsidered." *Journal of British Studies* 3 (May 1964): 57–84.

―――. *Pride's Purge: Politics in the Puritan Revolution.* Oxford: Oxford University Press, 1971.

―――. *Somerset in the Civil War and Interregnum.* Newton Abbot: David and Charles, 1973.

Van Tyne, Claude Halstead. *The Loyalists in the American Revolution.* 1902; reprint, Gloucester, Mass.: Peter Smith, 1959.

Villat, Louis. *La Révolution et l'Empire (1789–1815).* 2 vols. Paris: Presses universitaires de France, 1936.

Vovelle, Michel. *La Chute de la monarchie 1787–1792.* Paris: Le Seuil, 1972.

―――. *La mentalité révolutionnaire.* Paris: Editions sociales, 1985.

Wallon, Henri. *La Terreur: Etudes critiques sur l'histoire de la Révolution française.* 2 vols. Paris: Hachette, 1873.

Walzer, Michael L. *The Revolution of the Saints: A Study in the Origins of Radical Politics.* 1965; reprint, New York: Atheneum, 1971.

Wedgwood, C. V. *The Trial of Charles I.* London: Collins, 1964.

Weir, Robert M. "Who Shall Rule at Home: The American Revolution as a

Crisis of Legitimacy for the Colonial Elite." *Journal of Interdisciplinary History* 6 (Spring 1976): 679–700.

Welch, Cheryl B. *Liberty and Utility: The French Ideologues and the Transformation of Liberalism.* New York: Columbia University Press, 1984.

Willcox, William B. *Gloucestershire: A Study in Local Government, 1590–1640.* New Haven: Yale University Press, 1940.

Williams, Philip. *Crisis and Compromise: Politics in the Fourth Republic.* New York: Doubleday, 1966.

Woloch, Isser. *Jacobin Legacy: The Democratic Movement under the Directory.* Princeton: Princeton University Press, 1970.

Wood Gordon. *The Creation of the American Republic, 1776–1787.* New York: W. W. Norton, 1969.

———. "Conspiracy and the Paranoid Style: Causality and Deceit in the Eighteenth Century." *William and Mary Quarterly,* Third Series 39 (July 1982): 401–41.

Wood, Peter H. *Black Majority: Negroes in Colonial South Carolina from 1670 through the Stono Rebellion.* New York: Norton, 1974.

Woodward, C. Vann. *The Strange Career of Jim Crow.* 2d rev. ed. Oxford: Oxford University Press, 1955, 1966.

Wormuth, Francis D. *The Royal Prerogative 1603–1649.* Ithaca, N. Y.: Cornell University Press, 1939.

Woronoff, Denis. *La République bourgeoise, 1794–1799.* Paris: Le Seuil, 1972.

Young, Alfred, ed. *The American Revolution: Explorations in the History of American Radicalism.* Dekalb: Northern Illinois University Press, 1976.

———. "George Robert Twelves Hewes (1742–1840): A Boston Shoemaker and the Memory of the American Revolution." *William and Mary Quarterly,* Third Series 38 (October 1981): 561–623.

Zeldin, Theodore. *France, 1848–1945.* 2 vols. Oxford: Oxford University Press, 1973–1977.

Zuckerman, Michael. *Peaceable Kingdoms: New England Towns in the Eighteenth Century.* New York: Knopf, 1970.

Index